SWAHILI GRAM
INTRODUCTORY AND
INTERMEDIATE LEVELS

Sarufi ya Kiswahili cha Ngazi ya Kwanza na Kati

Oswald Almasi
Michael David Fallon
Nazish Pardhan Wared

University Press of America,® Inc.
Lanham · Boulder · New York · Toronto · Plymouth, UK

Copyright © 2014 by
University Press of America,® Inc.
4501 Forbes Boulevard
Suite 200
Lanham, Maryland 20706
UPA Acquisitions Department (301) 459-3366

10 Thornbury Road
Plymouth PL6 7PP
United Kingdom

British Library Cataloging in Publication Information Available

Library of Congress Control Number: 2014937163
ISBN: 978-0-7618-6381-6 (paperback : alk. paper)
eISBN: 978-0-7618-6382-3

Contents

Foreword

About this Book

This book is intended for University students who are interested in learning the Swahili language at the Introductory and Intermediate levels. This book consists of 40 teaching chapters, and each chapter is arranged in the following manner:

1. An Introduction of the main concepts that will be dealt with in the chapter.
2. Sections which present the chapter's material broken down into easier to understand concepts.
3. Examples for most Sections which help the student understand the concepts being taught.
4. Practice Exercises, so the student can begin to use the knowledge they have acquired.
5. A Vocabulary list of all new words taught in the chapter. After the new word has been encountered it will not appear in the Vocabulary of a following chapter but can be found at the back of the book in the Swahili Vocabulary Dictionary which is a complete dictionary of all the words used in this textbook. It is expected that the Vocabulary will be memorized by the students at their own speed.
6. Answers to Practice Exercises so students can confirm and correct the Practice Exercises they have just completed within the chapter.

Note on Vocabulary

This note is about how Swahili Vocabulary is presented and organized in this book. Firstly, all Swahili words, prefixes, infixes, suffixes and sentences are presented in italics, to more easily find and identify them. In the Vocabulary Section, when presenting a new Swahili noun the singular form of the noun is written first, followed by a forward slash (/) and then the Noun Class Prefix which is attached to make the noun plural. The Noun Class Prefix of course also helps in identifying which of the 6 main Noun Classes that the noun belongs to. Finally, the English translation is provided. For example the noun *daktari* (borrowed from the English word "doctor") would be found in the Vocabulary as follows:

daktari/ma-   doctor(s)

As you can see, the singular noun *daktari* comes first followed by the *ma-* which would make the noun *madaktari* which is the plural noun "doctors". The singular noun is always first so the Vocabulary can be in alphabetical order. However some nouns do not have a plural or their singular and plural forms are the same and so there would be no forward slash (/) or prefix. The 6 main Noun Classes and the formation of singular and plural nouns will be taught in their relevant chapters.

Acknowledgments and Dedication

There are many people and organizations the authors would like to thank: Atin Lal, Professor Lioba Moshi, Fatema Pardhan, Carolyn Luguya, Professor Grace B. Nyamongo, Ramadhan Ramadhan, Professor Grace Puja, Mohamed Yasin, Mohamed Noor, Professor Tom Ndege, Swahili Poet Said Nuweisr, Jeanne Guillaume formerly librarian for New College Library (Donald G. Ivey Library), National Swahili Council (BAKITA), Executive Officer for Tanzania Writer's Association (UWAVITA) Mr. Abasi Mkuwaje, The Department of Languages, Literatures and Linguistics at York University and The University of Toronto, for their advice, observations, assistance and continuing support.

We especially wish to thank Mary Almasi for her advice and loving support and Atta Almasi for assisting us with market research; Arash Wared for his knowledge of linguistic concepts and rules; Byron Court and Amabel Court for their technical knowledge and assistance in all matters both computer hardware and software related; Mr and Mrs. Gulam Pardhan for their wonderful hospitality in Tanzania.

This book is dedicated to all of our friends, families, and supporters who offered us all the support they could and put up with us when the going got tough. In addition each author has their own special dedication:

To my wonderful wife Mary Almasi for her patience and enduring love, my children Malkia, Kojo, Atta and Faustin who spent many nights wondering when their father would return, as well as Mzee Simon Kayoro who supported me when I needed his help.

—Professor Oswald Almasi

To Princess Carla for inspiring me with her determination and outright stubbornness, keeping me young in heart and mind, and making me realize taking the hard road has its own rewards.

—Michael David Fallon

To a wonderful husband Arash Wared for his optimism and never ending support. I would also like to extend my gratitude to my beautiful sister Fatema Pardhan, my parents and my in laws, the Pardhans and Wareds, for their constant enthusiasm and love.

—Nazish Pardhan Wared

Finally the authors wish to thank each other for the dedication and long hours working through every problem, for refusing to give up on this book or each other, and for forgiving each other.

Chapter 1

About the Swahili Language

The Swahili language or "Kiswahili" is discussed in relation to its history, geography, different dialects, and the spread of Kiswahili through the centuries. This chapter will also cover the status of the language in the world today and some aspects of cultural significance that the Swahili learner should be familiar with.

Kiswahili is a Bantu language that belongs to the Niger-Congo language family. The word Bantu means "people." The languages of Baganda in Uganda, Sotho in Lesotho, Zulu in South Africa and Kikuyu in Kenya are other examples of Bantu languages. Although these languages are not mutually intelligible, they are all derived from one common ancestral language and share some basic vocabulary, word building processes and sentence structure.[1] For example, the word for person in Kiswahili is *mtu* meaning "person" or *watu* meaning "people." Both the singular and plural forms of the word are very similar in many Bantu languages as shown in Table 1.1

TABLE 1.1
Table showing some Bantu languages

Bantu Language	Country	Singular	Plural
Baganda	Uganda	*omuntu*	*abantu*
Sotho	Lesotho	*motho*	*batho*
Zulu	South Africa	*umuntu*	*abantu*
Kikuyu	Kenya	*muntu*	*abato*

Kiswahili was originally spoken along the East African Coast from Southern Somalia to the Northern part of Mozambique and has existed for more than 1,000 years. The word "Swahili" has been derived from the Arabic word "Sahel" meaning "coast." The expansion of Swahili into the hinterland was facilitated by Coastal slave traders, merchants, missionaries and colonialists. The late Presidents Nyerere of Tanzania, Jomo Kenyatta of Kenya and Prime Minister Milton Obote of Uganda promoted Kiswahili during the struggle for independence (*uhuru*). President Nyerere promoted Swahili in many ways including the translation of two Shakespearean plays: The Merchant of Venice (*Mabepari wa Venice*) and Julius Caesar (*Juliasi Kaisari*). Nyerere also made Swahili the medium of instruction in elementary schools.

Currently Kiswahili is mainly spoken in Tanzania, Kenya and Uganda. In addition it is spoken to some extent in seven other countries or regions in East and Central Africa, namely, Rwanda, Burundi, the Eastern part of the Democratic Republic of the Congo, Southern Somalia, Northern Mozambique, Malawi and Northern Zambia which together have a Swahili speaking population of roughly 50 million. Outside the East and Central Africa Region, Kiswahili is spoken in Oman, some parts of Madagascar, South Africa and Djibouti.

Kiswahili is spoken in more than 15 dialects throughout East and Central Africa. The *Kiunguja* dialect of Zanzibar has been adopted as Standard Swahili since 1935 and is used by the media, as a medium of instruction in schools and in business transactions.

Other major dialects are *Kimvita, Kiamu, Kipemba* and *Kitumbatu* based in Mombasa, Lamu, Pemba and Unguja Islands respectively. Apart from these dialects, there are other dialects of people living in the interior of East and Central Africa, which tend to reflect the tribal languages of different Bantu speaking peoples.

As a consequence of interaction between the local people and foreigners, Kiswahili has many loan words from other languages such as Arabic, English, German, Portuguese, Persian and Hindi. It has been estimated that foreign words in the Swahili language make up approximately 30% of the vocabulary, with the majority coming from Arabic.[2] While it is true that Swahili uses many foreign words, it is also true to say that the Swahili people have adapted foreign words to meet their own needs. For example, borrowed words that have closed vowels (i.e. ending with consonants) have been changed so that they have open vowels (i.e. ending with a vowel). Also some loan words have completely changed their meaning. For example, the word *rafiki* (friend) is originally taken from the Arabic word "rafik" meaning "trusted one." Furthermore, it has been shown that the origin of some loan words cannot be traced to any particular language. In addition, Swahili has contributed words to the English vocabulary such as the word *safari,* which means "journey."

The great explorer, Sir Richard Francis Burton, who visited the East African Coast in the middle of the 19th Century, had this to say about the language:

> Kiswahili is both rich and poor. . . . It abounds in names of sensuous objects; there is a term for every tree, shrub, plant, grass, and bulb, and I have shown that the several ages of cocoa-nut are differently called. . . . Abounding in vowels and liquids, the language admits a vast volubility of utterances; in anger or excitement, the words flow like a torrent, and each dovetails into its neighbour until the whole speech becomes one vocabule.[3]

Kiswahili has attained an international status. The African Union, formerly the Organization of African Unity (OAU), has adopted Kiswahili as one of the official languages of Africa. For many years, major radio networks have been broadcasting Swahili programs. They include the BBC, Voice of America, Radio South Africa, Deutschewel (Germany), Radio Cairo, Radio Japan, Radio Beijing, All India Radio and Radio Moscow International. Many universities and colleges in Europe, Asia, North America and other parts of Africa have Swahili programs. Also, Swahili has been used in some North American movies such as Hotel Rwanda, the Last King of Scotland, the Lion King and Darwin's Nightmare. There are also several popular Swahili songs known throughout the world such as *Hakuna Matata* (No worries), *Malaika Nakupenda Malaika* (Angel, I love you Angel) and *Jambo Bwana* (Hello Mister). In addition, some English songs such as All Night Long (by Lionel Ritchie) and Liberian Girl (by Michael Jackson) have Swahili phrases in them.

Furthermore, there are hundreds of websites that deal with Swahili grammar, culture history and current news. The most ambitious initiatives to promote Kiswahili have been started in the United States including the world famous *Kamusi* Project which is managed by the Swahili Department at Yale University. Both Google and Microsoft have launched Swahili language Internet search engines to make Kiswahili accessible to the world.

Let us now discuss some cultural aspects, which anyone interested in studying the Swahili language should be familiar with. These aspects are Swahili greetings (see Chapter 4), oral traditions, expressions of gratitude, hospitality and clothing.

Unlike in the Western world, the Swahili people take their greetings very seriously, especially in the rural areas where the majority of the population resides. It is considered impolite to pass by someone without greeting him or her even though the person may be a complete stranger. However, this courtesy is not as commonly practiced in the cities. After initial greetings, information can be exchanged about other things such as work, school, family, business and so forth.

Greeting is a form of socialization designed to inform, educate and entertain especially in a countryside where there are only a few newspapers, radios, televisions and telephones. Furthermore, greetings help the community to conform to rigid social conventions. Just as each member of the community is pleased to hear good stories told about him or her, so one was sure that a disgraceful story would find the same treatment—the story of shame would inevitably be heard in every group and may be talked about as if it was an inquisition in a court of law.[4] Greetings are accompanied by a handshake using the right hand. The left hand is never used for a handshake while greeting. Neither can it be used for giving or receiving things because it is associated with cleaning oneself after visiting the bathroom (*choo*). If for some reasons one must use the left hand, due to a disability or if the right hand is occupied, one must apologize by saying *samahani*, which means "sorry."

The Swahili people have strong storytelling traditions since many rural residents do not have frequent access to books, newspapers and the internet. These stories are designed to teach good morals, pass customs and traditions from one generation to the next, inculcate speaking skills and for entertainment purposes.

Since many rural Swahili people live a communal lifestyle, everyone is expected to provide a helping hand to other community members. Therefore, it is less common for rural Swahili people to use expressions of gratitude when favors are exchanged. On the contrary, if they do not fulfill their responsibilities or if they misbehave, they are chastised, blamed and sometimes even punished. The word for expressing gratitude in Swahili is *asante* when thanking one person or *asanteni* when thanking more than one person.

Visitors to East and Central Africa always remember the hospitality of the Swahili people most of whom go out of their way to assist complete strangers. They invite visitors (*wageni*) not only to share meals (*karibu chakula*) but also to have tea (*karibu chai*). When a guest bids farewell, he/she is welcome to visit again (*karibu tena*).

The type of clothing used by the Swahili people varies from place to place depending on the weather. On the coast where it is hot, women wear *kanga* (a rectangular piece of cloth) and men wear *kanzu* (loose-fitting garments). Some traditional Muslim women cover themselves with *baibui* (a black loose-fitting garment which covers the entire body except the eyes). The *kanga* cloth is of particular significance because it has writings in Swahili which are designed to educate, inform and pass on words of wisdom from one generation to the next. This is why the *kanga* is referred to as "the cloth that speaks."

Notes

1. Thomas J. Hinnebusch, Sarah M. Mirza, S*wahili: A foundation for speaking reading and writing*, 2nd ed. (Lanham, MD: University Press of America, 1998), xvi.

2. Hinnebusch, Mirza, xvii-xviii.

3. Edward Rice, *Captain Sir Richard Francis Burton* (New York NY: Macmillan Publishing Co., 1990), 282.

4. G. Balamoan, *The Blue Nile Boy* (London, UK: Karia Press, 1989), 119.

Chapter 2

The Alphabet, Pronunciation and Common Mistakes

The Swahili language is now written in the modern Roman alphabet. In past times, before the colonization of East Africa in the 1890"s, any written Swahili would have been written using Swahili words but using the Arabic script and alphabet. As a result some words in modern Swahili retain an Arabic pronunciation and are spelled a specific way in order to evoke the original Arabic sound. A good example would be the combination of DH. The combination of DH in the word *fedha* (money) is NOT pronounced fed-ha, as most English speakers would attempt. Instead the "DH" sound is equivalent to the TH in "That" but NEVER as the TH in "thing." So *fedha* should sound like "fe-THat" but minus the "t" at the end, producing "fe-THa." Only 24 of the 26 letters in the modern Roman alphabet are used in Swahili, the letters Q and X are not used.

Vowels

Vowel sounds are the most important sounds to pronounce correctly as this is where most non-native speakers make mistakes. Here are examples on the correct pronunciation of vowel sounds.

A as in "bat" – *barua* (letter)
E as in "end" – *endelea* (continue, progress)
I as the "e" in "be" – *kiti* (chair)
O as in the "o" in "open" – *jambo* (hello)
U as the "u" in "student" – *babu* (grandfather)

Note the double "oo" in Swahili does NOT produce the same "uuu" sound as in English. The double "oo" in Swahili is simply a lengthened "o." The word "*kioo*" (glass, mirror) is NOT pronounced as "ki-uu" but as "ki-OO." Giving the double "oo" the "uuu" sound as in "pool" "fool" and "school" is a common mistake for English speakers. Simply make the "regular" sound for the letter "o" and stretch it for an extra half a second.

Stress

One thing to note before continuing, in Swahili stress ALWAYS falls on the second last syllable, as shown by the italicized syllable below. So, if we break up the previous Swahili words into syllables, we would get the following:

ba-*ru*-a (letter)
e-nde-*le*-a (continue, progress)
ki-ti (chair)
ja-mbo (hello)
ba-bu (grandfather)

In addition to the stress falling on the second last syllable, words that start with the letter "n" have a special rule when breaking the word up into syllables. When dealing with a word starting with the letter "n" and followed by another consonant the letter "n" either forms a separate syllable or part of another syllable based on the following rule. If the letters following the letter "n" can be broken down into one syllable ONLY, then the letter "n" is treated as a separate syllable.

n-chi (country)
n-ne (four)

However, if the letters following "n" can be broken into more than one syllable, then the letter "n" DOES NOT form a separate syllable, instead it is incorporated into the first syllable.

nde-ge (bird or plane)
nji-wa (dove)

Also note that the letter "m" can at times form its own syllable such as in *m*-to-to (child) or be part of another syllable such as in *mbo*-ga (vegetable).

Consonants

Consonants are the easiest sounds in Swahili, and always stay the same:

B as in "buck" or "bad" – *baba* (father)

C is never found alone, but is always found with H

CH as in "chocolate" – *chafu* (dirty)

D as in "drug" – *dawa* (drug, medicine)

F as in "fast" – *fahamu* (know, understand)

G as in "goose" – *gari* (vehicle). It is always a "hard" G as in "goose" or "gun" and never a "soft" G as in "gym" or "gentle."

H as in "hat"– *hali* (condition)

J as in "join" – *jambo* (hello)

K as in "kind" – *kaka* (brother)

L as in "love" – *lala* (sleep). In a few cases, native Swahili speakers interchange "L" and "R" so that "*lala*" becomes "*rara*." However this is considered poor Swahili and should not be done in Standard Swahili.

M as in "mother" – *mama* (mother)

N as in "nice" – *na* (and)

P as in "put" – *paka* (cat)

Q is never used in Swahili

R as in "rope" – *rafiki* (friend) Also see "L" above for the interchangeability of "L" and "R"

S as in "soup" – *soma* (read, study)

T as in "take" – *twiga* (giraffe)

V as in "vest" – *vita* (war)

W as in "wait" – *wapi*? (where?)

X is never used in Swahili

Y as in "yes" – *yai* (egg)

Z as in "zero" – *zawadi* (gift, present)

Swahili also has many letters found in combination that produce specific sounds. There are 3 broad categories of letter combinations, but only the 3rd category will be of some difficulty to English speakers. The combination letters will be introduced in capital letters below.

Category 1

Letter combinations in this category are the easiest for English speakers as they already exist in English and are pronounced exactly the same, for example:

CH as in "chocolate" – *chafu* (dirty)
NJ as in "enjoy" – *njaa* (hunger)
SH as in "shore" – *shule* (school)
TH as in "thing" – *thamani* (price, worth)
VY as in "envy" – *vyumba* (rooms)

Category 2

Letter combinations in this category only occur in English in compounded words, i.e. words made up of two nouns. In order to get the correct pronunciation in Swahili one must say the compounded word quickly, so as to get the combined letters to be pronounced as one sound as a Swahili speaker would. Listed below are some of the letter combinations that occur in Swahili.

BW as in "subway" – *bwana* (sir)
KW as in "backward" – *kweli* (true, truth)
MW as in "teamwork" – *mwalimu* (teacher)
NG as in "sunglory" – *nguo* (clothing, garment)
NY as in "lanyard" – *nyumba* (house)
PW as in "upward" – *pwani* (coast)

Category 3

These letter combinations are the most challenging for English speakers at first because they have NO equivalent sounds in English. Only listening to Swahili speakers and some practice will allow Swahili language learners to produce and recognize these sounds.

AA as in *baada* (after). AA is a voiced guttural sound taken directly from the 18th letter of the Arabic alphabet. However, even most native Swahili speakers do not pronounce it the "correct" Arabic way and instead pronounce it in much the same way as an English speaker would attempt to pronounce it. *"Baada"* (after) is pronounced as a lengthened "A" as in "aaa-partment" where the letter "a" is stretched for an extra half a second.

DH as in *fedha* (money). DH makes the TH sound from "THat" but NEVER the TH sound from "THing."

GH as in *ghali* (expensive). GH is a voiced guttural sound taken directly from the 19th letter of the Arabic alphabet. *"Ghali"* (expensive) is pronounced starting with the hard "G" sound from "gun" but flowing immediately into the "H" sound as in "house."

KH as in *khanga* (a piece of fabric). KH is a voiceless guttural sound taken directly from the 7th letter of the Arabic alphabet. Anyone who knows Arabic, Persian or Swahili can produce this sound.

NG' as in *ng'ombe* (cow/cattle). Please note the presence of an apostrophe in this case. When the apostrophe occurs a specialized sound is produced. The sound is closest to the NG in "singer" where air is pushed through the nose making a nasalized NG. A similar sound exists in Spanish with the letter ñ but without the "y" sound associated with that letter.

New Vocabulary

baada: after
baba: father(s)
babu: grandfather(s)
barua: letter(s)
bwana/ma-: sir(s), gentleman/men
chafu: dirty
chumba/vy-: room(s)
dawa: medicine(s), drug(s)
endelea: continue, progress
fahamu: understand
fedha: money, silver
gari/ma-: vehicle(s), car(s)
ghali: expensive
hali: condition, state
jambo: hello
kaka: brother(s)
khanga: piece of fabric
kioo/vi-: glass, mirror(s)

kiti/vi-: chair(s)
kweli: true, truth(s)
lala: sleep
mama: mother(s)
mboga: vegetable(s)
mwalimu/wa-: teacher(s)
na: and, with, by, also
-na-: present tense marker
nchi: country(ies), state(s)
ndege: plane(s), bird(s)
ng'ombe: cow(s), cattle
nguo: cloth(es), clothing, garment(s)
ni-: I
njaa: hunger(s), famine(s)
njiwa: dove(s)
nne: four
nyumba: house(s)
paka: cat(s)
pwani: coast(s)
rafiki: friend(s)
shule: school(s)
soma: read, study
thamani: price, value, worth
twiga: giraffe(s)
vita: war(s)
wapi?: where?
yai/ma-: egg(s)
zawadi: present(s), gift(s)

Simple Sentence Structure in Swahili

We will now introduce students to the construction of simple sentences in Swahili. All of the following concepts will be covered in detail in their relevant Chapters; the purpose here is for students to be able to distinguish the major "parts" of a Swahili sentence. The simple Swahili sentence is constructed using the acronym S.T.V.

S = Subject
T = Tense
V = Verb

Swahili uses a system of prefixes, suffixes and even infixes to communicate the required information instead of separate words as in English. In Swahili an entire sentence can consist of one word, if the sentence contains only one verb.

A simple sentence such as "I am studying" would be translated into Swahili as *Ninasoma.*

Deconstructing the above Swahili sentence we get *ni-na-soma*

Subject = NI - the subject of the sentence, in this case "I"
Tense = NA - the tense marker, in this case indicating the verb
    is in the present
Verb = SOMA - the verb, in this case "study"

Simple sentences in Swahili ALWAYS follow the structure S.T.V. – Subject, Tense, and Verb. More complicated Swahili sentences will of course contain more "parts" but for now simple Swahili sentence structure will be used in the opening Chapters of this book. The following Chapters will teach each of these "parts" of a Swahili sentence, the Subject, the Tense and the Verb.

Chapter 3

Personal Subject Prefixes, Personal Pronouns, and Their Negations

As you may recall, a simple Swahili sentence is constructed by using the STV rule discussed in Chapter 2. The STV rule is shown below:

Subject + Tense + Verb

In this chapter we will look at the first "spot" in a simple Swahili sentence, where the subject is located. In Swahili, the subject is denoted by a prefix which is then attached to a tense marker followed by a verb. When the subject being referred to is a human being, animal or an insect, the "spot" is taken by a Personal Subject Prefix. In this chapter, we will focus on Personal Subject Prefixes while Subject Prefixes dealing with things that are not humans, animals or insects will be covered in future Chapters.

Section A: Personal Subject Prefixes

Table 3.1 identifies who is the subject in a Swahili sentence i.e. who is "doing" the verb.

TABLE 3.1
Personal Subject Prefixes Table

Ni-	I	*Tu-*	We
U-	You (singular)	*M-*	You (plural)
A-	He/She	*Wa-*	They

Using Table 3.1, we can make the following simple sentences:

NI-na-soma = *Ninasoma.* – I am studying.
TU-na-soma = *Tunasoma.* – WE are studying.
U-na-soma = *Unasoma.* – YOU (singular) are studying.
M-na-soma = *Mnasoma.* – YOU (plural, literally YOU ALL)
    are studying.
A-na-soma = *Anasoma.* – HE/SHE is studying.
WA-na-soma = *Wanasoma.* – THEY are studying.

Note that *A-* stands for EITHER "he" or "she." If it is unclear whom the speaker is referring to, they may name the person, or add additional words to describe the person, "the man in the white shirt" or words such as "that woman." The best way to think of *A-* is as "the person." *Anasoma* then becomes "THE PERSON is studying" without assigning them any specific gender.

Also note that in Swahili there are two "types" of the word "you." There is a "you" addressed to one person, as in English, which is represented by the Personal Subject Prefix *U-* and there is a "you" for more than one person, which is represented by the Personal Subject Prefix *M-* which would most closely be translated in English as "you all."

Practice Exercise A

Let's do some practice using the Personal Subject Prefixes we have just learned. Fill in the blank spot with the correct Personal Subject Prefix from Table 3.1 that corresponds with the English word in capital letters inside the brackets.

1. _____-*najua.* (WE know.)
2. _____-*najua.* (THE PERSON knows.)
3. _____-*najua.* (THEY know.)
4. _____-*najua.* (I know.)
5. _____-*najua.* (YOU [pl. = plural] know.)
6. _____-*najua.* (YOU [sing. = singular] know.)
7. _____-*nasema.* (THE PERSON is speaking.)
8. _____-*nasema.* (I am speaking.)
9. _____-*nasema.* (WE are speaking)
10. _____-*nasema.* (YOU [sing.] are speaking.)

11. _____-*nasema.* (YOU [pl.] are speaking.)
12. _____-*nasema.* (THEY are speaking.)

Section B: Negation of Personal Subject Prefixes

So far, we have made some simple Swahili sentences in their affirmative form. Now we will look at making negative Personal Subject Prefixes. In other words, changing *"Ninasoma."* "I am studying." into "I am NOT studying."

TABLE 3.2
Negation of Personal Subject Prefixes Table

Si-	I (am not)	*Hatu-*	We (are not)
Hu-	You [singular] (are not)	*Ham-*	You [plural] (are not)
Ha-	He/She (is not)	*Hawa-*	They (are not)

In other words, *NI-* becomes *SI-*
TU- becomes *HATU-*
U- becomes *HU-*
M- becomes *HAM-*
A- becomes *HA-*
WA- becomes *HAWA-*

As you can see, most Personal Subject Prefixes are made negative by placing *H-* or *HA-* in front of them. The only exception is *NI-*, which instead becomes *SI-*.

Practice Exercise B

As in Practice Exercise A, please insert into the blank space the NEGATIVE Personal Subject Prefix that corresponds with the English word(s) in capital letters inside the brackets.

13. _____-*jui.* (WE do NOT know.)
14. _____-*jui.* (THE PERSON does NOT know.)
15. _____-*jui.* (THEY do NOT know.)

16. _____-*jui*. (I do NOT know.)
17. _____-*jui*. (YOU [pl.] do NOT know.)
18. _____-*jui*. (YOU [sing.] do NOT know.)
19. _____-*semi*. (THE PERSON is NOT speaking.)
20. _____-*semi*. (I am NOT speaking.)
21. _____-*semi*. (WE are NOT speaking.)
22. _____-*semi*. (YOU [sing.] are NOT speaking.)
23. _____-*semi*. (YOU [pl.] are NOT speaking.)
24. _____-*semi*. (THEY are NOT speaking.)

The disappearance of the tense marker (-*na*-) and the changing of the verb -*jua* to -*jui* and -*sema* to -*semi* will be explained in future Chapters. The most important concept to remember right now is the 6 Personal Subject Prefixes and how to make them negative.

Section C: Personal Pronouns and Their Negation

In addition to the Personal Subject Prefixes, Swahili also has 6 SEPERATE words that act as Personal Pronouns. These can be added to the sentence to reinforce and emphasise who is the subject of the sentence, the person "doing" the verb. For example, *Mimi* belongs with *ni*- from *ninasoma* which becomes *Mimi ninasoma* meaning literally, "I, I am studying." While this sort of construction would be unnecessary in English, it is perfectly acceptable in Swahili. Table 3.3 illustrates the 6 possible Personal Pronouns.

TABLE 3.3
Personal Pronouns Table

Mimi = I [goes with *Ni*-]	*Sisi* = We [goes with *Tu*-]
Wewe = You (singular) [goes with *U*-]	*Ninyi* = You (plural) [goes with *M*-]
Yeye = He/She [goes with *A*-]	*Wao* = They [goes with *Wa*-]

So, our previous sentences would now become:

Mimi ninasoma. – I, I am studying.
Sisi tunasoma. – WE, we are studying.
Wewe unasoma. – YOU, you are studying.
Ninyi mnasoma. – YOU (pl.), you (pl.) are studying.
Yeye anasoma. – THE PERSON, the person is studying.
Wao wanasoma. – THEY, they are studying.

These Personal Pronouns (*Mimi, Sisi* etc.) do NOT have to be used. *Ninasoma* is still a complete sentence and makes prefect sense to a Swahili speaker. However they are often used at the beginning of a sentence because it "sounds better" to Swahili ears, or for extra emphasis.

Practice Exercise C

Insert into the blank space the Personal Pronoun that corresponds with the English word in capital letters inside the brackets.

25. _____ *unajua.* (YOU[sing.], you[sing.] know.)
26. _____ *ninajua.* (I, I know.)
27. _____ *wanajua.* (THEY, they know.)
28. _____ *anajua.* (HE/SHE [THE PERSON], he/she knows.)
29. _____ *tunajua.* (WE, we know.)
30. _____ *mnajua.* (YOU [pl.], you [pl.] know.)
31. _____ *ninapika.* (I, I am cooking.)
32. _____ *wanapika.* (THEY, they are cooking.)
33. _____ *unapika.* (YOU [sing.], you[sing.] are cooking.)
34. _____ *anapika.* (THE PERSON, the person is cooking.)
35. _____ *mnapika.* (YOU [pl.], you [pl.] are cooking.)
36. _____ *tunapika.* (WE, we are cooking.)
37. _____ *wanauliza.* (THEY, they are asking.)
38. _____ *unauliza.* (YOU[sing.], you[sing.] are asking.)
39. _____ *ninauliza.* (I, I am asking.)
40. _____ *tunauliza.* (WE, we are asking.)
41. _____ *mnauliza.* (YOU [pl.], you [pl.] are asking.)
42. _____ *anauliza.* (HE/SHE, he/she is asking.)

Negative Sentences with Personal Pronouns

Whether a sentence is affirmative or negative, no changes are made to the Personal Pronouns. They can be added to the sentence to reinforce and emphasise who is the subject of the sentence, for example:

Mimi ninasoma. – I, I am studying.

The negation of which is simply:

Mimi sisomi. – I, I am not studying.

New Vocabulary

a-: "He/She" Personal Subject Prefix
ha-: "He/She" negative Personal Subject Prefix
ham-: "You (pl.)" negative Personal Subject Prefix
hatu-: "We" negative Personal Subject Prefix
hawa-: "They" negative Personal Subject Prefix
hu-: "You" negative Personal Subject Prefix
jua: the verb "know"
jui: the negative of the verb "know" in the present tense
m-: "You (pl.)" Personal Subject Prefix
mimi: "I" personal pronoun
-na-: an infix, present tense marker, placing the verb in the present
ni-: "I" Personal Subject Prefix
ninyi: "You all" personal pronoun
pika: the verb "cook"
sema: the verb "speak" or "say"
semi: the negative of the verb "speak" or "say" in the present tense
si-: "I" negative Personal Subject Prefix
sisi: "We" personal pronoun
soma: the verb "study" or "read"
somi: the negative of the verb "study" or "read" in the present tense
tu-: "We" Personal Subject Prefix
u-: "You" Personal Subject Prefix
uliza: the verb "ask"
wa-: "They" Personal Subject Prefix
wao: "They" personal pronoun

wewe: "You" personal pronoun
yeye: "He/She" (The person) personal pronoun

Key to Exercises

Answers to Practice Exercise A

1. *TUnajua.* (WE know.)
2. *Anajua.* (THE PERSON knows.)
3. *WAnajua.* (THEY know.)
4. *NInajua.* (I know.)
5. *Mnajua.* (YOU [pl.] know.)
6. *Unajua.* (YOU [sing.] know.)
7. *Anasema.* (THE PERSON is speaking.)
8. *NInasema.* (I am speaking.)
9. *TUnasema.* (WE are speaking.)
10. *Unasema.* (YOU [sing.] are speaking.)
11. *Mnasema.* (YOU [pl.] are speaking.)
12. *WAnasema.* (THEY are speaking.)

Answers to Practice Exercise B

13. *HATUjui.* (WE do NOT know.)
14. *HAjui.* (THE PERSON does NOT know.)
15. *HAWAjui.* (THEY do NOT know.)
16. *SIjui.* (I do NOT know.)
17. *HAMjui.* (YOU [pl.] do NOT know.)
18. *HUjui.* (YOU [sing.] do NOT know.)
19. *HAsemi.* (THE PERSON is NOT speaking.)
20. *SIsemi.* (I am NOT speaking.)
21. *HATUsemi.* (WE are NOT speaking.)
22. *HUsemi.* (YOU [sing.] are NOT speaking.)
23. *HAMsemi.* (YOU [pl.] are NOT speaking.)
24. *HAWAsemi.* (THEY are NOT speaking.)

Answers to Practice Exercise C

25. *Wewe unajua.* (YOU [sing.], you [sing.] know.)
26. *Mimi ninajua.* (I, I know.)
27. *Wao wanajua.* (THEY, they know.)

28. *Yeye anajua.* (HE/SHE [THE PERSON], he/she knows.)
29. *Sisi tunajua.* (WE, we know.)
30. *Ninyi mnajua.* (YOU [pl.], you [pl.] know.)
31. *Mimi ninapika.* (I, I am cooking.)
32. *Wao wanapika.* (THEY, they are cooking.)
33. *Wewe unapika.* (YOU [sing.], you [sing.] are cooking.)
34. *Yeye anapika.* (THE PERSON, the person is cooking.)
35. *Ninyi mnapika.* (YOU [pl.], you [pl.] are cooking.)
36. *Sisi tunapika.* (WE, we are cooking.)
37. *Wao wanauliza.* (THEY, they are asking.)
38. *Wewe unauliza.* (YOU [sing.], you [sing.] are asking.)
39. *Mimi ninauliza.* (I, I am asking.)
40. *Sisi tunauliza.* (WE, we are asking.)
41. *Ninyi mnauliza.* (YOU [pl.], you [pl.] are asking.)
42. *Yeye anauliza.* (HE/SHE, he/she is asking.)

Chapter 4

Swahili Greetings

The Swahili people of East and Central Africa take their greetings seriously. This chapter introduces the most commonly used Swahili greetings. It also discusses expressions that are associated with the Swahili culture.

Section A: Calling out *Hodi*

The Swahili people use the word *Hodi* (May I come in?) when they approach someone's house. When *Hodi* is used in this context, it is the equivalent of ringing the doorbell in the Western world. The visitor continues to call out *Hodi* until he/she gets a response from her/his host. The response to *Hodi* is:

Karibu. – Welcome.

If there is more than one person visiting, the response is:

Karibuni. – Welcome all.

The suffix *-ni* denotes the plural form of *Karibu*. But in other contexts, the suffix *-ni* can mean "in" or "at" (See Chapter 10). If permission to enter someone's premises is denied, the host responds by saying:

Hakuna hodi. – You may not come in.

The word *Hodi* is also used when one approaches a river or a well to request for permission to come nearer to the river or well. Due to the lack of potable water, many people in rural areas in East and Central Africa do laundry or bathe in rivers or use water from wells.

If one wants to pass through a crowd, one may also call out *Hodi*. In this case, the word *Hodi* means "May I pass?" The response to this kind of *Hodi* is also *Karibu*. Sometimes instead of using *Hodi* in asking for permission to pass through a crowd, the word *Samahani* which means "Excuse me" is used. The response to *Samahani* is *Bila Samahani* or "No excuse needed."

Greeting:
    Hodi? – May I come in?
Response:
    Karibu. – Welcome.
Greeting:
    Hodi? – May I come in?
Response:
    Hakuna hodi. – You may not come in.
Greeting:
    Samahani. – Excuse me.
Response:
    Bila samahani. – No excuse needed.

Practice Exercise A

Fill in the blanks.

1. When a person approaches somebody's house he/she calls out _____.
2. If the host wants to welcome the visitor, he/she responds by saying _____.
3. If more than one person is visiting, the host responds by saying _____.
4. If the host does not want the visitor to enter the house he/she responds by saying_____.
5. When someone wants to pass through a crowd, the person may say _____ or _____.

Section B: Greetings

After a visitor enters the premises, greetings are exchanged. The most common Swahili greetings are *Jambo* (affair, matter, thing) and *Habari* (the news).

Jambo Greetings

Before discussing *Jambo* Greetings, it is important to recall the negative forms of Personal Subject Prefixes as taught in Chapter 3.

If you want to greet one person, you must combine the Negative Personal Subject Prefix for the Second Person singular, which is *HU-* (You [sing.] not) with *Jambo* to form:

Hujambo? – You do not have a matter?

The other person responds by combining the Negative Personal Subject Prefix of the First Person Singular, which is *Si-* (I not) with *Jambo* to form:

Sijambo. – I am fine. (Literally means "I do not have a matter.")

If the person being greeted is a woman (*bibi*), one would greet her by saying:

Hujambo bibi? – How are you madam?

If the greeter is a man (*bwana*), the lady would respond by saying:

Sijambo bwana. – I am fine sir.

When greeting more than one person, the greeter would combine the Negative Personal Subject Prefix of Second Person Plural, which is *Ham-* (you [pl.] not) with *Jambo* to form:

Hamjambo? – You (pl.) do not have a matter?

The response to *Hamjambo?* is:

Hatujambo. – We are fine. (Literally means "We do not have a matter.")

Combining the Negative Personal Subject Prefix of First Person Plural *Hatu-* (we [pl.] not) with the word *Jambo* is how we arrive at the response *Hatujambo*.

If a teacher (*mwalimu*) is greeting his/her students (*wanafunzi*), he/she would say:

Hamjambo wanafunzi? – How are you students?

The students would respond by saying:

Hatujambo mwalimu. – We are fine teacher.

By following the examples above, the *Jambo* greeting can also be used to inquire about a person(s) who are not in the vicinity. When inquiring about a single person who is not present, the greeter would combine the Negative Personal Subject Prefix of Third Person Singular, which is *Ha-* (he/she not) with *Jambo* to form:

Hajambo? – How is he/she? (Literally means "He/She does not have a matter?")

The response would be:

Hajambo. – He/She is fine. (Literally means "He/She does not have a matter.")

If one is enquiring about Third Person Plural, one would ask:

Hawajambo? – How are they? (Literally means "They do not have a matter?")

The response would be:

Hawajambo. – They are fine. (Literally means "They do not have a matter.")

As you can see from the Third Person examples above, when a Third Person is inquired about, whether singular or plural, the answer stays in the Third Person.

The *Jambo* greeting is the only form of greeting which may be preceded by the word *Je* which is designed to alert the person or persons being greeted that a question is about to be asked (You will learn more about *Je* in Chapter 16 on Question Words). For example, instead of just saying:

Watoto hawajambo? – How are the children?

One would begin by saying:

Je, watoto hawajambo? – How are the children?

The response would still be:

Watoto hawajambo. – The children are fine.

Please note that the *jambo* greeting and the response to the *jambo* greeting allows for the word order to be reversed. Therefore, the example above can be posed as:

Hawajambo watoto? – How are the children?

The response would be:

Hawajambo watoto. – The children are fine.

Practice Exercise B

Translate into Swahili.

6. Dad and mom are fine.
7. The children are fine.
8. Teacher is fine.
9. The youth is fine.
10. Grandfather is fine.
11. Is the lady fine?
12. Are you (pl.) fine?
13. You (sing.) are fine.
14. We are fine.
15. How is Joanna?

Choose the correct response to the *Jambo* Greetings from the two responses found in the bracket.

16. *Peter and Anna (hajambo, hawajambo).*
17. *Walimu (hujambo, hawajambo).*
18. *Mkulima (hajambo, hatujambo).*
19. *Polisi (pl.) (sijambo, hawajambo).*
20. *Mtoto (hawajambo, hajambo).*
21. *Mfanyakazi (hujambo, hajambo).*
22. *Wapishi (hujambo, hawajambo).*
23. *Wanafunzi (hawajambo, hajambo).*
24. *Madaktari (hajambo, hawajambo).*
25. *Mimi na John (hawajambo, hatujambo).*

Section C: *Habari* Greetings

As stated previously, the word *Habari* means "The News." When greeting another person, the greeter says:

Habari? – What is your (sing.) news?

When greeting more than one person, the greeter says:

Habarini? – What is your (pl.) news?

As stated earlier in this Chapter, the suffix *-ni* denotes the plural form of *Habari.*

With this type of greeting one can ask about "The News" of anything after the initial greetings have been exchanged.

Examples:
Habari za leo? – The news of today?
Habari za watoto? – The news about the children?
Habari za asubuhi? – The news of the morning?
Habari za kazi? – The news about work?

The response to the *Habari* Greeting always contains the word *Nzuri* meaning "Good" or "Fine." If something is wrong, the respondent is expected to say *Nzuri* first and then provides an explanation afterwards about what is amiss by using the word *lakini* which means "but." Upon hearing the sad news, the greeter is expected to express sorrow by saying either *Pole sana* meaning "I feel very sorry for you (sing.)." or *Poleni sana* "I feel very sorry for you (pl.). " The response to *Pole* or *Poleni* is one of the following: *Nimeshapoa.* meaning "I have already recovered." *Tumeshapoa.* meaning "We have already recovered." *Ameshapoa.* meaning "He/She has already recovered." or *Wameshapoa.* meaning "They have already recovered." depending on who is being referred to. This response is followed by *Asante sana* meaning "Thank you very much." or *Asanteni* if more than one person is being thanked.

Example:

Kojo:

Hujambo Christine? – How are you Christine?

Christine:

Sijambo Kojo. Habari za kazi? – I am fine Kojo. What is the news about work?

Kojo:

Nzuri sana. Watoto hawajambo? – Very good. How are the children?

Christine:

Hawajambo, lakini Alexi ni mgonjwa. – They are fine, but Alex is sick.

Kojo:

Pole sana. – I am very sorry for you (sing.)/I am sorry to hear that.

Christine:

Ameshapoa. Asante sana. – He has already recovered. Thank you very much.

Practice Exercise C

Translate into English.

26. *Habari za masomo?*
27. *Habari za asubuhi?*
28. *Habari za babu?*
29. *Habari za safari?*
30. *Habari za mwalimu?*
31. *Habari za mkulima?*

32. *Habari za wasichana?*
33. *Habari za kazi?*
34. *Habari za madaktari?*
35. *Habari za Kanada?*

Section D: Other forms of Swahili Greetings

Apart from *Habari* and *Jambo* Greetings, there are other forms of greetings which the student of Swahili should be familiar with. These are: *Shikamoo, Salama, Hali gani, Mambo* and Arabic Greetings.

Shikamoo Greetings

This type of greeting is meant to show respect and is reserved for people such as parents, grandparents, uncles and aunts, older siblings, teachers as well as people in authority.

The word *Shikamoo* means "Hello" or "Accept my respect." During the era of the slave trade on the East African Coast and Zanzibar, slaves used to greet their masters using this form of greeting. The response to *Shikamoo* is *Marahaba* meaning "Hello" or "Delightful." When greeting more than one person one could say, *Shikamooni*. Again, the suffix -*ni* denotes the plural form. However, the response to *Shikamooni* is still *Marahaba*.

Salama Greetings

The word *Salama* means peaceful. One can greet another person by just saying:

Salama? – Is it peaceful?

The other person responds by saying:

Salama sana. – Very peaceful.

There is no plural form for this type of greeting. Thus, when greeting more than one person, one should still say:

Salama? – Is it peaceful?

Hali gani Greetings

The word *Hali* means "Condition" and *gani?* means "what?" When greeting someone, the greeter could say:

Hali gani? – What is your condition?

The response is:

Njema. – I am fine.

If more than one person is being greeted, the same greeting and response would apply.

Mambo Greetings

The word *Mambo* is the plural of *Jambo*, which means "things, matters, and affairs." This is a recent form of greeting used mostly by young people. The person using this form of greeting would just ask:

Mambo? – What's up?

The other responds by saying:

Poa. – Cool.

Arabic Greetings

It is common on the East African Coast for Swahili speakers to greet each other in Arabic. It is a sign of being educated if someone greets others using a foreign language! Swahili speakers commonly use the following Arabic greetings:

Salam alekum? – How are you? Literally means "Peace be upon you all."

The other person would respond by saying:

Alekum salam. – I am well. Literally means "Upon you all be peace."

Another form of Arabic greeting is *Sabalkheri*. One person would greet another by saying:

> *Sabalkheri.* – Good morning.

The response to *Sabalkheri* is the same, which is *Sabalkheri*.

Masalkheri is yet another form of Arabic greeting which means "Good Evening," and the response is *Masalkheri*.

Handshakes

A handshake constitutes part of Swahili greetings. When greeting each other, the Swahili people always shake hands. For reasons already explained (See Chapter 1), the right hand rather than the left is used for greetings, and foreigners are expected to do likewise. Greeting someone without offering or returning a handshake is considered disrespectful. Also, while relatives and acquaintances of both genders may shake hands while greeting each other, it is considered inappropriate behaviour for a man to shake a lady's hand especially if she is someone's wife unless she offers her hand to the person greeting her.

Kwa heri

After greetings are exchanged, the Swahili people, like others, say goodbye to each other at the end of the conversation by saying:

> *Kwa heri.* – Goodbye.

The other person responds by saying:

> *Kwa heri ya kuonana.* – Goodbye till we meet each other again.

An alternative response to *Kwa heri* is:

> *Karibu tena.* – Come again.

When saying "Goodbye" to more than one person, the phrase *Kwa herini* is used, again, the suffix *-ni* denoting the plural form.

Practice Exercise D

Provide appropriate responses to the following greetings.

36. *Salam alekum?*
37. *Salbakheri.*
38. *Masalkheri.*
39. *Shikamoo?*
40. *Kwa heri.*
41. *Salama?*
42. *U hali gani?*
43. *Mambo?*
44. *Pole.*
45. *Poleni.*

Indicate whether or not the following statements are True or False by writing the letters T or F at the end of the statement.

46. A handshake is part of Swahili greeting.
47. The right hand is always offered for a handshake.

New Vocabulary

alekum salam: I am well
ameshapoa: He/She has already recovered
asante: thank you
asubuhi: morning(s)
bibi: lady(ies), grandmother(s)
bila samahani: No excuse needed
daktari/ma-: doctor(s)
gani?: what?, which?, how?
habari: news, what news?
habarini?: What is your (pl.) news?
hakuna: there is nothing
hajambo?: how is he/she?
hamjambo?: you (pl.) are fine?
hatujambo: we are fine
hawajambo?: how are they?
hodi?: may I come in?
hujambo?: you (sing.) are fine?

jambo/mambo: thing(s), matter(s), affair(s)
je?: well, how about?
Kanada: Canada
karibu: near, nearby, nearly, close, welcome (sing.)
karibuni: welcome (pl.)
kazi: work, job(s)
kijana/vi-: youth(s), young person(s)
kuonana: meet each other
kwa heri: goodbye (sing.)
kwa herini: goodbye (pl.)
lakini: but, nevertheless
leo: today
marahaba: hello, delightful
masalkheri: good evening
mfanyakazi/wa-: worker(s)
mgonjwa/wa-: sick person(s), patient(s)
mkulima/wa-: farmer(s)
mpishi/wa-: cook(s), chef(s)
msichana/wa-: girl(s)
mtoto/wa-: child(ren)
mwanafunzi/wa-: student(s)
ni: is/are
-ni: denotes plural form
nimeshapoa: I have already recovered
njema: fine
nzuri: good
poa: cool, calm, peaceful, feel better
pole: sorry (sing.)
poleni: sorry (pl.)
polisi: police
sabalkheri: good morning
safari: journey(s), safari trip(s)
salam alekum: How are you?
salama: peaceful, safe
samahani: excuse me, sorry
sana: very
shikamoo: Hello (said to an elder)
shikamooni: Hello (pl.) (said to elders)
sijambo: I am fine

somo/ma-: academic subject(s)
tena: again, furthermore, besides
tumeshapoa: We have already recovered
wameshapoa: They have already recovered
ya: of
za: of

Key to Exercises

Answers to Practice Exercise A

1. *Hodi.*
2. *Karibu.*
3. *Karibuni.*
4. *Hakuna hodi.*
5. *Hodi* or *Samahani.*

Answers to Practice Exercise B

6. *Baba na mama hawajambo.*
7. *Watoto hawajambo.*
8. *Mwalimu hajambo.*
9. *Kijana hajambo.*
10. *Babu hajambo.*
11. *Je, bibi hajambo?*
12. *Hamjambo?*
13. *Hujambo.*
14. *Hatujambo.*
15. *Je, Joanna hajambo?*
16. *Hawajambo.*
17. *Hawajambo.*
18. *Hajambo.*
19. *Hawajambo.*
20. *Hajambo.*
21. *Hajambo.*
22. *Hawajambo.*
23. *Hawajambo.*
24. *Hawajambo.*
25. *Hatujambo.*

Answers to Practice Exercise C

26. What is the news about studying?
27. What is the morning's news?
28. What is the news about grandfather?
29. What is the news about the journey?
30. What is the news about the teacher?
31. What is the news about the farmer?
32. What is the news about the girls?
33. What is the news about work?
34. What is the news about the doctors?
35. What is the news about Canada?

Answers to Practice Exercise D

36. *Aleykum salam.*
37. *Salbakheri.*
38. *Masalkheri.*
39. *Marahaba.*
40. *Kwa heri ya kuonana/Karibu tena.*
41. *Salama.*
42. *Njema.*
43. *Poa.*
44. *Nimeshapoa* or *Ameshapoa.*
45. *Tumeshapoa* or *Wameshapoa.*
46. True.
47. True.

Chapter 5

Present and Future Tenses and Their Negations

In this chapter, we will learn how to make simple sentences using verbs in the present tense and future tense. In Swahili, a particular tense marker denotes each tense. The present tense marker is *-na-* and the future tense marker is *-ta-*. The hyphens (-) before and after the tense marker indicate that something has to be added before and after the tense marker. As mentioned in Chapter 3, the Personal Subject Prefix comes before the first hyphen and the verb comes after the second hyphen (STV rule). We will now learn how simple sentences using tense markers are constructed.

Section A: The Present Tense

The present tense is used to show an action that is in progress at the present moment or an action that takes place on a daily basis. As mentioned above, the present tense is expressed by the tense marker *-na-*. Sentences using present tense markers are constructed in the following manner.

Personal Subject Prefix + Present Tense Marker + Verb

There are six Personal Subject Prefixes in Swahili. Please refer to Chapter 3 for more details. The present tense marker is always *-na-*. There are many verbs in Swahili as you may have seen in previous chapters, and you will see many more in this chapter.

If we want to make a simple sentence such as "I am playing," we do it as follows. We take the Personal Subject Prefix for "I" which is *ni-*. We then attach this to the present tense marker *-na-* and we get *nina-*. Finally, we attach this to the verb "play" which is *cheza* and we get *Ninacheza* which means "I am playing."

Using the same method of construction with other Personal Subject Prefixes and Bantu verbs (see below for more information on different categories of verbs), we get:

U-na-soma. – You (sing.) are reading.
A-na- andika. – He/She is writing.
Tu-na-kimbia. – We are running.
M-na-cheka. – You (pl.) are laughing.
Wa-na-nunua. – They are buying.

The important thing to notice here is that in all these sentences, *-na-* is the present tense marker and it does not change.

We will now briefly mention verbs in Swahili. Swahili verbs can be divided into three categories: verbs of Bantu origin, Arabic verbs and Monosyllabic verbs. Monosyllabic verbs are Bantu verbs; however, since they have special rules, they will be treated as a separate category. It is important to remember these categories of verbs as they will have their own rules governing the construction of affirmative and negative sentences. In the present tense, verbs of Bantu origin and Arabic verbs follow the same rules in affirmative sentences. The verbs discussed so far in Section A are all verbs of Bantu origin. Below are some examples of verbs of Arabic origin.

Ni-na-kubali. – I am accepting.
U-na-fikiri. – You (sing.) are thinking.
A-na-rudi. – He/She is returning.

Please note the way to distinguish Bantu verbs from Arabic verbs is by looking at the last vowel of the verb. The last vowel of a Bantu verb is always the letter *a* while Arabic verbs never end with the letter *a* and instead end with either *e*, *i* or *u*.

Monosyllabic verbs are treated slightly differently. Monosyllabic verbs have a *ku-* infinitive marker prefixed to the verb and this is retained in affirmative present tense sentences for all Monosyllabic verbs except *pa*.

The most common Monosyllabic verbs are listed below:

la (eat)
pa (give)
wa (become)
nywa (drink)
nya (rain)
chwa (setting of the sun)
ja (come)
fa (die, perish)
cha (rising of the sun)

Sentences using present tense markers with Monosyllabic verbs are constructed as follows:

Ni-na-kula. – I am eating.
U-na-kunywa. – You (sing.) are drinking.
A-na-kuja. – He/She is coming.

Practice Exercise A

Translate the following sentences into English.

1. *Mnasoma.*
2. *Wanaandika.*
3. *Anapika.*
4. *Tunaruka.*
5. *Anapenda chakula.*
6. *Unaishi Kanada.*
7. *Watu wanakuja.*
8. *Mgonjwa anakunywa dawa.*
9. *Mama anapika.*
10. *Babu anafikiri.*

Section B: Present Tense Negation

When negating a simple present tense sentence, we need to negate the Personal Subject Prefix, the present tense marker and the verb. In present tense sentences, the Personal Subject Prefix is always negated by substituting it with a Negative Personal Subject Prefix (see Chapter 3), and the present tense marker is always negated by deleting it; however each of the three categories of verbs is negated differently. This is illustrated below:

Negative Personal Subject Prefix + ~~Present Tense Marker~~ + Negated Verb

Negated Bantu Verbs

With verbs of Bantu origin, negation of the verb is done by changing the last vowel of the verb, which is *a*, to the letter *i*. If we want to negate a present tense sentence containing a Bantu verb, such as, *Ninacheza* "I am playing," we do it as follows. We substitute the Personal Subject Prefix for "I" which is *ni-* with the Negative Personal Subject Prefix which is *si-*. We then delete the present tense marker *-na-*. Since the present tense marker is deleted, the Negative Personal Subject Prefix is directly attached to the negated verb. As mentioned above, since the last vowel of the Bantu verb changes to the letter *i*, the verb "play" which is *cheza* would become *-chezi*. The complete negation of *Ninacheza* "I am playing" would be *Sichezi* "I am not playing."

Here are more examples:

> *Ninapika.* – I am cooking.
> *Sipiki.* – I am not cooking.
> *Unasoma.* – You (sing.) are reading.
> *Husomi.* – You (sing.) are not reading.

Negated Arabic Verbs

The negation of present tense sentences containing Arabic verbs is done in the same way as sentences containing verbs of Bantu origin, except that Arabic verbs retain their last vowel in their negated verb i.e. the Arabic verb remains unchanged.

Examples:

> *Ninarudi.* – I am returning.
> *Sirudi.* – I am not returning.
> *Unafahamu.* – You (sing.) understand.
> *Hufahamu.* – You (sing.) do not understand.

Negated Monosyllabic Verbs

The negation of present tense sentences containing Monosyllabic verbs is also done in the same way as sentences containing regular Bantu verbs, except that Monosyllabic verbs drop their infinitive *ku-* in their negated form. Also note that the last vowel of Monosyllabic verbs change to *i* as seen in other negated Bantu verbs.

Examples:

> *Ninakula.* – I am eating.
> *Sili.* – I am not eating.
> *Unakunywa.* – You (sing.) are drinking.
> *Hunywi.* – You (sing.) are not drinking.

Practice Exercise B

Translate the following into English.

11. *Hatufahamu.*
12. *Hawanywi.*
13. *Hakubali kwenda Kenya.*
14. *Hawali samaki.*
15. *Daktari haji.*
16. *Huandiki.*
17. *Mama harudi leo.*
18. *Mtoto hafikiri.*
19. *Msichana hali samaki.*
20. *Sisomi katika Chuo Kikuu cha Toronto.*

Section C: The Future Tense

The future tense is used to show an action that will take place in the future. As mentioned previously, the future tense is expressed by the tense marker *-ta-*. Sentences using future tense markers are constructed in the following manner.

Personal Subject Prefix + Future Tense Marker + Verb

If we want to make a simple sentence such as "I will play," we do it as follows. We take the Personal Subject Prefix for "I" which is *ni-*. We then attach this to the future tense marker *-ta-* and we get *nita-*. Finally, we attach this to the verb "play" which is *cheza* and we get *Nitacheza* which means "I will play."

Using the same method of construction with other Personal Subject Prefixes and Bantu verbs, we get:

U-ta-soma. – You (sing.) will read.
A-ta-andika. – He/She will write.
Tu-ta-kimbia. – We will run.
M-ta-cheka. – You (pl.) will laugh.
Wa-ta-nunua. – They will buy.

The important thing to notice here is that in all these sentences, *-ta-* is the future tense marker and it does not change.

In the future tense, verbs of Bantu origin and Arabic verbs follow the same rules in affirmative sentences. Below are some examples of verbs of Arabic origin.

Ni-ta-kubali. – I will accept.
U-ta-fikiri. – You (sing.) will think.
A-ta-rudi. – He/She will return.

Monosyllabic verbs retain their infinitive marker *ku-* in sentences using future tense markers.

Ni-ta-kula. – I will eat.
U-ta-kunywa. – You (sing.) will drink.
A-ta-kuja. – He/She will come.

Practice Exercise C

Translate the following sentences into English.

21. *Mtasoma barua.*
22. *Wataandika.*
23. *Atapika.*
24. *Tutaruka katika ndege.*
25. *Atapenda zawadi.*
26. *Utaishi Kanada.*

27. *Watu watakuja katika duka.*
28. *Mgonjwa atakufa.*
29. *Kaka atanunua nguo.*
30. *Mama atapika samaki.*

Section D: Future Tense Negation

It is very simple to negate future tense sentences. The only change that occurs is that the Personal Subject Prefix is substituted with Negative Personal Subject Prefix. The future tense marker and each of the three categories of verbs remain the same. This is illustrated below:

Negative Personal Subject Prefix + Future Tense Marker + Verb

If we want to negate a future tense sentence containing a Bantu verb, such as, *Nitacheza* "I will play," we do it as follows. We substitute the Personal Subject Prefix for "I" which is *ni-* with the Negative Personal Subject Prefix which is *si-*. We then attach it to the future tense marker -*ta-* to get *sita-*. We finally attach this to the verb "play" which is *cheza* and the complete negation of *Nitacheza* "I will play" would be *Sitacheza* "I will not play."

Here are more examples of negation of future tense sentences containing verbs of Bantu origin.

> *Nitapika.* – I will cook.
> *Sitapika.* – I will not cook.
> *Utasoma.* – You (sing.) will read.
> *Hutasoma.* – You (sing.) will not read.

Here are examples of negation of future tense sentences containing verbs of Arabic origin.

> *Watarudi.* – They will return.
> *Hawatarudi.* – They will not return.
> *Mtafahamu.* – You (pl.) will understand.
> *Hamtafahamu.* – You (pl.) will not understand.

Here are examples of negation of future tense sentences containing Mono-syllabic verbs. Please note that the infinitive *ku-* is retained.

> *Nitakula.* – I will eat.
> *Sitakula.* – I will not eat.
> *Utakunywa.* – You (sing.) will drink.
> *Hutakunywa.* – You (sing.) will not drink.

Practice Exercise D

Translate the following into English.

31. *Hatutafahamu.*
32. *Watoto hawatakunywa.*
33. *Hatakubali.*
34. *Hawatakufa.*
35. *Daktari hatakuja.*
36. *Hutaenda katika soko.*
37. *Mama hatarudi leo.*
38. *Mtoto hatafikiri.*
39. *Thomas hatakula samaki.*
40. *Sitasoma leo.*

New Vocabulary

andika: write
cha: rising of the sun
chakula/vya-: food(s)
cheka: laugh
cheza: play
chuo/vy- kikuu/vi-: university(ies)
chwa: setting of the sun
duka/ma-: shop(s)
enda: go, move
fa: die
fikiri: think
ishi: live
ja: come
katika: in, into, inside, at
kimbia: run
kubali: accept, agree

la: eat
mtu/wa-: person(s)
nunua: buy
nya: rain
nywa: drink
pa: give
panda: love, like
rudi: return, come back
ruka: jump, fly
samaki: fish(es)
soko/ma-: market(s)
wa: be, exist

Key to Exercises

Answers to Practice Exercise A

1. You (pl.) are reading.
2. They are writing.
3. He/She is cooking.
4. We are flying.
5. He/She loves food.
6. You (sing.) are living in Canada.
7. The people are coming.
8. The patient is drinking medicine.
9. Mother is cooking.
10. Grandfather is thinking.

Answers to Practice Exercise B

11. We don't understand.
12. They are not drinking.
13. He/She is not agreeing to go to Kenya.
14. They are not eating fish.
15. The doctor is not coming.
16. You (sing.) are not writing.
17. Mother is not returning today.
18. The child is not thinking.
19. The girl is not eating fish.
20. I am not studying at the University of Toronto.

Answers to Practice Exercise C

21. You (pl.) will read a letter.
22. They will write.
23. He/She will cook.
24. We will fly in an airplane.
25. He/She will love the gift(s).
26. You (sing.) will live in Canada.
27. People will come in the shop.
28. The patient will die.
29. Brother will buy clothes.
30. Mother will cook fish.

Answers to Practice Exercise D

31. We will not understand.
32. The children will not drink.
33. He/She will not agree.
34. They will not die.
35. The doctor will not come.
36. You (sing.) will not go inside the market.
37. Mother will not return today.
38. The child will not think.
39. Thomas will not eat fish.
40. I will not study today.

Chapter 6

Simple Past and Past Perfect Tenses and Their Negations

In this chapter, we will learn how to make simple sentences using verbs in the simple past tense and past perfect tense. In Swahili, a particular tense marker denotes each tense. The simple past tense marker is *-li-* and the past perfect tense marker is *-me-*. The hyphens (-) before and after the tense marker indicate that something has to be added before and after the tense marker. As mentioned in Chapter 3, the Personal Subject Prefix comes before the first hyphen and the verb comes after the second hyphen (STV rule). We will now learn how simple sentences using tense markers are constructed.

Section A: The Simple Past Tense

The simple past tense is used to show an action that took place in the past. As mentioned previously, the simple past tense is expressed by the tense marker *-li-*. Sentences using simple past tense markers are constructed in the following manner.

Personal Subject Prefix + Simple Past Tense Marker + Verb

If we want to make a simple sentence such as "I played," we do it as follows. We take the Personal Subject Prefix for "I" which is *ni-*. We then attach this to the simple past tense marker *-li-* and we get *nili-*. Finally, we attach this to the verb "play" which is *cheza* and we get *Nilicheza* which means "I played."

Using the same method of construction with other Personal Subject Prefixes and Bantu verbs, we get:

U-li-soma. – You (sing.) read.
A-li-andika. – He/She wrote.
Tu-li-kimbia. – We ran.
M-li-cheka. – You (pl.) laughed.
Wa-li-nunua. – They bought.

The important thing to notice here is that in all these sentences, *-li-* is the simple past tense marker and it does not change.

In the simple past tense, verbs of Bantu origin and Arabic verbs follow the same rules in affirmative sentences. Below are some examples of verbs of Arabic origin.

Ni-li-kubali. – I accepted.
U-li-fikiri. – You (sing.) thought.
A-li-rudi. – He/She returned.

Monosyllabic verbs retain their infinitive marker *ku-* in sentences using simple past tense markers.

Ni-li-kula. – I ate.
U-li-kunywa. – You (sing.) drank.
A-li-kuja. – He/She came.

Practice Exercise A

Translate the following sentences into English.

1. *Mlisoma barua.*
2. *Walipanda mazao.*
3. *Alisikitika sana.*
4. *Tuliruka.*
5. *Alipenda zawadi.*
6. *Uliishi Ujerumani.*
7. *Watu walikuja katika duka.*
8. *Mgonjwa alipona.*
9. *Alinunua baiskeli.*
10. *Mama alipika samaki.*

Section B: Simple Past Tense Negation

It is also fairly easy to negate simple past tense sentences. In simple past tense sentences, the Personal Subject Prefix is always negated by substituting it with a Negative Personal Subject Prefix. The simple past tense marker is always negated by substituting it with the negative simple past tense marker which is *-ku-*. Bantu and Arabic verbs remain unchanged in their negated form; however, the infinitive marker *ku-* is dropped in negated Monosyllabic verbs. This is illustrated below:

Negative Personal Subject Prefix +
Negated Simple Past Tense Marker + Verb

If we want to negate a simple past tense sentence containing a Bantu verb, such as, *Nilicheza* "I played," we do it as follows. We substitute the Personal Subject Prefix for "I" which is *ni-* with the Negative Personal Subject Prefix which is *si-*. We then attach it to the negative simple past tense marker *-ku-* to get *siku-*. We finally attach this to the verb "play" which is *cheza* and the complete negation of *Nilicheza* "I played" would be *Sikucheza* "I did not play."

Here are more examples of negation of simple past tense sentences containing verbs of Bantu origin.

Nilipika. – I cooked.
Sikupika. – I did not cook.
Ulisoma. – You (sing.) read.
Hukusoma. – You (sing.) did not read.

Here are examples of negation of simple past tense sentences containing verbs of Arabic origin.

Walikubali. – They accepted.
Hawakukubali. – They did not accept.
Mlifahamu. – You (pl.) understood.
Hamkufahamu. – You (pl.) did not understand.

Here are examples of negation of simple past tense sentences containing Monosyllabic verbs. Please note that the infinitive *ku-* is deleted, the *-ku-*

that appears in the sentences below is the negative simple past tense marker.

> *Nilikula.* – I ate.
> *Sikula.* – I did not eat
> *Ulikunywa.* – You (sing.) drank.
> *Hukunywa.* – You (sing.) did not drink.

Practice Exercise B

Translate the following into English.

11. *Hatukufahamu.*
12. *Watoto hawakunywa.*
13. *Hakukubali.*
14. *Hawakula.*
15. *Daktari hakuja.*
16. *Hukununua.*
17. *Mama hakurudi leo.*
18. *Mtoto hakufikiri.*
19. *Thomas hakula nyama.*
20. *Sikusoma katika Chuo Kikuu cha Washington.*

Section C: The Past Perfect Tense

The past perfect tense is used to show an action that took place in the past and the resulting state of that action still exists, or a simple present action which is complete.

The past perfect tense is expressed by the tense marker *-me-*. Sentences using past perfect tense markers are constructed in the following manner.

Personal Subject Prefix + Past Perfect Tense Marker + Verb

If we want to make a simple sentence such as "I had played," we do it as follows. We take the Personal Subject Prefix for "I" which is *ni-*. We then attach this to the past perfect tense marker *-me-* and we get *nime-*. Finally, we attach this to the verb "play" which is *cheza* and we get *Nimecheza* which means "I have played."

Using the same method of construction with other Personal Subject Prefixes and Bantu verbs, we get:

U-me-soma. – You (sing.) have read.
A-me-fariki. – He/She is dead.
Tu-me-kimbia. – We have run.
M-me-cheka. – You (pl.) have laughed.
Wa-me-nunua. – They have bought.

The important thing to notice here is that in all these sentences, *-me-* is the past perfect tense marker and it does not change.

In the past perfect tense, verbs of Bantu origin and Arabic verbs follow the same rules in affirmative sentences. Below are some examples of verbs of Arabic origin.

Ni-me-kubali. – I have accepted.
U-me-fikiri. – You (sing.) have thought.
A-me-rudi. – He/She has returned.

Monosyllabic verbs retain their infinitive marker *ku-* in sentences using past perfect tense markers.

Ni-me-kula. – I have eaten.
U-me-kunywa. – You (sing.) have drunk.
A-me-kuja. – He/She has come.

Practice Exercise C

Translate the following sentences into English.

21. *Wahariri wamemaliza kazi.*
22. *Wamepanda nyanya.*
23. *Amepoza chai.*
24. *Mwalimu amechanganya kemikali.*
25. *Amelala.*
26. *Umeishi Marekani.*
27. *Watu wamekuja katika kiwanja cha michezo.*
28. *Mgonjwa amekunywa dawa.*
29. *Amenunua kompyuta.*
30. *Bibi amepika mayai.*

Section D: Past Perfect Tense Negation

There are two different ways of negating past perfect tense sentences. In past perfect tense sentences, the Personal Subject Prefix is always negated by substituting it with a Negative Personal Subject Prefix. The past perfect tense marker is negated by substituting it with either the negative past perfect tense marker which is *-ja-* if the action could still take place, or the negative simple past tense marker *-ku-* if there is no possibility that the action could still take place. Bantu and Arabic verbs remain unchanged in their negated form; however, the infinitive marker *ku-* is dropped in negated Monosyllabic verbs.

Negative Personal Subject Prefix + Negated Past Perfect Tense Marker/Negated Simple Past Tense Marker + Verb

If we want to negate a past perfect tense sentence containing a Bantu verb, such as, *Nimecheza* "I have played," we do it as follows. We substitute the Personal Subject Prefix for "I" which is *ni-* with the Negative Personal Subject Prefix which is *si-*. We then attach either the negative past perfect tense marker *-ja-* to get *sija-* OR the negative simple past tense marker *-ku-* to get *siku-* . We finally attach this to the verb "play" which is *cheza* and the complete negation of *Nimecheza* "I have played" would be *Sijacheza* "I have not played yet "OR *Sikucheza* "I did not play."

Here are more examples of negation of past perfect tense sentences containing verbs of Bantu origin.

> *Nimepika.* – I have cooked.
> *Sijapika.* – I have not yet cooked OR
> *Sikupika.* – I did not cook.
> *Umesoma.* – You (sing.) have read.
> *Hujasoma.* – You (sing.) have not yet read OR
> *Hukusoma.* – You (sing.) did not read.

Here are examples of negation of past perfect tense sentences containing verbs of Arabic origin.

Wamekubali. – They have accepted.
Hawajakubali. – They have not yet accepted OR
Hawakukubali. – They did not accept.
Mmefahamu. – You (pl.) have understood.
Hamjafahamu. – You (pl.) have not yet understood OR
Hamkufahamu. – You (pl.) did not understand.

Here are examples of negation of past perfect tense sentences containing Monosyllabic verbs. Please note that the infinitive *ku-* is deleted.

Nimekula. – I have eaten.
Sijala. – I have not yet eaten OR
Sikula. – I did not eat.
Umekunywa. – You (sing.) have drunk.
Hujanywa. – You (sing.) have not yet drunk OR
Hukunywa. – You (sing.) did not drink.

Practice Exercise D

Translate the following into English.

31. *Hawajafahamu.*
32. *Watoto hawakula.*
33. *Hajakubali.*
34. *Hakulima.*
35. *Balozi hajaja.*
36. *Hujamaliza mtihani.*
37. *Mama hajapika.*
38. *Rafiki hajafika.*
39. *Tatu hakula kuku.*
40. *Sijasoma katika Chuo Kikuu cha Toronto.*

New Vocabulary

baiskeli: bicycle(s)
balozi/ma-: ambassador(s)
chai: tea
changanya: mix
fariki: die
fika: arrive

kemikali: chemical(s)
kiwanja/vi- cha/vya michezo: stadium(s)
kompyuta: computer(s)
kuku: chicken(s)
lima: cultivate
maliza: complete, finish
Marekani: The United States of America
mhariri/wa-: editor(s)
mtihani/mi-: examination(s)
nyama: meat
nyanya: tomato(es), grandmother(s)
panda: climb, plant
pona: cure, heal
poza: cool off
sikitika: regret
Ujerumani: Germany
zao/ma-: crop(s)

Key to Exercises

Answers to Practice Exercise A

1. You (pl.) read a letter.
2. They planted crops.
3. He/She regretted very much.
4. We flew.
5. He/She loved the gift(s).
6. You (sing.) lived in Germany.
7. People came in the shop.
8. The patient was cured.
9. He/She bought bicycle(s).
10. Mother cooked fish.

Answers to Practice Exercise B

11. We did not understand.
12. The children did not drink.
13. He/She did not agree.
14. They did not eat.
15. The doctor did not come.

16. You (sing.) did not buy.
17. Mother did not return today.
18. The child did not think.
19. Thomas did not eat meat.
20. I did not study at University of Washington.

Answers to Practice Exercise C

21. The editors have completed the work.
22. They have planted tomatoes.
23. He/She has cooled off the tea.
24. The teacher has mixed the chemical(s).
25. He/She has slept.
26. You (sing.) have lived in America.
27. People have come to the stadium.
28. The patient has drunk (taken) the medicine.
29. He/She has bought a computer(s).
30. Grandmother has cooked eggs.

Answers to Practice Exercise D

31. They have not yet understood.
32. The children did not eat.
33. He/She has not yet agreed.
34. He/She did not cultivate.
35. The ambassador has not yet come.
36. You (sing.) have not yet completed the exam.
37. Mother has not yet cooked.
38. The friend has not yet arrived.
39. Tatu did not eat chicken.
40. I have not yet studied at University of Toronto.

Chapter 7

The Swahili Noun Class System: M-/WA- and M-/MI-

Most languages in the world, with English being the main exception, classify nouns into different groups known as noun classes. Historically, the division of nouns into noun classes in Swahili was based on how the East African people perceived the world. For instance, they grouped human beings into one class, animals into another class, sharp and elongated objects into another class and so on. As time passed, the East African region came into increasing contact with the outside world initially due to trade expansion and later, colonialism. This contact caused the Swahili language to borrow new words from other languages such as English, German, Portuguese, Arabic, Hindi and so forth. The increase in Swahili vocabulary brought about the need to revise and expand the noun classes. Currently, nouns are classified into 8 noun classes. Listed below are the names of the noun classes and a brief description of what they contain. We will learn more details about each noun class in the chapters to follow.

1. M-/WA- class contains human beings.
2. M-/MI- class contains trees, plants, etc.
3. JI-/MA- class contains fruits, parts of plants, etc. It also contains mass nouns and collectives.
4. KI-/VI- class contains objects useful to humans and artifacts, etc.
5. N- class contains words borrowed from other languages, names of animals and relationship nouns, etc.

6. U- class contains household objects, names of countries, abstract nouns and qualities.
7. PA- class contains locatives.
8. KU- class contains verbal nouns.

Section A: The M-/WA- Class

This is one of the few noun classes in Swahili in which most nouns refer to one particular type of thing. In this noun class, most nouns refer to human beings. It is important to remember that **not** all nouns referring to human beings are contained in this class. We will come across some nouns referring to human beings while studying the JI-/MA-, KI-/VI- and N- classes in upcoming chapters.

Most nouns in the M-/WA- class are denoted by the agreement prefix *m-* in the singular form, which changes to *wa-* in the plural form. Listed below are some examples:

mtu – person
watu – people
mganga – doctor, shaman
waganga – doctors, shamans
mgeni – visitor, guest
wageni – visitors, guests
mgonjwa – sick person
wagonjwa – sick people
mpishi – chef
wapishi – chefs
mtoto – child
watoto – children
mtumishi – servant
watumishi – servants
mfanyakazi – worker
wafanyakazi – workers
mzee – old person
wazee – old people
Mzee is also used as a term of respect for someone older than
     you are.

There are two exceptional nouns in the M-/WA- class that do not refer to humans. These nouns refer to animals and insects in a general sense. They are:

mdudu – insect
wadudu – insects
mnyama – animal
wanyama – animals

You will see in an upcoming chapter that the specific names of animals and insects are found in the N- class.

The M-/WA- class also contains many nouns that are denoted by the agreement prefix *mw-* in the singular form. These nouns also take the agreement prefix *wa-* in the plural form. With these nouns, when the agreement prefix *mw-* in the singular form is removed, we remain with a stem noun that begins with a vowel. For example, in a noun such as *mw-alimu* (teacher), when the agreement prefix *mw-* is removed, we remain with the stem noun *-alimu* (meaning knowledge). When such a noun is pluralized, the plural contains two vowels occurring together i.e *mw-alimu* (teacher) changes to become *wa-alimu* (teachers) in the plural form. Since it is difficult to pronounce words that have vowels adjacent to each other, the Swahili language has developed the following merger rules:

a + a becomes "a"
a + e becomes "e"
a + i becomes "e"

Hence, when *mw-alimu* changes into plural, we would expect it to become *wa-alimu* but based on the above rule, it becomes *walimu* (since a + a becomes a).

Another example would be a noun such as *mw-izi* (thief). When *mw-izi* changes into plural, we would expect it to become *wa-izi*, but based on the rule above, it becomes *wezi* (since a + i becomes e).Here are more examples of nouns that begin with the agreement prefix *mw-* in the singular form and follow the merger rule.

mwanafunzi – student
wanafunzi – students
mwana – child

wana – children
mwenyeji – inhabitant
wenyeji – inhabitants

Other words that need a special mention are compound nouns. Here are some common compound nouns:

mwanamke – woman
wanawake – women
mwanaume – man
wanaume – men
mwanasiasa – politician
wanasiasa – politicians

Since a compound noun is made of two nouns, when changing the compound noun into its plural form, we have to pluralize both of its two component nouns individually. When *mwanamke* is changed into plural, we have to pluralize both of its 2 component nouns, *mwana* and *mke*. When *mw-ana* changes into plural, we would expect it to become *wa-ana*, but based on the rules that we have studied, it becomes *wana* (since a + a becomes a). *Mke* is a regular noun whose prefix begins with *m-* in the singular form and changes to *wa-* in the plural form to become *wake*. Hence, *mwanamke* changes to become *wanawake* in the plural form.

Please note that when the word *mwana* is used in compounds nouns, it does not retain its original meaning of "a child." Also note that the plural form of the noun *siasa* remains unchanged from its singular form because it belongs to the N- Class. You will learn more about the N- Class in Chapter 9.

Nationalities and some occupations also fall under the M-/WA- noun class. However, they do not follow the merger rules explained above. For example, the noun *Mw-amerika* (American) in the plural becomes *Wa-amerika* (Americans). As you can see, the adjacent vowels remain together and are not merged into one vowel. Here are more examples of nationalities:

Mwafrika – African
Waafrika – Africans
Mwarabu – Arab
Waarabu – Arabs

Mfaransa – French person
Wafaransa – French people
Mholanzi – Dutch person
Waholanzi – Dutch people
Mhindi – Indian
Wahindi – Indians
Mchina – Chinese person
Wachina – Chinese people

Here are some examples of occupations:

mkulima – farmer
wakulima – farmers
mchoraji – artist
wachoraji – artists
mwimbaji – singer
waimbaji – singers

Practice Exercise A

Translate the following into their plural in Swahili.

1. student
2. teacher
3. girl
4. patient
5. guest
6. hunter
7. insect
8. boy
9. worker
10. chef

Practice Exercise B

Change the following plurals into singulars.

11. *wanyama*
12. *wenyeji*
13. *wakulima*

14. *wazee*
15. *wanawake*

Practice Exercise C

Translate the following nationalities and occupations into Swahili.
16. Italians
17. Russians
18. Iranian
19. Spanish people
20. Nigerian
21. worker
22. players
23. farmers
24. chef
25. writers

Section B: The M-/MI- Class

Unlike the M-/WA- class, the nouns in the M-/MI- class do not refer to one particular type of thing. This noun class contains mostly trees and plants. It also contains natural phenomena, some parts of the body and many other nouns which do not appear to have much in common with other nouns in this class.

Most nouns in the M-/MI- class are denoted by the agreement prefix *m-* in the singular form, which changes to *mi-* in the plural form. Listed below are some examples:

mti – tree
miti – trees
mmea – plant
mimea – plants
mbuyu – Baobab tree
mibuyu – Baobab trees
mkono – hand
mikono – hands
mguu – leg
miguu – legs

mchezo – game
michezo – games
mtihani – examination
mitihani – examinations
mto – pillow, river
mito – pillows, rivers
moto – a fire
mioto – fires
moyo – heart
mioyo – hearts

The M-/MI- class also contains many nouns, which are denoted by the agreement prefix *mw-* in the singular form. These nouns also take the agreement prefix *mi-* in the plural form. Listed below are some examples:

mwaka – year
miaka – years
mwezi – month, moon
miezi – months, moons
mwili – body (of living thing)
miili – bodies (of living things)
mwisho – conclusion
miisho – conclusions
mwembe – mango tree
miembe – mango trees
mwiba – thorn
miiba – thorns

Please observe that there is no difference in appearance between the singular nouns that begin with the agreement prefix *mw-* in the singular form in M-/WA- class and M-/MI- class. Therefore, in order to determine which agreement prefix the noun must take in the plural form, the meaning must be known. If the meaning is a descriptive of a human being, or the word for animal (*mnyama*) or insect (*mdudu*) the plural will begin with *wa-,* otherwise, the plural will begin with *mi-*.

Practice Exercise D

Change the following singulars into plurals.

26. *mkono*
27. *mguu*
28. *mlima*
29. *mji*
30. *mwaka*
31. *mwili*
32. *mwiba*
33. *moyo*
34. *mkate*
35. *mzigo*

Practice Exercise E

Translate the following into English.

36. *mifereji*
37. *misitu*
38. *miezi*
39. *milango*
40. *mitaa*

New Vocabulary

mbuyu/mi-: baobab tree(s)
mchezaji/wa-: actor(s), dancer(s), player(s), athlete(s)
mchezo/mi-: game(s), play(s)
Mchina/wa-: Chinese person(s)
mchoraji/wa-: artist(s)
mdudu/wa-: insect(s)
Mfaransa/wa-: French person(s)
mfereji/mi-: ditch(es)
mganga/wa-: doctor(s), shaman(s)
mgeni/wa-: visitor(s), guest(s)
mguu/mi-: leg(s), by foot
Mhindi/wa-: Indian(s)
Mhispania/wa-: Hispanic(s)

Mholanzi/wa-: Dutch person(s)
mji/mi-: city(ies), town(s)
mkate/mi-: bread(s)
mke/wa-: wife(ves)
mkono/mi-: hand(s)
mlango/mi-: door(s)
mlima/mi-: mountain(s)
mlimaji/wa-: farmer(s)
mmea/mi-: plant(s)
Mnijeria/wa-: Nigerian(s)
mnyama/wa-: animal(s)
moto/mi-: fire(s)
moyo/mi-: heart(s)
Mrusi/wa-: Russian(s)
msitu/mi-: forest(s)
mtaa/mi-: street(s)
mti/mi-: tree(s)
mto/mi-: pillow(s), river(s)
mtumishi/wa-: servant(s), steward(s)
mvulana/wa-: boy(s)
Mwafrika/wa-: African(s)
mwaka/miaka: year(s)
Mwamerika/wa-: American(s)
mwana/wa-: child(ren)
mwanamke/wanawake: woman/women
mwanasiasa/wa-: politician(s)
mwanaume/wa-: man/men
mwandishi/wa-: writer(s), author(s)
Mwarabu/wa-: Arab(s)
mwembe/miembe: mango tree(s)
mwenyeji/wa-: inhabitant(s), host(s)
mwezi/miezi: month(s), moon(s)
mwiba/mi-: thorn(s)
mwili/mi-: body(ies)
mwimbaji/wa-: singer(s)
mwindaji/wa-: hunter(s)
Mwirani/wa-: Iranian(s)
mwisho/miisho: end(s), conclusion(s)
Mwitali/wa-: Italian(s)

mwizi/wezi: thief(ves)
mzee/wa-: elder(s), old person(s)
mzigo/mi-: luggage(s)

Key to Exercises

Answers to Practice Exercise A

1. *wanafunzi*
2. *walimu*
3. *wasichana*
4. *wagonjwa*
5. *wageni*
6. *wawindaji*
7. *wadudu*
8. *wavulana*
9. *wafanyakazi*
10. *wapishi*

Answers to Practice Exercise B

11. *mnyama*
12. *mwenyeji*
13. *mkulima*
14. *mzee*
15. *mwanamke*

Answers to Practice Exercise C

16. *Waitali*
17. *Warusi*
18. *Mwirani*
19. *Wahispania*
20. *Mnijeria*
21. *mfanyakazi*
22. *wachezaji*
23. *walimaji*
24. *mpishi*
25. *waandishi*

Answers to Practice Exercise D

26. *mikono*
27. *miguu*
28. *milima*
29. *miji*
30. *miaka*
31. *miili*
32. *miiba*
33. *mioyo*
34. *mikate*
35. *mizigo*

Answers to Practice Exercise E

36. ditches
37. forests
38. months
39. doors
40. streets

Chapter 8

Swahili Noun Classes: JI-/MA- Class and KI-/VI- Class

This chapter will focus on two more noun classes in the Swahili noun class system namely the JI-/MA- class and KI-/VI- class. We will begin with the JI-/MA- class.

Section A: The JI-/MA- Class

There are some categories of nouns, which generally fall under the JI/ MA- noun class. This includes names of fruits, some parts of plants, some parts of the body, one's status or occupation. It also includes non-countable nouns, some abstract nouns, collectives and a special category of nouns called the augmentatives.

This class is often referred to as the JI-/MA- class since some nouns in this class have the prefix JI- in the singular form, which may either change to MA- in the plural form or have MA- added to it. You may also come across some nouns, which contain JI- in the singular form but contain an irregular plural prefix. Other nouns in this class have no prefix in the singular form but contain MA- in the plural form. Below are the main categories that exist in the JI-/MA- class.

1. These nouns contain the prefix JI- in the singular form, which changes to MA- in the plural form:

    jicho – eye
    macho – eyes
    jiwe – stone

mawe – stones
jifya – earth
mafya – hearths

Exception nouns

There are some nouns that fall into this category that contain the prefix JA- in the singular form which change to MA- in the plural form:

jambo – matter
mambo – matters

2. These nouns contain the prefix JI- in the singular form to which MA- is added in the plural form:

jibu – answer
majibu – answers
jina – name
majina – names
jimbo – province
majimbo – provinces

3. These nouns contain JI- in the singular form but contain irregular plural prefix:

jino – tooth
meno – teeth
jiko – stove
meko – stoves

4. These nouns have no prefix in the singular form but contain MA- in the plural form:

gari – car
magari – cars
dirisha – window
madirisha – windows
daraja – bridge
madaraja – bridges
gazeti – newspaper

magazeti – newspapers
jani – leaf
majani – leaves
wazo – thought
mawazo – thoughts

5. These nouns do not have a singular form. They only appear in the plural form and are denoted by the prefix MA

maji – water
maziwa – milk
mafuta – oil
matata – trouble

Practice Exercise A

Change the following nouns from singular to plural where applicable.

1. *tunda*
2. *tawi*
3. *jua*
4. *ua*
5. *majivu*
6. *pera*
7. *figa*
8. *jini*
9. *jembe*
10. *mazungumzo*

Translate the following sentences into Swahili.

11. They asked questions.
12. He/She got (encountered) problems.
13. The officers will come tomorrow.
14. We will buy pineapples.
15. I want an egg.

Here are a few categories of nouns that generally fall under the JI-/MA- class:

- Names of fruits, some parts of plants and some parts of the body which occur in pairs or a set:

    chungwa – orange
    machungwa – oranges
    nanasi – pineapple
    mananasi – pineapples
    jani – leaf
    majani – leaves
    gogo – tree-trunk
    magogo – tree-trunks
    sikio – ear
    masikio – ears
    jicho – eye
    macho – eyes

- Nouns indicating one's status or occupation:

    bwana – mister/sir
    mabwana – misters/sirs
    rais – president
    marais – presidents
    dereva – driver
    madereva – drivers
    daktari – doctor
    madaktari – doctors

- Non-countable nouns are shown below. These nouns only appear in the plural form:

    maji – water
    maziwa – milk
    mafuta – oil

- Some abstract nouns are also included in this noun class. The singular and plural form of the noun may be the same or may be different:

    wazo – thought
    mawazo – thoughts

tatizo – problem
matatizo – problems
mazungumzo – conversation
mazungumzo – conversations
matata – trouble
matata – troubles

Note: This class can be used to collectivize or augment nouns. These concepts will be taught in Chapter 38.

Change the following occupation nouns from singular to plural.

16. *Waziri*
17. *Jambazi*
18. *Rubani*
19. *Nabii*
20. *Nesi*

Section B: The KI-/VI- class

Most nouns in this class refer to household objects or languages. A few nouns in this class refer to parts of the body and some animals. This class is the easiest class in Swahili to use as far as singulars and plurals are concerned. Most nouns in this class have the prefix KI- in the singular form which changes to VI- in the plural form. A minority of nouns in this class have the prefix CH- in the singular form which changes to VY- in the plural form. However, not all nouns beginning with CH- belong to the KI-/VI- class.

1. These nouns contain the prefix KI- in the singular form which changes to VI- in the plural form:

kiatu – shoe
viatu – shoes
kiazi – potato
viazi – potatoes
kidonge – pill
vidonge – pills
kijiko – spoon
vijiko – spoons

kisu – knife
visu – knives
kitabu – book
vitabu – books

2. These nouns contain the prefix CH- in the singular form which changes
    to VY- in the plural form:

    chombo – tool, utensil
    vyombo – tools, utensils
    chumba – room
    vyumba – rooms
    chakula – food
    vyakula – food
    choo – lavatory
    vyoo – lavatories

Practice Exercise B

Change the following nouns from plural to singular where applicable.

21. *vituo*
22. *vyura*
23. *viungo*
24. *vyuma*
25. *viumbe*
26. *vyama*
27. *vyandarua*
28. *vinyozi*
29. *vitanda*
30. *vioo*

Translate the following sentences into Swahili.

31. You will need matches.
32. The barbers are cutting hair.
33. We used a mosquito net over the bed.
34. He/She broke an ankle.
35. We arranged a meeting.

Here are a few categories of nouns that belong to the KI-/VI- class:

- Household objects, some parts of the body and some animals:

  kijiko – spoon
  vijiko – spoons
  kisu – knife
  visu – knives
  chakula – food
  vyakula – food
  kiuno – waist
  viuno – waists
  kiboko – hippopotamus
  viboko – hippopotami
  kifaru – rhino
  vifaru – rhinos

- Also, the names of languages belong to this class and they only exist in the singular form.

  Kiswahili – Swahili
  Kiingereza – English
  Kifaransa – French
  Kireno – Portuguese
  Kiarabu – Arabic

- Nouns that show incapacity or subordinate status belong here:

  kiziwi – deaf person
  viziwi – deaf people
  kipofu – blind person
  vipofu – blind people
  kijana – youth
  vijana – youths
  kibarua – labourer
  vibarua – labourers

Note: This class can be used to make diminutive nouns. This concept will be taught in Chapter 38.

How would you say the following languages in Swahili?

36. Hindi
37. Spanish
38. Chinese
39. Maasai language
40. Persian/Farsi

New Vocabulary

chama/vy-: political party(ies)
chandarua/vy-: mosquito net(s), veil(s)
chombo/vy-: vessel(s), tool(s), utensil(s)
choo/vy-: lavatory(ies)
chuma/vy-: steel, iron
chungwa/ma-: orange(s)
chura/vy-: frog(s)
daraja/ma-: bridge(s)
dereva/ma-: driver(s)
dirisha/ma-: window(s)
figa/ma-: hearth(s)
gazeti/ma-: newspaper(s), magazine(s)
gogo/ma-: tree trunk(s)
hitaji: need
jambazi/ma-: gangster(s)
jani/ma-: leaf(ves)
jembe/ma-: hoe(s)
jibu/ma-: answer(s)
jicho/macho: eye(s)
jifya/ma-: hearth(s)
jiko/meko: stove(s), kitchen(s)
jimbo/ma-: province(s)
jina/ma-: name(s)
jini/ma-: spirit(s)
jino/meno: tooth/teeth
jiwe/mawe: stone(s)
jua/ma-: sun(s)
juu ya: over, above, about
kata: cut
kesho: tomorrow

Kiajemi: Persian/Farsi, Persian/Farsi language
Kiarabu: Arabic, Arabic language
kiatu/vi-: shoe(s)
kiazi/vi-: potato(es)
kibarua/vi-: labourer(s)
kibiriti/vi-: match(es) – for lighting a fire
kiboko/vi-: hippopotamus(mi)
Kichina: Chinese, Chinese language
kidonge/vi-: pill(s)
Kifaransa: French, French language
kifaru/vi-: rhino(s)
kifundo/vi-: ankle(s)
Kihindi: Hindi, Hindi language
Kihispania: Spanish, Spanish language
Kiingereza: English, English language
kijiko/vi-: spoon(s)
kikao/vi-: meeting(s)
Kimaasai: Maasai, Maasai language
kinyozi/vi-: barber(s)
kipofu/vi-: blind person(s)
Kireno: Portuguese, Portuguese language
kisu/vi-: knife(ves)
Kiswahili: Swahili, Swahili language
kitabu/vi-: book(s)
kitanda/vi-: bed(s)
kituo/vi-: stop(s), station(s)
kiumbe/vi-: organism(s)
kiungo/vi-: body joint(s)
kiuno/vi-: waist(s)
kiziwi/vi-: deaf person(s)
mafuta: fat, oil
maji: water
majivu: ashes
matata: trouble
maziwa: milk
mazungumzo: conversation(s)
nabii/ma-: prophet(s)
nanasi/ma-: pineapple(s)
nesi/ma-: nurse(s)

ofisa/ma-: officer(s), official(s)
panga: rent, arrange
pata: get, receive
pera/ma-: guava(s)
rais/ma-: president(s)
rubani/ma-: pilot(s)
sikio/ma-: ear(s)
swali/ma-: question(s)
taka: want
tatizo/ma-: problem(s)
tawi/ma-: branch(es)
tumia: use, spend, exploit
tunda/ma-: fruit(s)
ua/ma-: flower(s)
unywele/nywele: hair(s)
vunja: break
waziri/ma-: minister(s)
wazo/ma-: thought(s)

Key to Exercises

Answers to Practice Exercise A

1. *atunda*
2. *matawi*
3. *majua*
4. *maua*
5. *majivu*
6. *mapera*
7. *mafiga*
8. *majini*
9. *majembe*
10. *mazungumzo*
11. *Waliuliza maswali.*
12. *Alipata matatizo.*
13. *Maofisa watakuja kesho.*
14. *Tutanunua mananasi.*
15. *Ninataka yai.*
16. *Mawaziri*

17. *Majambazi*
18. *Marubani*
19. *Manabii*
20. *Manesi*

Answers to Practice Exercise B

21. *kituo*
22. *chura*
23. *kiungo*
24. *chuma*
25. *kiumbe*
26. *chama*
27. *chandarua*
28. *kinyozi*
29. *kitanda*
30. *kioo*
31. *Utahitaji vibiriti.*
32. *Vinyozi wanakata nywele.*
33. *Tulitumia chandarua juu ya kitanda.*
34. *Alivunja kifundo.*
35. *Tulipanga kikao.*
36. *Kihindi*
37. *Kihispania*
38. *Kichina*
39. *Kimaasai*
40. *Kiajemi*

Chapter 9

Swahili Noun Classes: N- and U-

This chapter will focus on two more noun classes in the Swahili noun class system namely the N- class and the U- class. We will begin with the N- class.

Section A: The N- Class

The N- class contains words mostly borrowed from other languages primarily English and Arabic. It also contains names of animals and relationship nouns. Due to the large number of borrowed words in Swahili, the N- class is the largest of all the noun classes. However, although the majority of borrowed words are contained in the N- class, some borrowed words can be found in other noun classes.

Nouns in the N- class are identical in both their singular and plural forms and therefore do not have singular or plural prefixes. The only way that singular and plural nouns are distinguished in this class is by the agreement that the noun takes with the subject prefix, object infix etc. Noun class agreements will be taught in future chapters. Here are a few categories of nouns that belong to the N- class:

1. Nouns borrowed from other languages:

   baiskeli – bicycle(s)
   meza – table(s)
   barabara – road(s)
   barafu – ice
   kahawa – coffee

kalamu – pen(s), pencil(s)
inchi – inch(es)
dakika – minute(s)
bunduki – gun(s)
askari – guard(s)
polisi – police

2. Names of animals:

simba – lion(s)
twiga – giraffe(s)
pundamilia – zebra(s)
paka – cat(s)
mbwa – dog(s)
inzi – fly(ies) (any sort)
samaki – fish
farasi – horse(s)
nguruwe – pig(s)

3. Relationship nouns:

baba – father(s)
mama – mother(s)
dada – sister(s)
kaka – brother(s)
bibi – grandmother(s)
shangazi – paternal aunt(s)
rafiki – friend(s)
ndugu – relative(s)

There are some nouns in the N- class which do not belong to any of the categories listed above:

ndizi – banana(s)
nyumba – house(s)
chumvi – salt
chupa – bottle(s)
simu – telephone(s)
mboga – vegetable(s)
takataka – garbage

Practice Exercise A

Identify the noun classes to which the following nouns belong.

1. *mtoto*
2. *mama*
3. *ua*
4. *pesa*
5. *sigara*
6. *mgeni*
7. *kijiko*
8. *kikombe*
9. *sabuni*
10. *nyoka*

Section B: The U- class

Most nouns belonging to this class are abstract nouns, uncountable nouns and names of some countries. Almost all nouns in this class have the letter U- as a prefix when in singular form however a few nouns begin with the letter W- in the singular form. Here are a few categories of nouns which belong to the U- Class:

1. Abstract nouns:

    utata – complication, complexity
    ufalme – kingship
    uzee – old age
    utoto – childhood
    Uislamu – Islam
    Ukristo – Christianity
    ujana – youthfulness
    uvivu – laziness
    umoja – unity
    wingi – plenty
    uhuru – freedom
    urefu – length, depth, height
    uchofu – tiredness
    ulaghai – deceitfulness
    ulinganifu – harmony
    ulinzi – security, defence

ujamaa – relationship, socialism
uchoyo – greed
upendo – love
ukimwi – AIDS

Many of the above nouns are made from adjectives (example: *uvivu* from *vivu*, lazy), nouns from other noun classes (example: *ujamaa* from *jamaa*, relative) and some verbs (example: *upendo* from *penda*, love). Since they are abstract nouns, they do not have a plural form.

2. Uncountable nouns:

ugali – corn meal porridge
ubongo – brain matter
uboho – bone marrow
wali – rice
umeme – electricity

3. Names of countries or regions:

Ulaya – Europe
Uchina – China
Unguja – Zanzibar
Uingereza – Great Britain
Uhindi – India
Uarabuni – Arabia
Umaasai – Maasailand (the land of the Maasai tribe)

Since the above nouns are names of countries, they also do not have a plural form.

4. Nouns which have plural forms:

Nouns in this category have different ways of forming their plurals as listed below.

•   The plural form is made by dropping the first letter of the noun as shown in the examples below:

ukuta – wall
kuta – walls
unywele – hair

nywele – hairs
ukumbi – lounge
kumbi – lounges
ukoja – necklace
koja – necklaces
utambi – wick
tambi – wicks
ushanga – bead
shanga – beads

- If after dropping the letter u, the noun begins with d, g or z, then the letter *n-* is prefixed to the noun.

  udevu – beard
  ndevu – beards
  uduvi – shrimp
  nduvi – shrimps
  ugimbi – beer
  ngimbi – beers

- If after dropping the letter u, the noun begins with b or v, then the letter *m-* is prefixed to the noun.

  ubao – plank
  mbao – planks
  ubawa – wing
  mbawa – wings
  ubinja – whistle
  mbinja – whistles

- If after dropping the letter u, the remaining part of the noun is Mono-syllabic, the letters *nyu-* are prefixed to the noun.

  uzi – thread
  nyuzi – threads
  uso – face
  nyuso – faces
  ua – courtyard
  nyua – courtyards
  uma – fork
  nyuma – forks

- If the noun begins with the letter w, the letter w is dropped and the letters *ny-* are prefixed to the noun.

  waadhi – sermon
  nyaadhi – sermons
  wadhifa – position
  nyadhifa – positions
  wavu – net
  nyavu – nets
  waraka – document
  nyaraka – documents

- Some nouns in the U- Class take the plural prefix of the JI-/MA-class after dropping their first letter *u-*.

  uamuzi – judgment
  maamuzi – judgments
  uangalizi – management
  maangalizi – management styles
  ubainisho – clear evidence
  mabainisho – clear evidence

There are some exceptions to the above rules. Example:

  ulimi – tongue
  ndimi – tongues

Practice Exercise B

Change the following nouns from singular to plural.

11. *ukoo*
12. *Urusi*
13. *wakati*
14. *ukali*
15. *utajiri*
16. *wino*
17. *ufa*
18. *udongo*
19. *upana*

20. *ufunguo*
21. *ubavu*
22. *uwingu*
23. *wingu*
24. *uwongo*
25. *ukosefu*

New Vocabulary

askari: guard(s), soldier(s)
barabara: road(s)
barafu: ice
bunduki: gun(s)
chumvi: salt
chupa: bottle(s)
dada: sister(s)
dakika: minute(s)
farasi: horse(s)
inchi: inch(es)
inzi: fly(ies) (any sort)
jamaa: relative(s)
kahawa: coffee
kalamu: pen(s), pencil(s)
kikombe/vi-: cup(s)
mbwa: dog(s)
meza: table(s)
ndizi: banana(s)
ndugu: relative(s)
nguruwe: pig(s)
nyoka: snake(s)
pesa: money
pundamilia: zebra(s)
sabuni: soap(s), detergent(s)
shangazi: paternal aunt(s)
sigara: cigarette(s)
samba: lion(s)
simu: telephone(s)

takataka: garbage
ua/ny-: courtyard(s)
uamuzi/maamuzi: decision(s), judgement(s)
uangalizi/maangalizi: management, management styles
Uarabuni: Arabia
ubainisho/bainisho: clear evidence
ubao/m-: plank(s), board(s)
ubavu/m-: rib(s)
ubawa/m-: wing(s)
ubinja/m-: whistle(s)
uboho: bone marrow
ubongo: brain matter
Uchina: China
uchofu: tiredness
uchoyo: greed
udevu/ndevu: beard(s)
udongo: dirt, soil
uduvi/nduvi: shrimp(s)
ufa/ny-: crack(s), fault(s)
ufalme: kingship
ufunguo/funguo: key(s)
ugali: corn meal porridge
ugimbi/ngimbi: beer(s)
Uhindi: India
uhuru: freedom, independence
Uingereza: Great Britain
Uislamu: Islam
ujamaa: relationship, socialism
ujana: youthfulness
ukali: fierceness
ukimwi: AIDS
Ukristo: Christianity
ukoja/koja: necklace(s)
ukoo/koo: family(ies)
ukosefu: deficit, shortage(s)
ukumbi/kumbi: lounge(s), meeting hall(s)
ukuta/kuta: wall(s)

ulaghai: deceitfulness
Ulaya: Europe
ulimi/ndimi: tongue(s)
ulinganifu: harmony
ulinzi: security, defence
uma/ny-: fork(s)
Umaasai: Maasailand
umeme: electricity, lightning
umoja: unity
Unguja: Zanzibar
upana: width
upendo: love
urefu: length, depth, height, distance
Urusi: Russia
ushanga/shanga: bead(s)
uso/ny-: face(s)
utajiri: wealth
utambi/tambi: wick(s)
utata: complication, complexity
utoto: childhood
uvivu: laziness
uwingu/mbingu: sky(ies)
uwongo/ma-: lie(s)
uzee: old age
uzi/ny-: thread(s), string(s)
vivu: lazy
waadhi/nyaadhi: sermon(s)
wadhifa/nyadhifa: position(s)
wakati/nyakati: time(s), moment(s)
wali: rice
waraka/nyaraka: document(s)
wavu/nyavu: net(s)
wingi: plenty
wingu/ma-: cloud(s)
wino: ink

Key to Exercises

Answers to Practice Exercise A

1. M-/WA- class
2. N- class
3. JI-/MA- class
4. N- class
5. N- class
6. M-/WA- class
7. KI-/VI- class
8. KI-/VI- class
9. N- class
10. N- class

Answers to Practice Exercise B

11. *koo*
12. *Urusi*
13. *nyakati*
14. *ukali*
15. *utajiri*
16. *wino*
17. *nyufa*
18. *udongo*
19. *upana*
20. *funguo*
21. *mbavu*
22. *mbingu*
23. *mawingu*
24. *maongo*
25. *ukosefu*

Chapter 10

Swahili Noun Classes: PA- and KU- and Noun Class Agreement

This chapter will focus on two more noun classes in the Swahili noun class system namely the PA- Class and KU- class. In addition, the subject prefix agreement for all Swahili noun classes will be taught.

Section A: The PA- (Mahali Class)

Although this noun class contains only one noun i.e. *mahali* which means "location(s)," it is by far the most complicated of all noun classes as far as its agreements are concerned. Location in Swahili takes three types of agreements depending on the type of location.

The letter "P" denotes definite location;
The letter "K" denotes indefinite location or area; and
The letter "M" denotes inside location.

The agreements for the PA- Class will be taught in Section C. In Swahili, it is very simple to translate phrases containing information about a location. You simply add the locative suffix *-ni* at the end of the noun. This can be used to translate the prepositions "in," "on" or "at," depending on the context in English. Below are some examples:

kabati – cupboard
kabatini – in the cupboard
nyumba – house

nyumbani – in/at the house
njia – road
njiani – on/in the road
shule – school
shuleni – in/at school

Also, the locative suffix *-ni* can be replaced with the preposition *katika* placed in front of the noun, when translating the prepositions "in" or "at." For example:

kabatini – in the cupboard
katika kabati – in the cupboard

There are some instances where the locative suffix *-ni* cannot be used to replace the preposition *katika*. *Katika* must be used with compound nouns which contain a noun and an adjective as well as nouns constructed using the *-a* of Association as shown below:

chuo kikuu – university
katika chuo kikuu – in/at the university
shirika la uma – public institution
katika shirika la uma – in/at the public institution

Practice Exercise A

Translate the following into Swahili.

1. at work
2. on the bed
3. in the bag
4. at the petrol station
5. in the Indian Ocean
6. in the world
7. on the river bank
8. on the tower
9. at the shop
10. in university

Section B: KU- Class

In Swahili, the KU- Class is only used with verbs and is used to form infinitives or gerunds. In English, an infinitive is the preposition "to" plus the verb (i.e. to go, to eat, to work etc). An infinitive can be used as a verb complement in a sentence (verbal infinitive) or as the subject of a sentence (verbal noun). A gerund is a verb form that ends in -ing. A gerund carries the same meaning as a present tense participle or can be used as the subject of a sentence (verbal noun). Below are some examples:

Infinitive - Verbal Infinitive
Ninapenda kusoma. – I like to read.

Gerund - Present tense participle
Ninapenda kusoma. – I like reading

Infinitive - Verbal Noun
Kusoma ni kuzuri. – To read is good.

Gerund - Verbal Noun
Kusoma ni kuzuri. – Reading is good.

Verbal nouns are nouns in the KU- Class and take agreements according to this class. This will be taught in the following section.

Although the negation of the KU- Class is rarely used, infinitives or gerunds in the KU- Class are negated by inserting the infix *-to-* between the infinitive *ku-* marker and the verb. Below are some examples for Bantu and Arabic verbs:

kusoma – read/reading
kutosoma – not to read/not reading
kulala – to sleep/sleeping
kutolala – not to sleep/not sleeping
kudharau – to ignore/ignoring
kutodharau – not to ignore/not ignoring

Below are some examples for Monosyllabic verbs. Please note that Monosyllabic verbs retain their *ku-* infinitive marker when negated.

kula – to eat/eating
kutokula – not to eat/not eating
kupa – to give/giving
kutokupa – not to give/not giving

Practice Exercise B

Change the following verbs into their infinitives and then negate them.

11. *panda*
12. *amka*
13. *ruka*
14. *imba*
15. *iba*

Translate the following sentences into Swahili.

16. You (sing.) want to sleep.
17. He/She does not like to cultivate.
18. We finished swimming.
19. Cheating is not good.
20. They want not to bargain

Section C: Subject Prefix Agreement

In this section, we will learn how the noun classes taught previously are used in a sentence. In Swahili, the noun dominates the sentence and when used with a verb, the Subject Prefix has to agree with the noun. Subject prefixes for the M-/WA- Class (Personal Subject Prefixes and their negations) were taught in Chapter 3. We will be focusing on the remaining noun classes in this section.

TABLE 10.1
Chart for Subject Prefixes and their Negations

	Noun Class	Affirmative Subject Prefix	Negative Subject Prefix
Singular	M - 1st person singular	*ni-*	*si-*
	2nd person singular	*u-*	*hu-*
	3rd person singular	*a-*	*ha-*
Plural	WA - 1st person plural	*tu-*	*hatu-*
	2nd person singular	*m-*	*ham-*
	3rd person singular	*wa-*	*hawa-*
Singular	M-	*u-*	*hau-*
Plural	MI-	*i-*	*hai-*
Singular	JI-	*li-*	*hali-*
Plural	MA-	*ya-*	*haya-*
Singular	KI-	*ki-*	*haki-*
Plural	VI-	*vi-*	*havi-*
Singular	N-	*i-*	*hai-*
Plural	N-	*zi-*	*hazi-*
Singular	U-	*u-*	*hau-*
Plural	U-	*zi-*	*hazi-*
	PA-	*pa-*	*hapa*
	KU-	*ku-*	*haku-*
	M-	*m-*	*ham-*
	KU-	*ku-*	*kuto-*

Below are examples of Subject Prefix Agreements for all noun classes except Personal Subject Prefix Agreements which were covered in Chapter 3.

Mti ulianguka. – The tree fell down.
Miti ilianguka. – The trees fell down.
Yai halinuki. – The egg does not smell bad.
Mayai hayanuki. – The eggs do not smell bad.
Kitabu kimeanguka. – The book has fallen down.
Vitabu vimeanguka. – The books have fallen down.
Pete inameremeta. – The ring is shining.
Pete zinameremeta. – The rings are shining.
Ukuta hautasimama. – The wall will not stand.
Kuta hazitasimama. – The walls will not stand.
Mahali pananuka. – The place smells bad (definite location).
Mahali pananuka. – The places smell bad (definite location).
Mahali kunanuka. – The place smells bad (indefinite location).
Mahali kunanuka. – The places smell bad (indefinite location).
Mahali mnanuka. – The place smells bad (inside location).
Mahali mnanuka. – The places smell bad (inside location).
Kuandika kuzuri. – The writing is good.
Kuandika kuzuri. – The writings are good.

As you can see from Table 10.1 and the examples, the PA- and KU-Class keep the same subject prefixes when changing from singular to plural. Also, several noun classes share their affirmative and/or negative subject prefixes as shown in Table 10.2

TABLE 10.2
Shared Affirmative and Negative Subject Prefixes

	Noun Class	Affirmative Subject Prefix	Negative Subject Prefix
Singular	M-/MI-	*u-*	*hau-*
Singular	U-	*u-*	*hau-*
Singular	M-/WA- 2nd person sing.	*u-*	*hu-*
Plural	M-/MI-	*i-*	*hai-*
Singular	N-	*i-*	*hai-*
Plural	N-	*zi-*	*hazi-*
Plural	U-	*zi-*	*hazi-*

It is also important to note that although nouns referring to humans, animals and insects may exist in other noun classes, they still take agreement with the M-/WA- Class. Exceptions to this rule will be taught in Chapter 38.

Daktari atafika. – The doctor will arrive.
Madaktari watafika. – The doctors will arrive.
Simba hajalala. – The lion has not yet slept.
Simba hawajalala. – The lions have not yet slept.
Kipofu atakula. – The blind person will eat.
Vipofu watakula. – The blind people will eat.

Also, note that all countries take agreement with the singular N-class even though some of them exist in the U- Class. As you can see in the example below the Subject Prefix is *i-* which is for the singular N-class, even though the word *Urusi* belongs in the U- class.

Urusi imeendelea. – Russia has progressed.

Lastly, if the inanimate noun(s) being referred to is/are unknown, the sentence will take agreement with the N- Class. For example:

Itanukia. – It will smell good.
Zitanukia. – They will smell good.

Practice Exercise C

Change the following singular sentences into plural when applicable.

21. *Ndoo imejaa maji.*
22. *Mti unanukia.*
23. *Gari halitasimama.*
24. *Ndege anaruka.*
25. *Mahali pameanguka.*
26. *Unywele uling"aa.*
27. *Kipofu anajenga nyumba.*
28. *Kitanda kimesimama.*
29. *Kucheka ni kubaya.*
30. *Mwanafunzi alimwaga mafuta.*

Translate the following sentences into English.

31. *Ndoo zimejaa maji.*
32. *Miti inanukia.*
33. *Magari hayatasimama.*
34. *Ndege wanaruka.*
35. *Mahali pameanguka.*
36. *Nywele ziling"aa.*
37. *Vipofu wanajenga nyumba.*
38. *Vitanda vimesimama.*
39. *Kucheka ni kubaya.*
40. *Wanafunzi walimwaga mafuta.*

New Vocabulary

amka: wake up
anguka: fall
Bahari ya Hindi: Indian Ocean
-baya: bad
danganya: cheat
dharau: ignore, despise
dunia: world(s), the Earth
iba: steal
imba: sing
jaa: fill
jenga: build
kabati/ma-: cupboard(s), locker(s)
mahali: place(s)
meremeta: shine, glitter
mfuko/mi-: bag(s), pocket(s), sack(s)
mnara/mi-: tower(s)
mwaga: spill, pour
ndoo: bucket(s)
ng"aa: shine
njia: way(s), method(s), road(s), path(s)
nuka: smell bad, stink
nukia: smell good, scent
ogelea: swim, wash
patina: haggle, bargain
pete: ring(s)

petroli: petrol, gasoline
shirika/ma- la/ya uma: public institution(s)
si: is not/are not
simama: stand
ukingo/kingo: riverbank(s)
-zuri: good, beautiful

Key to Exercises

Answers to Practice Exercise A

1. *kazini*
2. *kitandani*
3. *mfukoni*
4. *katika kituo cha petroli*
5. *katika Bahari ya Hindi*
6. *duniani*
7. *ukingoni*
8. *mnarani*
9. *dukani*
10. *katika chuo kikuu*

Answers to Practice Exercise B

11. *kupanda – kutopanda*
12. *kuamka – kutoamka*
13. *kuruka – kutoruka*
14. *kuimba – kutoimba*
15. *kuiba – kutoiba*
16. *Unataka kulala.*
17. *Hapendi kulima.*
18. *Tulimaliza kuogelea.*
19. *Kudanganya si kuzuri.*
20. *Wanataka kutopatana.*

Answers to Practice Exercise C

21. *Ndoo zimejaa maji.*
22. *Miti inanukia.*
23. *Magari hayatasimama.*

24. *Ndege wanaruka.*
25. *Mahali pameanguka.*
26. *Nywele ziling"aa.*
27. *Vipofu wanajenga nyumba.*
28. *Vitanda vimesimama.*
29. *Kucheka ni kubaya.*
30. *Wanafunzi walimwaga mafuta.*
31. The buckets have been filled with water.
32. The trees smell good.
33. The vehicles will not stop.
34. The birds are flying.
35. The place (definite) has fallen down.
36. The hairs were shining.
37. The blind people are building the house(s).
38. The beds have stood upright.
39. To laugh is bad/ Laughing is bad.
40. The students spilled oil.

Chapter 11

Object Infixes

In this chapter we will learn how Noun Class agreement applies when the noun from that class is the object of the sentence. The Object Infix can be used to replace or to reinforce the noun that is the object of the sentence. There are no exact rules of when Object Infixes should be used. Generally, the Object Infix is used when one wants to emphasize the object of the sentence or when a demonstrative or a possessive is present. It is also more commonly used when referring to living things as the object of the sentence. Object Infixes, no matter which class they are from, are always placed between the tense marker and the verb and can be used with any tense marker either positive or negative. As you can see in Table 11.1, there is no Negative Object Infix.

As you can see from Table 11.1, the PA- and KU- Class keep the same Subject Prefixes when changing from singular to plural. Also note that several noun classes use the same Object Infix.

Section A: M-/WA- Class Object Infixes

When discussing Object Infixes in the M-/WA- class, it should be noted that the 1st person singular (*ni-*), the 1st person plural (*tu-*) and 3rd person plural (*wa-*) use their Personal Subject Prefix as their Object Infix (See Chapter 3 for Personal Subject Prefixes). 2nd person singular and plural and 3rd person singular have Object Infixes that are not the same as their Personal Subject Prefixes. As mentioned above, Object Infixes are always placed between the tense marker and the verb as shown by the formula:

Agreement Subject Prefix + Tense Marker + Object Infix + Verb

TABLE 11.1
Object Infix Chart

Noun Class		Object Infix	English Translation
Singular	M - 1st person singular	-ni-	me
	2nd person singular	-ku-	you (sing.)
	3rd person singular	-m(w)-	him/her
Plural	WA - 1st person plural	-tu-	us
	2nd person plural	-wa-	you (pl.)
	3rd person plural	-wa-	them
Singular	M-	-u-	it
Plural	MI-	-i-	them
Singular	JI-	-li-	it
Plural	MA-	-ya-	them
Singular	KI-	-ki-	it
Plural	VI-	-vi-	them
Singular	N-	-i-	it
Plural	N-	-zi-	them
Singular	U-	-u-	it
Plural	U-	-zi-	them
	PA-	-pa-	it/them
	KU-	-ku-	it/them
	M-	-m(w)-	it/them
	KU-	-ku-	it/them

Therefore the sentence "He will see me" would be *A* + *ta* + *ni* + *ona*. = *Ataniona*.

There are a few rules which apply when using Object Infixes for the M-/WA- class. Notice that the Object Infix for the 3rd person singular (him/her) has the letter *w* in brackets in Table 11.1. This is because when a verb beginning with a vowel is used the Object Infix becomes -*mw*- as shown in the example below.

I will see him/her. – *Nitamwona*.

Of course, if the verb in the Swahili sentence does not start with a vowel then the Object Infix for the 3rd person singular (him/her) is simply -*m*- as shown in the following example.

I will answer him/her. – *Nitamjibu.*

The Object Infix for 2nd person singular which is *-ku-* should not be confused with either the infinitive *-ku-* used with verbs or with the negative tense marker *-ku-* which is used to negate the simple past tense marker *-li-*. For example:

I loved you. – *Nilikupenda.*

If the sentence was made negative it would become:

I did not love you. – *Sikukupenda.*

The first *-ku-* in the above negative sentence is the negative tense marker *-ku-* which is used to negate the simple past tense marker *-li-*, while the second *-ku-* is the Object Infix for 2nd person singular.

Note that there are rules used to ensure there is no confusion between the Object Infixes for the 2nd person plural "you (pl.)" and 3rd person plural "them" which are both translated in Swahili as *-wa-*. The sentence *Niliwaona* could mean either "I saw you (pl.)" or "I saw them"

To avoid confusion, the Object Infix *-wa-* is generally taken to refer to the 3rd person plural "them." When someone wishes to refer to the 2nd person plural "you (pl.)" there are three possible ways to indicate this. The most common way is to take the sentence *Niliwaona* which could mean either "I saw you (pl.)" or "I saw them" and change the sentence to the following:

Niliwaoneni. – I saw you (pl.).

As you can see the Subject Prefix, Tense marker and Object Infix are all left the same. The difference is with the verb, in this case *ona*, which has had the final vowel *a* changed to *e* and the suffix *-ni* attached. All Bantu verbs will have their final vowel *a* changed to *e*. If the verb is of Arabic origin, its final vowel will remain unchanged. The suffix *-ni* must be added to all Bantu and Arabic verbs.

The second way of making the sentence is by the use of the Personal Pronoun *ninyi.*

Niliwaona ninyi. – I saw you (pl.).

The final way of making the sentence is by the use of the Object Infix -*ku*- for the 2nd person singular, but then indicating that the sentence refers to plural by the inclusion of the suffix -*ni*. This last construction is the least common in Swahili.

Nilikuoneni. – I saw you (pl.).

Lastly, it is important to note that even though some nouns referring to humans, animals and insects may exist in other noun classes, they still take the Object Infixes with the M-/WA- Class.

Mgonjwa alimshukuru daktari. – The patient thanked the doctor.
Mgonjwa aliwashukuru madaktari. – The patient thanked the doc-
    tors.
Nilimshauri kijana. – I advised the youth.
Niliwashauri vijana. – I advised the youths.

Practice Exercise A

Translate into Swahili.

1. They are helping us.
2. They chased the chickens.
3. He met her.
4. We will not help you (sing.).
5. I visited the prophet.
6. I have answered you (pl.).
7. She likes him.
8. The cat will chase the rats.
9. They forgave the children.
10. I did not ask you (sing.).
11. We do not know them.
12. Our government helps the blind people.
13. You (pl.) pushed me.
14. She killed the mosquito.
15. You (sing.) bought the cats.

Section B: The Other Noun Classes

Object Infixes for all the other noun classes are exactly the same as their Agreement Subject Prefixes. Below are a few examples:

Tuliula mkate. – We ate the (loaf of) bread.
Tuliila mikate. – We ate the (loaves of) bread.
Hatukuula mkate. – We did not eat the (loaf of) bread.
Hatukuila mikate. – We did not eat the (loaves of) bread.
Ulilifungua sanduku. – You (sing.) opened the box.
Uliyafungua masanduku. – You (sing.) opened the boxes.
Hukulifungua sanduku. – You (sing.) did not open the box.
Hukuyafungua masanduku. – You (sing.) did not open the boxes.
Nimekivunja kiti. – I have broken the chair.
Nimevivunja viti. – I have broken the chairs.
Sikukivunja kiti. – I have not broken the chair.
Sikuvivunja viti. – I have not broken the chairs.
Atainunua baiskeli. – He will buy the bicycle.
Atazinunua baiskeli. – He will buy the bicycles.
Hatainunua baiskeli. – He will not buy the bicycle.
Hatazinunua baiskeli. – He will not buy the bicycles.
Wanaulima uwanja. – They are cultivating the field.
Wanazilima nyanja. – They are cultivating the fields.
Hawaulimi uwanja. – They are not cultivating the field.
Hawazilimi nyanja. – They are not cultivating the fields.
Tulipatembelea mahali. – We visited the place (definite).
Tulipatembelea mahali. – We visited the places (definite).
Hatukupatembelea mahali. – We did not visit the place (definite).
Hatukupatembelea mahali. – We did not visit the places (definite).
Tulikutembelea mahali. – We visited the place (indefinite).
Tulikutembelea mahali. – We visited the places (indefinite).
Hatukukutembelea mahali. – We did not visit the place (indefinite).
Hatukukutembelea mahali. – We did not visit the places (indefinite).
Tulimtembelea mahali. – We visited the place (inside).
Tulimtembelea mahali. – We visited the places (inside).
Hatukumtembelea mahali. – We did not visit the place (inside).
Hatukumtembelea mahali. – We did not visit the places (inside).
Tutakupenda kusoma. – We will like the reading.
Tutakupenda kusoma. – We will like the readings.
Hatutakupenda kusoma. – We will not like the reading.
Hatutakupenda kusoma. – We will not like the readings.

Note that when referring to the PA- Class (inside), the Object Infix has the letter *w* in brackets in Table 11.1. This is because when a verb beginning with a vowel is used the Object Infix becomes -*mw*-. Also, when the Object Infixes for the PA- Class are present, it is optional to use the noun *mahali*.

Lastly, if the inanimate noun(s) being referred to is/are unknown, the Object Infix from the N- Class is used. For example:

Niliinunua. – I bought it.
Nilizinunua. – I bought them.

Practice Exercise B

Translate into Swahili.

16. The pen has stained the shirt.
17. The insects damaged the crops.
18. He will weed the garden.
19. I have read the book.
20. The fire burned the place (definite).
21. He is building the stone wall.
22. The water will fill the hole.
23. I have agreed with the writing.
24. The saw will cut the tree.
25. I cooked it.

Section C: More information on Object Infixes

Some sentences have two objects. When this occurs, one of the objects in the sentence has to be represented by a proper noun, because a Swahili verb phrase can only take one object infix. If one of the objects is a living thing, the living thing is represented by an object infix while the non-living thing is referred to by its proper noun. Also, often object infixes are used with prepositional verb typology which will be taught in Chapter 26.

Nitamsimulia hadithi. – I will tell him/her the story.

When two objects that are non-living are in a sentence, then the noun that is the direct object provides the object infix.

Nilikiona kitabu mfukoni. – I saw the book in the bag.

When a Monosyllabic verb is used with an Object Infix, then the infinitive *ku-* is dropped from the verb phrase. This rule applies no matter which tense marker is being used.

Niliyanywa maji. – I drank the water.

While it was stated that there are no exact rules of when Object Infixes should be used, there are three verbs in Swahili that must always take an Object Infix. Furthermore the Object Infix taken for these three verbs must always be from the M-/WA- Class.[1] These three verbs are listed below:

ambia – tell
ita – call
pa – give

Alimwambia kila kitu. – He/She told him/her everything.
Tumewaita jirani. – We have called the neighbours.
Nilikupa mkate. – I gave you the bread.

Practice Exercise C

Translate the following sentences into Swahili.

26. She gave me the pen.
27. The students gave the doorman the broom.
28. The shopkeeper has called the police.
29. I heard the stone smashing the window.
30. The beggar told me that he needed money.

New Vocabulary

ambia: tell
bawabu/ma-: doorman/doormen
bustani: garden(s), park(s)
chafua: make dirty
choma: roast, burn
fungua: open, unlock
hadithi: story(ies)
haribu: destroy, spoil, damage

ita: call
jaza: fill
jibu: answer
jirani/ma-: neighbour(s)
kila kitu: everything
kimbiza: chase
kuta: meet
kuwa: that
mbu: mosquito(es)
msumeno/mi-: saw(s)
mwenye duka/wenye duka: shopkeeper(s)
mwombaji/wa-: beggar(s)
ona: see, feel
palilia: weed, hoe
panya: mouse(s), rat(s)
saidia: help
samehe: forgive, pardon
sanduku/ma-: box(es), suitcase(s)
serikali: government(s)
shati/ma-: shirt(s)
shauri: advise
shukuru: thank
sikia: listen, hear, feel
simulia: narrate, tell a story
sukuma: push
tembelea: visit
tundu/ma-: hole(s), nest(s)
ua: kill
ufagio/fagio: brush(es), broom(s)
uwanja/nyanja: field(s), open area(s)

Key to Exercises

Answers to Practice Exercise A

1. *Wanatusaidia.*
2. *Waliwakimbiza kuku.*
3. *Alimkuta.*
4. *Hatutakusaidia.*

 5. *Nilimtembelea nabii.*
 6. *Nimewajibuni* or *Nimewajibu ninyi* or *Nimekujibuni.*
 7. *Anampenda.*
 8. *Paka atawakimbiza panya.*
 9. *Waliwasamehe watoto.*
10. *Sikukuuliza.*
11. *Hatuwajui.*
12. *Serikali yetu inawasaidia vipofu.*
13. *Mlinisukuma.*
14. *Alimwua mbu.*
15. *Uliwanunua paka.*

Answers to Practice Exercise B

16. *Kalamu imelichafua shati.*
17. *Wadudu waliyaharibu mazao.*
18. *Ataipalilia bustani.*
19. *Nimekisoma kitabu.*
20. *Moto ulipachoma.*
21. *Anaujenga ukuta wa mawe.*
22. *Maji yatalijaza tundu.*
23. *Nimekukubali kuandika.*
24. *Msumeno utaukata mti.*
25. *Niliipika.*

Answers to Practice Exercise C

26. *Alinipa kalamu.*
27. *Wanafunzi walimpa bawabu ufagio.*
28. *Mwenye duka amewaita polisi.*
29. *Nililisikia jiwe linavunja dirisha.*
30. *Mwombaji aliniambia kuwa alihitaji fedha.*

Note

1. Peter M. Wilson, *Simplified Swahili*, New ed. (Harlow, UK: Longman Group UK Limited, 1985), 110.

Chapter 12

Possessives

Possessives, "*vimilikishi*" in Swahili, are words which show owner-ship. In Swahili, possessives have to agree with "what is being pos-sessed" rather than the possessor, as is the case in English. There are two main ways of showing ownership in Swahili. The first one is by using Possessive Suffixes and the second way is by using the -*a* of Asso-ciation.

Section A: Possessive Suffixes

There are six Possessive Suffixes, which are shown in Table 12.1 in singular and plural forms:

TABLE 12.1
Possessive Suffixes

Singular		Plural	
-*angu*	mine	-*etu*	our, ours
-*ako*	your, yours	-*enu*	your, yours
-*ake*	hers, his, its	-*ao*	their, theirs

In order to use Possessive Suffixes shown in Table 12.1 to denote ownership, it is necessary to explain how this is done by first listing the Noun Classes (See Chapters 7, 8, 9, 10) with their respective Possessive Prefixes in singular and plural forms as shown in Table 12.2.

TABLE 12.2
Possessive Prefixes

Singular/Plural	Noun Class	Possessive Prefix
Singular	M-	*w-*
Plural	WA-	*w-*
Singular	M-	*w-*
Plural	MI-	*y-*
Singular	JI-	*l-*
Plural	MA-	*y-*
Singular	KI-/CH-	*ch-*
Plural	VI-/VY-	*vy-*
Singular	N-	*y-*
Plural		*z-*
Singular	U-	*w-*
Plural		*z-*
Singular	PA-	*p-* (specific place) *kw-* (indefinite place) *mw-* (inside place)
Plural		*p-* *kw-* *mw-*
Singular	KU-	*kw-*
Plural		*kw-*

The way to make words denoting ownership in Swahili is by taking the Possessive Prefix and combining it with the Possessive Suffix (See Table 12.1 and 12.2). For example, if the thing to be owned is a single bicycle (*baiskeli*), which is in the N- Noun Class, we take the Possessive Prefix for this noun in singular which is *y-* (See Table 12.2) and combine it with any of the Possessive Suffixes, "*-angu*" (mine), "*-etu*" (ours) etc.

(See Table 12.1) depending on who owns the bicycle. If I own the bicycle, then I would combine the Possessive Prefix *y*- with the Possessive Suffix "*-angu*" to form "*yangu*" (mine.) We would therefore have:

baiskeli yangu – my bicycle
baiskeli zangu – my bicycles

As you can see the word "*baiskeli*" (bicycle) is the same in both singular and plural. In the second sentence "*baiskeli*" is known to be in the plural because of the "*z*-" from the word "*zangu*." The "*z*-" Possessive Prefix is taken from the N- Noun Class plural column.

If I want to say "My child" I would combine the Possessive Prefix *w*- in the M-/WA- Noun Class with "*-angu*" to form "*wangu*" (mine). In this case we would therefore have:

mtoto wangu – my child
watoto wangu – my children

Note that in the M-/WA- Noun Class, the noun itself indicates whether it is singular or plural; the singular word for the noun is not the same as the plural word, i.e. "*mtoto*" versus "*watoto*." Therefore the possessive form "*wangu*" stays the same in both singular and plural because the Possessive Prefix for singular and plural for this Noun Class is the same (See Table 12.2).

Ownership of an object from the M-/MI- Class, for example, such as one tree (*mti*) would require the combination of the Possessive Prefix *w*- in the singular with "*-angu*" to form "*wangu*" (mine).

mti wangu – my tree

If there is more than one tree, I would combine *y*- in the plural with "*-angu*" to form "*yangu*" (mine).

miti yangu – my trees

By following the procedure used above, we can show ownership of things in the remaining Noun Classes using the Possessive Suffix "*-angu*":

Examples:

> *kitabu changu* – my book
> *vitabu vyangu* – my books
> *jina langu* – my name
> *majina yangu* – my names
> *nyumba yangu* – my house
> *nyumba zangu* – my houses
> *ukuta wangu* – my wall
> *kuta zangu* – my walls
> *mahali pangu* – my place (specific)
> *mahali pangu* – my places (specific)
> *mahali kwangu* – my place (indefinite)
> *mahali kwangu* – my places (indefinite)
> *mahali mwangu* – my place (inside)
> *mahali mwangu* – my places (inside)
> *kusoma kwangu* – my reading
> *kusoma kwangu* – my readings

By referring to Table 12.1 and Table 12.2, ownership can be shown by combining the Possessive Prefixes of things in different Noun Classes with the any of the Possessive Suffixes "*-ako*" (your, yours) sing., "*-enu*" (your, yours) pl., "*-ake*" (hers/his/its), "*-ao*" (theirs), and "*-etu*" (ours).

Examples:

> *mtoto wako* – your (sing.) child
> *watoto wako* – your (sing.) children
> *mahali penu* – your (pl.) place
> *mahali penu* – your (pl.) places
> *kusoma kwake* – her/his reading
> *kusoma kwake*   – her/his readings
> *nyumba yao* – their house
> *nyumba zao* – their houses
> *kitabu chetu* – our book
> *vitabu vyetu* – our books

From the examples shown above, it is apparent that possessives in Swahili take agreements with what is being possessed rather than the possessor as we have pointed out in the first paragraph of this chapter.

As a general rule, nouns denoting humans, animals and insects, which are found in Noun Classes other than M-/WA-, still take agreements with the M-/WA- Class (See Chapter 7). However, there is an exception to this rule when it comes to showing possessive forms with any nouns in the N- Noun Class which denote relationships such as the following:

mama – mother
baba – father
dada – sister
kaka – brother
binamu – cousin/nephew
jamaa – relative
rafiki – friend
bibi/nyanya – grandmother
babu – grandfather
shangazi – paternal aunt
shemeji – brother/sister in-law
ndugu – relative

Possessive forms with these nouns take agreement with the Possessive Prefixes in the N- Noun Class which are "*y-*" in the singular and "*z-*" in the plural and NOT with "*w-*" in the M-/WA- Noun Class in both singular and plural (See Table 12.2). For example, with the noun "*dada*" (sister) we combine *y-* in the singular with "*-angu*" to form "*yangu*" (mine), thus we get:

dada yangu – my sister

If I have more than one sister, I would combine the Possessive Prefix "*z-*" in the plural with the Possessive Suffix "*-angu*" to form "*zangu*" (mine). Thus we get:

dada zangu – my sisters

Examples:

dada yangu – my sister
dada zangu – my sisters
kaka yangu – my brother

kaka zangu – my brothers
shangazi yangu – my aunt
shangazi zangu – my aunts
rafiki yangu – my friend
rafiki zangu – my friends

Practice Exercise A

Translate the following into Swahili.

1. My house
2. Her/his house
3. Your (sing.) books
4. Your (pl.) book
5. Your teacher
6. Her/his father
7. Her/his mother
8. Their books
9. Her/his flowers
10. Their places
11. My sister
12. My grandmother
13. Our university
14. My father
15. Our school
16. My place
17. Our reading
18. Their house
19. My reading
20. Our classroom

There are a few special cases where whole words and Possessive Suffixes can be combined into one word. For example, "*mwenzi*" (a companion) or "*wenzi*" (companions) can be combined with the Possessive Suffixes shown in Table 12.1. The construction of the possessive using "*mwenzi*" and "*wenzi*" result in the dropping of the final "*i.*"

Examples:

Singular:

> *mwenzi* + *-angu* = *mwenzangu* – my companion
> *mwenzi* + *-ako* = *mwenzako* – your (sing.) companion
> *mwenzi* + *-ake* = *mwenzake* – her/his companion
> *mwenzi* + *-etu* = *mwenzetu* – our companion
> *mwenzi* + *-enu* = *mwenzenu* – your (pl.) companion
> *mwenzi* + *-ao* = *mwenzao* – their companion

Plural:

> *wenzi* + *-angu* = *wenzangu* – my companions
> *wenzi* + *-ako* = *wenzako* – your (sing.) companions
> *wenzi* + *-ake* = *wenzake* – her/his companions
> *wenzi* + *-etu* = *wenzetu* – our companions
> *wenzi* + *-enu* = *wenzenu* – your (pl.) companions
> *wenzi* + *-ao* = *wenzao* – their companions

Translate into English.

> 21. *Mwenzangu anasoma Kiswahili.*
> 22. *Mwenzako jina lake nani?*
> 23. *Mwenzetu anasoma Kiswahili.*
> 24. *Mwenzao alikwenda Montreal.*
> 25. *Wenzetu waliandika barua.*
> 26. *Wenzangu wanakaa hapa.*
> 27. *Wenzake wanaangalia sinema.*
> 28. *Mtoto wangu anacheza na wenzake.*
> 29. *Mwenzenu anasoma chuo kikuu.*
> 30. *Wenzetu walinunua Kamusi ya Kiswahili.*

Note on Word order: As you can see the personal possessive word comes immediately AFTER the noun they qualify, no matter which class the noun is from. The position immediately after the noun is ALWAYS reserved for the personal possessive if one is present in the sentence. If personal possessives, adjectives, demonstratives etc occur in the sentence there is a particular word order that must be followed, which is:

Noun, personal possessive, adjective, quantity and demonstrative.[1]

Proper word order will be discussed again in future Chapters.

Section B: The *-a* of Association

The second way of showing ownership in Swahili is by using the *-a* of Association. This is done by combining the Possessive Prefixes as listed in Table 12.2 with the *-a* of Association. For example, if we want to show that John owns a chair (*kiti*), we combine "*ch-*" in the singular with the "*-a*"of Association to form "*cha*" (of). Thus we get:

kiti cha John – John's chair

As we can see in the example above, the word order in Swahili is a complete reversal of the word order in English. The thing being possessed comes first, in this case *kiti* (chair). Next comes the *-a* of Association (*cha*), which links the possessed thing with the possessor, and the person doing the possessing (John) comes last.

If John owns more than one chair, we combine "*vy-*" in the plural with the "*-a*" of Association to form "*vya*" (of). Thus we get:

viti vya John – John's chairs

Examples:

 mtoto wa mwalimu – the teacher's child
 watoto wa mwalimu – the teacher's children
 mti wa baba yangu – my father's tree
 miti ya baba yangu – my father's trees
 jina la mwalimu – the teacher's name
 majina ya mwalimu – the teacher's names
 kitabu cha mtoto – the child's book
 vitabu vya mtoto – the child's books
 nyumba ya mtu – the person's house
 nyumba za mtu – the person's houses
 ua la dada yangu – my sister's flower
 maua ya dada yangu – my sister's flowers
 mahali pa nyanya – grandmother's place
 mahali pa nyanya – grandmother's places

Practice Exercise B

Circle the correct Possessive forms, which agree with the nouns in the following sentences.

Example: *mtoto (ya, wa) mwalimu.*

The correct answer to be circled is "*wa.*"

31. *Nyumba (ya, wa) familia yangu.*
32. *Mwanafunzi (ya, wa) Chuo Kikuu cha Toronto.*
33. *Mti (wa, za) baba yangu.*
34. *Miti (za, ya) baba yangu.*
35. *Nyumba (sing.) (wa, ya) baba yake.*
36. *Kitabu (ya, cha) mama yangu.*
37. *Vitabu (za, vya) watoto.*
38. *Kusoma kwa wanafunzi (ya, wa) Kiswahili.*
39. *Ua (ya, la) shangazi yangu.*
40. *Darasa (ya, la) watoto.*
41. *Kitabu (ya, cha) rafiki yangu.*
42. *Vitabu (vya, za) darasa letu.*
43. *Kuandika (la, kwa) wanafunzi wa Kiingereza.*
44. *Nyumba (pl.) (ya, za) wafanyakazi.*
45. *Darasa (ya, la) wanafunzi wa Kiswahili.*
46. *Madarasa (za, ya) wanafunzi wa chuo kikuu.*
47. *Kompyuta (pl.) (la, za) watoto wa shule.*
48. *Mahali (la, pa) kusoma Kiswahili.*
49. *Kuandika (za, kwa) mtoto.*
50. *Ua (la, wa) bibi.*

More practice exercises on possessive forms.

Translate into Swahili.

51. The teacher's book.
52. My sister's bicycle.
53. Her/his companions are studying in Africa.
54. Her/his sister went to New York.
55. Heather is reading her Swahili book.
56. What is your companion's name?
57. My brother.

58. My brother's friend.
59. Our books.
60. Their children.

Note on Word Order: As noted in Section A the personal possessive has a particular position in a Swahili sentence and there is a particular word order that must be followed which was:

Noun, personal possessive, adjective, quantity and demonstrative.

However, the *-a* of Association has its own special word order that must be followed, which is:

Noun being possessed, adjective, quantity, demonstrative, the *-a* of Association, and finally the possessor.

If, for example, an adjective were not used in the sentence, quantity would take the position of the adjective, but otherwise word order stays the same as above.

Section C: Reading Practice

Read the following passage and then answer the questions, which follow:

Bwana na bibi Thompson wanakaa katika Mji wa Toronto. Bwana Thompson ni daktari wa Hospitali ya Watoto. Mama Thompson ni mwalimu. Yeye anafundisha katika shule ya sekondari. Bwana na bibi Thompson wana watoto sita. Majina ya watoto wao ni Paul, Jonathan, Joshua, Mary, Alex na Joanna. Paul, Jonathan na Mary wanasoma Chuo Kikuu cha Toronto. Wanakwenda chuoni kwa baiskeli kwa sababu wanakaa karibu na chuo. Joshua, Alex na Joanna wanasoma shule ya sekondari. Wao wanakwenda shuleni kwa motokaa ya mama yao. Wanafunzi wenzao wanakwenda shuleni kwa miguu kwa sababu wanakaa karibu na shule.

Practice Exercise C

Answer the following questions in Swahili.

61. *Bwana na bibi Thompson na watoto wao wanakaa katika mji gani?*

62. *Bwana na bibi Thompson wana watoto wangapi?*
63. *Paul, Jonathan na Mary wanasoma wapi?*

Answer the following questions with *Ndiyo* (Yes) or *Hapana* (No).

64. *Alex, Joshua na Joanna wanasoma shule ya sekondari.*
65. *Alex, Joshua na Joanna wanakwenda shuleni kwa baiskeli.*
66. *Bwana Thompson anafanya kazi katika Hospitali ya Watoto.*
67. *Mama Thompson anafundisha sekondari.*
68. *Bwana Thompson na familia yake wanakaa katika Mji wa Dar-es-Salaam.*
69. *Alex, Joshua na Joanna wanakwenda shuleni kwa motokaa.*
70. *Wanafunzi wenzao wanakwenda shuleni kwa miguu.*

New Vocabulary

Afrika: Africa
-ake: hers/his/its
-ako: your, yours (sing.)
angalia: watch, look
-angu: mine
-ao: theirs
binamu: cousin(s)
darasa/ma-: classroom(s), class(es), grade(s)
-enu: your, yours (pl.)
-etu: ours
familia: family(ies)
fanya: do, make
fundisha: teach
hapa: here
hapana: no
hospitali: hospital(s)
kaa: live, stay, sit
kamusi: dictionary(ies)
kimilikishi/vi-: possessive(s)
-kuu: main
kwa: by, to/by means of, for, with, on
kwa sababu: by reason of, because
motokaa: car(s)

mwenzake: her/his companion
mwenzako: your (sing.) companion
mwenzangu: my companion
mwenzao: their companion
mwenzenu: your (pl.) companion
mwenzetu: our companion
mwenzi/wenzi: friend(s), colleague(s), companion(s)
nani?: who?
ndiyo: yes
-ngapi?: how many?
sekondari: secondary
shemeji: brother/sister-in-law(s)
sinema: cinema(s)
sita: six
wana: they have
wenzake: her/his companions
wenzako: your (sing.) companions
wenzangu: my companions
wenzao: their companions
wenzenu: your (pl.) companions
wenzetu: our companions

Key to Exercises

Answers to Practice Exercise A

1. *Nyumba yangu*
2. *Nyumba yake*
3. *Vitabu vyako*
4. *Kitabu chenu*
5. *Mwalimu wako*
6. *aba yake*
7. *Mama yake*
8. *Vitabu vyao*
9. *Maua yake*
10. *Mahali pao*
11. *Dada yangu*
12. *Bibi yangu*
13. *Chuo chetu*

14. *Baba yangu*
15. *Shule yetu*
16. *Mahali pangu*
17. *Kusoma kwetu*
18. *Nyumba yao*
19. *Kusoma kwangu*
20. *Darasa letu*
21. My companion studies Swahili.
22. What is the name of your companion?
23. Our companion is studying Swahili.
24. Their companion went to Montreal.
25. Our companions wrote a letter.
26. My companions reside here.
27. His/Her companions are watching a movie.
28. My child is playing with his/her companions.
29. Your (pl.) companion is studying at the university.
30. Our companions bought a Swahili Dictionary.

Answers to Practice Exercise B

31. *ya*
32. *wa*
33. *wa*
34. *ya*
35. *ya*
36. *cha*
37. *vya*
38. *wa*
39. *la*
40. *la*
41. *cha*
42. *vya*
43. *kwa*
44. *za*
45. *la*
46. *ya*
47. *za*
48. *pa*
49. *kwa*

50. *la*
51. *Kitabu cha mwalimu.*
52. *Baiskeli ya dada yangu.*
53. *Wenzake wanasoma Afrika.*
54. *Dada yake alikwenda New York.*
55. *Heather anasoma kitabu chake cha Kiswahili.*
56. *Mwenzako jina lake nani?*
57. *Kaka yangu.*
58. *Rafiki ya kaka yangu.*
59. *Vitabu vyetu.*
60. *Watoto wao.*

Answers to Practice Exercise C

61. *Toronto.*
62. *Sita.*
63. *Chuo Kikuu cha Toronto.*
64. *Ndiyo.*
65. *Hapana.*
66. *Ndiyo.*
67. *Ndiyo.*
68. *Hapana.*
69. *Ndiyo.*
70. *Ndiyo.*

Note

1. Wilson, 76.

Chapter 13

Adjectives

In Swahili, any word, phrase or clause used to qualify a noun or to explain the noun is considered an adjective. Therefore adjectives in Swahili are not just simple adjectives as in English, but instead include phrases and clauses that can be used as adjectives. Adjectives in Swahili are divided into several categories, each of which has its own set of rules.

1. Adjectives that take agreement and the agreement prefix is attached to an adjective "stem" which starts with a vowel.
2. Adjectives that take agreement and the agreement prefix is attached to an adjective stem which starts with a consonant.
3. Exception adjectives that take agreement but do not follow the usual agreement of other adjectives.
4. Invariable adjectives which are of Arabic origin and do not take any agreement with the noun they qualify.
5. Compound adjectives made from nouns, verbs and other words in Swahili and combined with the -a of Association.

Section A: Vowel Stem Adjectives

Adjectives that must take agreement fall into two categories, adjectives that start with vowels and adjectives that start with consonants. We will begin with adjectives that take agreement and start with vowels. Table 13.1 shows the agreement taken by adjective stems that begin with either *a*, *e*, *i*, *o*, or *u*, the letter y is not considered a vowel in Swahili.

Table 13.1 must be memorized as the specific rules depend on the noun class and the vowel stem of the adjective.

TABLE 13.1
Vowel Stem Adjectives

		-angavu	*-ekundu*	*-ingine*	*-ororo*	*-unganifu*
Sing.	M-	*mwangavu*	*mwekundu*	*mwingine*	*mwororo*	*munganifu*
Pl.	WA-	*waangavu*	*wekundu*	*wengine*	*waororo*	*waunganifu*
Sing.	M-	*mwangavu*	*mwekundu*	*mwingine*	*mwororo*	*munganifu*
Pl.	MI-	*myangavu*	*myekundu*	*mingine*	*myororo*	*miunganifu*
Sing.	JI-	*langavu*	*jekundu*	*lingine*	*lororo*	*liunganifu*
Pl.	MA-	*maangavu*	*mekundu*	*mengine*	*mororo*	*maunganifu*
Sing.	KI-	*changavu*	*chekundu*	*kingine*	*chororo*	*kiunganifu*
Pl.	VI-	*vyangavu*	*vyekundu*	*vingine*	*vyororo*	*viunganifu*
Sing.	N-	*nyangavu*	*nyekundu*	*nyingine*	*nyororo*	*nyunganifu*
Pl.	N-	*nyangavu*	*nyekundu*	*nyingine*	*nyororo*	*nyunganifu*
Sing.	U-	*mwangavu*	*mwekundu*	*mwingine*	*mwororo*	*munganifu*
Pl.	U-	*nyangavu*	*nyekundu*	*nyingine*	*nyororo*	*nyunganifu*
	PA-	*pangavu*	*pekundu*	*pengine*	*pororo*	*punganifu*
	KU-	*kuangavu*	*kwekundu*	*kwingine*	*kororo*	*kuunganifu*
	M-	*muangavu*	*mwekundu*	*mwingine*	*mororo*	*munganifu*
	KU-	*kuangavu*	*kwekundu*	*kwingine*	*kororo*	*kuunganifu*

The adjective stem *-ema* meaning "good" or "kind" takes a special agreement when agreeing with nouns from the N- Class. Instead of *nyema* which would be expected from the N- Class in Table 13.1 the stem *-ema* actually takes the agreement *njema*. For example:

Safari njema! – Good journey! (Meaning, *I wish you a good journey!*)

Practice Exercise A

Translate the following sentences into Swahili.

1. The piece of wood is thin.
2. The owl is a very watchful bird.

3. The wall was bare.
4. People will not buy many houses next year.
5. The wicked person ran far away.

Section B: Consonant Stem Adjectives

TABLE 13.2
Consonant Stem Adjectives

	Noun Class	*-zuri*	*-baya*
Singular	M-	*mzuri*	*mbaya*
Plural	WA-	*wazuri*	*wabaya*
Singular	M-	*mzuri*	*mbaya*
Plural	MI-	*mizuri*	*mibaya*
Singular	JI-	*zuri*	*baya*
Plural	MA-	*mazuri*	*mabaya*
Singular	KI-	*kizuri*	*kibaya*
Plural	VI-	*vizuri*	*vibaya*
Singular	N-	*nzuri*	*mbaya*
Plural	N-	*nzuri*	*mbaya*
Singular	U-	*mzuri*	*mbaya*
Plural	U-	*nzuri*	*mbaya*
	PA-	*pazuri*	*pabaya*
	KU-	*kuzuri*	*kubaya*
	M-	*mzuri*	*mbaya*
	KU-	*kuzuri*	*kubaya*

In general adjectives with consonant stems follow Table 13.2, however when consonant stem adjectives must agree with nouns from the N-Class then the following rules apply.

1. When a consonant stem adjective beginning with the letters d, g, j, y, or z is used to describe a noun from the N- Class then the prefix *n-* is necessary.

2. When a consonant stem adjective beginning with the letter b is used to describe a noun from the N- Class then the prefix *m-* must be used.
3. All other consonant stem adjectives do not take agreement when describing nouns from the N- Class.

In addition a few adjective stems take special agreements. The adjective stem *-refu* (long, tall) has a special agreement when agreeing with nouns from the N- Class. The adjective stem *-refu* takes the modified form of *ndefu* when following nouns from the N- Class. For example:

Meza ndefu – The long table

The adjective stem *-pya* (new) has some special agreements. Mentioned below are the noun class agreements that do not follow the regular pattern. All other noun class agreements follow the regular agreements in Table 13.2

Singular JI- becomes *jipya*
Singular N- becomes *mpya*
Plural N- becomes *mpya*
Plural U- becomes *mpya*

Practice Exercise B

Translate the following sentences into English.

6. *Mimi nitaandika mtihani mgumu.*
7. *Bibi alipika chakula kitamu.*
8. *Ndizi kubwa zinatoka Afrika Kusini.*
9. *Debe tupu haliachi kuvuma.*
10. *Watu wanene watarudi kesho kufanya mazoezi.*

Section C: Exception Adjectives

There are four commonly used adjectives in Swahili which do not follow the usual agreement of other adjectives as taught above. These adjectives are *-ote* which means "all" or "whole," *-o -ote* which means "any," *-enye* which means "having," and *-enyewe* which means "-self." Except for the M-/WA- class all other noun class agreements are easy to remember because they follow the same agreement as used with the *-a* of Association.

Table 13.3 shows the Noun Class agreement of every Noun Class with the adjectives *-ote, -o -ote*, *-enye* and *-enyewe*.

TABLE 13.3
Exception Adjectives

Noun Class	*-ote*	*-o -ote*	*-enye*	*-enyewe*
M - 1st Person (Sing.)	*wote*		*mwenye*	*mwenyewe*
WA- 1st Person (Pl.)	*sote*		*wenye*	*wenyewe*
M - 2nd Person (Sing.)	*wote*		*mwenye*	*mwenyewe*
WA- 2nd Person (Pl.)	*nyote*		*wenye*	*wenyewe*
M - 3rd Person (Sing.)	*wote*	*ye yote*	*mwenye*	*mwenyewe*
WA- Person (Pl.)	*wote*	*wo wote*	*wenye*	*wenyewe*
M- Singular	*wote*	*wo wote*	*wenye*	*wenyewe*
MI- Plural	*yote*	*yo yote*	*yenye*	*yenyewe*
JI - Singular	*lote*	*lo lote*	*lenye*	*lenyewe*
MA- Plural	*yote*	*yo yote*	*yenye*	*yenyewe*
KI- Singular	*chote*	*cho chote*	*chenye*	*chenyewe*
VI- Plural	*vyote*	*vyo vyote*	*vyenye*	*vyenyewe*
N- Singular	*yote*	*yo yote*	*yenye*	*yenyewe*
N- Plural	*zote*	*zo zote*	*zenye*	*zenyewe*
U- Singular	*wote*	*wo wote*	*wenye*	*wenyewe*
U- Plural	*zote*	*zo zote*	*zenye*	*zenyewe*
PA-	*pote*	*po pote*	*penye*	*penyewe*
KU-	*kote*	*ko kote*	*kwenye*	*kwenyewe*
M-	*mote*	*mo mote*	*mwenye*	*mwenyewe*
KU-	*kote*	*ko kote*	*kwenye*	*kwenyewe*

When the adjectives *-ote* or *-o -ote* are included in a sentence with other adjectives it is important to note the word order. Since the adjectives *-ote* or *-o -ote* deal with quantity they usually come as the last adjective, unless an adjective is used as a predicate then the predicate adjective must always come last.

Chukua vitabu vikubwa vyekundu vyote. – Take all the big red books.
Vitabu vikubwa vyote ni vyekundu. – All the big books are red.
Chukua vitabu vikubwa vyekundu vyo vyote. – Take any of the big red books.
Vitabu vikubwa vyo vyote ni vyekundu. – Any of the big books are red.

When the words *cho chote* are used without reference to any noun then the meaning is understood to be "any object at all" as it agrees with the missing noun *kitu* meaning "thing."

When the adjective *-enye* is used in a sentence then it must be followed by either a noun or an infinitive verb.

Kandili yenye mafuta mengi. – The lantern with a lot of oil
Helikopta yenye kufika. – The arriving helicopter

When the adjective *-enye* is included in a sentence with other adjectives it is important to note the word order. The adjective *-enye* must come after all adjectives, including *-ote* and *-o -ote*.

Kitambaa chepesi cho chote chenye tundu kimetupwa.
Any light cloth with a hole has been thrown out.

When the adjective *-enyewe* is used in a sentence it must follow a noun, verb or a pronoun.

Msichana mwenyewe alitaka kuolewa. – The girl herself wanted to get married.
Alifanya mwenyewe. – He/She himself/herself did it.
Mimi mwenyewe sikwenda kazini. – I myself did not go to work.

When the adjective *-enyewe* is included in a sentence with other adjectives it is important to note the word order. The adjective *-enyewe* must come after all adjectives, including *-ote* and *-o -ote*.

Kitambaa chepesi chote chenyewe kimetupwa. – The whole light cloth itself has been thrown out.

Also note that the word *mwenyewe* is used as a noun to mean "owner," and *wenyewe* as "owners."

Practice Exercise C

Translate the following sentences into English.

11. *Askari wote wa Kanada watarudi mwaka ujao.*
12. *Thurea yenyewe imeanguka.*
13. *Mchango wo wote utawasaidia wateswa wa mafuriko.*
14. *Mchinjaji mwenye kisu kikali kikubwa amelala.*
15. *Karoti zote katika mfuko zimeoza.*

Section D: Invariable Adjectives

Invariable adjectives are adjectives that do not take agreement with the nouns that they qualify. There are a large number of adjectives that belong to this category, and many are of foreign origin, mostly Arabic, although some are also of Bantu origin. Invariable adjectives follow the same rules for word order as Variable adjectives. Here are some of the more common Invariable adjectives:

madhubuti – precise, reliable
sawa – equal
safi – clean
karimu – generous
maskini – poor
tajiri – rich
bure – useless
kila – each, every
rahisi – easy
tayari – ready
ghali – expensive
bora – better, best
imara – firm, stable
hodari – brave, serious
maalumu – special
butu – blunt (referring to anything that can be sharpened: pencil, knife)
gubigubi – covered from head to toe (usually clothing or blanket)

kame – barren, arid (referring to land)
chepechepe – wet, moist, soaked

Practice Exercise D

Translate the following sentences into Swahili.

16. The doctor himself covered the sick person completely.
17. We do not want to wear moist clothes.

Section E: Compound Adjectives

Compound adjectives are made from nouns, verbs and other words in Swahili. The construction of compound adjectives is always done by placing the *-a* of Association in front of the word being changed into a compound adjective and must take agreement with the noun being described. The *-a* of Association is used to join two words together to indicate a relationship between them. Below are some examples of compound adjectives:

maji ya moto – hot water
mwili wa baridi – cold body
mahali pa hatari – dangerous place
sehemu ya siri – secret area
duka la mipira   – football shop
maktaba ya karibu – nearby library

Note that sometimes the meaning of the compound adjective is different from the original meaning of the noun, for example:

The Swahili word *bure* means "useless" however when it becomes a compound adjective *-a bure* it takes the meaning of "free" (without cost).

In addition to using two nouns to form a compound adjective there are other ways of forming compound adjectives, for example:

Using verbs in the infinitive form:

kaanga – fry
-a kukaanga – fried

bembeleza – sooth
-a kubembeleza – soothing

Using a verb in the Prepositional form (see Chapter 26) which expresses the purpose of something:

makasi ya kunyolea – haircutting scissors
chumba cha kusomea – reading room
nyumba ya kufikia wageni – guest arriving house (guest house)

To express directions in Swahili and indicate gender the *-a* of Association is also used:

-a kulia – right
chandarua cha kulia – rightside mosquito net
-a kushoto – left
gurudumu la kushoto – leftside tire
-a kike – female
bidhaa za kike – products for women
-a kiume – male
mapambo ya vito ya kiume – men's jewellery

The *-a* of Association can be used to form compound adjectives that describe what "type" of thing something is, for example:

-a kitoto – childish
harakati za kitoto – childish activities
-a kizamani – ancient
magofu ya kizamani – ancient ruins
-a kizungu – European
kofia ya kizungu – European hat

Practice Exercise E

Translate the following sentences into English.

18. *Watoto wengi wa kisasa wamekwenda chuo kikuu.*
19. *Gauni la kijani lilipotea.*
20. *Mwelekeo wa kusumbua si mzuri.*

New Vocabulary

-a kike: female, feminine

-a kitoto: childish

-a kiume: male

-a kizamani: ancient

-a kizungu: European

-a kulia: right

-a kushoto: left

acha: stop, quit, permit

Afrika Kusini: South Africa

-angalifu: watchful, careful

-angavu: clear, shining

baridi: cold

bembeleza: sooth

bidhaa: product(s), merchandise

bora: better, best

bundi: owl(s)

bure: useless

butu: blunt (referring to anything that can be sharpened: pencil, knife)

chepechepe: wet, moist, soaked

cho chote: any object at all

chukua: take, carry

debe/ma-: tin(s), can(s)

-ekundu: red

-ema: good, kind

-embamba: thin, narrow

-enye: having, using

-enyewe: -self

-epesi: light (in weight), quick

funika: cover, disguise

gauni/ma-: gown(s), dress(es)

gofu/ma-: ruin(s), wreck(s)

gubigubi: covered from head to toe (usually clothing or blanket)

-gumu: difficult, hard

gurudumu/ma-: tire(s), wheel(s)

harakati: activity(ies), struggle(s)

hatari: danger(s), emergency(ies)

helikopta: helicopter(s)

hodari: clever, brave, serious
imara: firm, stable
-ingi: many
-ingine: another
kaanga: fry
kali: sharp, fierce
kame: barren, arid (referring to land)
kandili: lamp(s), lantern(s)
karimu: generous
karoti: carrot(s)
kijani: green
kila: each, every
kipande/vi-: piece(s)
kisasa: modern, up-to-date
kitambaa/vi-: cloth(s)
kito/vi-: jewel(s), precious stone(s)
kitu/vi-: thing(s)
kofia: hat(s), crown(s)
-kubwa: big, large
maalumu: special
madhubuti: precise, reliable
mafuriko: flood(s)
makasi: shears, scissors
makasi ya kunyolea: haircutting scissors
maktaba: library(ies)
maskini: poor
mbali: far, far away
mchango/mi-: contribution(s), donation(s)
mchinjaji/wa-: butcher(s)
mpira/mi-: football(s)
mteswa/wa-: victim(s)
mwaka ujao: next year
mwelekeo/mi-: attitude(s), tendency(ies)
mwenyewe/wenyewe: owner(s)
nene: fat
-o -ote: any
olewa: get married (for women only)
-ororo: soft, smooth
-ote: all, whole

-ovu: wicked, evil
oza: rot, give in marriage (for women only)
pambo/ma-: ornament(s), decoration(s)
potea: lose, disappear
-pya: new
rahisi: easy, simple, cheap
-refu: long, tall
safi: clean
sawa: equal (to/in)
sehemu: part(s), fraction(s), area(s), portion(s)
siri: secret
sumbua: disturb, annoy
tajiri: rich
tamu: sweet, delicious
tayari: ready
thurea: chandelier(s)
toka: come from, until
tupa: throw away, abandon
tupu: empty
uchi: bare, naked
-unganifu: connecting
vaa: wear, put on
vuma: make noise
zoezi/ma-: exercise(s)

Key to Exercises

Answers to Practice Exercise A

1. *Kipande cha mti ni chembamba.*
2. *Bundi ni ndege mwangalifu sana.*
3. *Ukuta ulikuwa uchi.*
4. *Watu hawatanunua nyumba nyingi mwaka ujao.*
5. *Mtu mwovu alikimbia kwenda mbali.*

Answers to Practice Exercise B

6. I will write a difficult exam.
7. Grandmother cooked delicious food.
8. Large bananas come from South Africa.
9. An empty tin does not cease to make noise.
10. The obese people will return tomorrow to do exercises.

Answers to Practice Exercise C

11. All Canadian soldiers will return next year.
12. The chandelier itself has fallen down.
13. Any donation will help flood victims.
14. The butcher with the big sharp knife has slept.
15. All carrots in the bag are rotten.

Answers to Practice Exercise D

16. *Daktari mwenyewe alimfunika mgonjwa gubigubi.*
17. *Hatutaki kuvaa nguo chepechepe.*

Answers to Practice Exercise E

18. Many children of modern times have gone to University.
19. The green dress was lost.
20. The disturbing attitude is not good.

Chapter 14

Demonstratives

Demonstratives are used to refer to entities that the speaker wishes to identify and are usually used to state their distance from the speaker. Demonstratives must agree with the noun they qualify and can be used as either adjectives or pronouns. There are two types of demonstratives: Demonstrative of Proximity (this, these) and Demonstrative of Distance (that, those). When referring back to someone or something that has already been discussed in proximity or distance, the Demonstrative of Reference for Proximity and the Demonstrative of Reference for Distance are used respectively.

Section A: Demonstrative of Proximity

The Demonstrative of Proximity (this, these) denotes someone or something that is close to the speaker. The Demonstrative of Proximity is formed by:

> Letter "*h-*" + Vowel of the affirmative subject prefix +
> Affirmative subject prefix

As you can see in Table 14.1, all the Demonstratives of Proximity begin with the letter "*h-*" and end with the affirmative subject prefix of that particular noun class. The intermediate vowel is a duplicate of the vowel from the affirmative subject prefix. The only exceptions are the singular M-/WA- Class and the inside locative for the PA- Class. The Demonstrative of Proximity for the M-/WA- Class for the 1st person and 2nd person singular and plural do not exist. We would expect the 3rd person sing. to be formed using the affirmative subject prefix *a-* but it instead uses *-yu* to become *huyu*. Since the affirmative subject prefix for the inside locative for the PA- Class *m(w)-* does not have a vowel, the vowel *u* is used.

TABLE 14.1
Demonstrative of Proximity Table

Noun Class		Letter 'h-'		Duplicated vowel		Affirmative Subject Prefix		Demonstrative Of Proximity
M-	1st Person	*h-*		-		*ni-*		-
	2nd Person	*h-*		-		*u-*		-
	3rd Person	*h-*		*-u-* (exception)		*a-*		*huyu*
WA-	1st Person	*h-*		-		*tu-*		-
	2nd Person	*h-*		-		*m-*		-
	3rd Person	*h-*	+	*-a-*	+	*wa-*	=	*hawa*
M-		*h-*	+	*-u-*	+	*u-*	=	*huu*
MI-		*h-*	+	*-i-*	+	*i-*	=	*hii*
JI-		*h-*	+	*-i-*	+	*li-*	=	*hili*
MA-		*h-*	+	*-a-*	+	*ya-*	=	*haya*
KI-		*h-*	+	*-i-*	+	*ki-*	=	*hiki*
VI-		*h-*	+	*-i-*	+	*vi-*	=	*hivi*
N-		*h-*	+	*-i-*	+	*i-*	=	*hii*
N-		*h-*	+	*-i-*	+	*zi-*	=	*hizi*
U-		*h-*	+	*-u-*	+	*u-*	=	*huu*
U-		*h-*	+	*-i-*	+	*zi-*	=	*hizi*
PA-		*h-*	+	*-a-*	+	*pa-*	=	*hapa*
KU-		*h-*	+	*-u-*	+	*ku-*	=	*huku*
M-		*h-*		*-u-* (exception)		*m(w)-*	=	*humu*
KU-		*h-*	+	*-u-*	+	*ku-*	=	*huku*

Here are few examples using the Demonstrative of Proximity:

> *Ua hili ni zuri.* – This flower is nice.
> *Maua haya ni mazuri.* – These flowers are nice.
> *Paka huyu alilala.* – This cat was asleep.
> *Paka hawa walilala.* – These cats were asleep.

As taught in previous chapters, below is the word order when demonstratives are used:

> Noun, personal possessive, adjective,
> quantity, demonstrative and possessive.

Example:

> *Visu vyangu vikubwa vitano hivi vya kale.* – These five big ancient knives of mine.

Practice Exercise A

Translate the following sentences into Swahili.

1. These green apples.
2. These tall boys are running.
3. This old building was destroyed.
4. These long rivers.
5. This young fat lion has been asleep.
6. This beautiful place is the presidential palace.
7. These long readings are lovely.
8. These short walls are black.
9. These utensils of ours are from France.
10. This cloth of the neighbour will not dry.

Section B: Demonstrative of Reference for Proximity

When the Demonstrative of Proximity is used to refer to someone or something that has already been discussed, we use the Demonstrative of Reference for Proximity. The Demonstrative of Reference for Proximity is formed by:

First syllable of Demonstrative of Proximity + Relative particle

As you can see in Table 14.2, all the Demonstratives of Reference for Proximity begin with the first syllable of Demonstrative of Proximity for that particular noun class. This first syllable is attached to the relative particle for that particular noun class. The only exception is the singular M-/WA- Class. The Demonstrative of Reference for Proximity for the M-/WA- Class for the 1st person and 2nd person singular and plural do not exist. We would expect the 3rd person sing. to be formed using the relative particle *-ye-* but it instead uses *-yo* to become *huyo*.

Here are few examples using the Demonstrative of Reference for Proximity.

> *Hilo ua ni zuri.* – This (referred to) flower is nice.
> *Hayo maua ni mazuri.* – These (referred to) flowers are nice.
> *Huyo paka alilala.* – This (referred to) cat was asleep.
> *Hao paka walilala.* – These (referred to) cats were asleep

As you can see from the examples above, the Demonstrative of Reference for Proximity usually precedes the noun it refers to. However, the Demonstrative of Reference for Proximity is placed immediately after the noun when there is an adjective. For example:

> *Ua hilo jeupe ni zuri.* – This (referred to) white flower is nice.
> *Maua hayo meupe ni mazuri.* – These (referred to) white flowers
>   are nice.

When a Demonstrative of Reference for Proximity is used with a personal possessive and an adjective, the personal possessive is placed immediately after the noun. The Demonstrative of Reference for Proximity follows the personal possessive and finally, the adjective follows the Demonstrative of Reference for Proximity.

> *Ua langu hilo jeupe ni zuri.* – This (referred to) white flower of
>   mine is nice.
> *Maua yangu hayo meupe ni mazuri.* – These (referred to) white
>   flowers of mine are nice.

TABLE 14.2
Demonstrative of Reference for Proximity Table

Noun Class		First Syllable of demonstrative of proximity		Relative Particle		Demonstrative Of Reference for Proximity
M-	1st Person	-		-ye-		-
	2nd Person	-		-ye-		-
	3rd Person	hu-		-ye- (exception)		huyo
WA-	1st Person	-		-o-		-
	2nd Person	-		-o-		-
	3rd Person	ha-	+	-o-	=	hao
M-		hu-	+	-o-	=	huo
MI-		hi-	+	-yo-	=	hiyo
JI-		hi-	+	-lo-	=	hilo
MA-		ha-	+	-yo-	=	hayo
KI-		hi-	+	-cho-	=	hicho
VI-		hi-	+	-vyo-	=	hivyo
N-		hi-	+	-yo-	=	hiyo
N-		hi-	+	-zo-	=	hizo
U-		hu-	+	-o-	=	huo
U-		hi-	+	-zo-	=	hizo
PA-		ha-	+	-po-	=	hapo
KU-		hu-	+	-ko-	=	huko
M-		hu-		-mo-	=	humo
KU-		hu-	+	-ko-	=	huko

Practice Exercise B

Translate the following sentences into Swahili.

11. These (referred to) projects started last year.
12. This (referred to) elbow of mine is hurting.
13. This (referred to) near place (indefinite) is not safe.
14. These (referred to) heavy blankets are theirs.
15. This (referred to) mountaineer is not wise.
16. This (referred to) green plant will grow next week.
17. This (referred to) singing is bad.
18. The (referred to) secondary school did not buy these tables of yours.
19. These (referred to) truths are self-evident.
20. This (referred to) food of the relative smells good.

Section C: Demonstrative of Distance (that, those)

The Demonstrative of Distance (that, those) denotes someone or something that is far from the speaker. The Demonstrative of Distance is formed by:

Affirmative subject prefix + "le"

As you can see in Table 14.3, all the Demonstratives of Distance begin with the affirmative subject prefix of that particular noun class. The affirmative subject prefix is followed by the suffix -*le*. The only exception is the singular M-/WA- Class. The Demonstrative of Distance for the M-/WA- Class for the 1st person and 2nd person singular and plural do not exist. We would expect the 3rd person sing. to be formed using the affirmative subject prefix *a-* but it instead uses *yu-* to become *yule*.

Here are few examples using the Demonstrative of Distance:

Ua lile ni zuri. – That flower is nice.
Maua yale ni mazuri. – Those flowers are nice.
Paka yule alilala. – That cat was asleep.
Paka wale walilala. – Those cats were asleep.

TABLE 14.3
Demonstrative of Distance Table

Noun Class		Affirmative Subject Prefix	Suffix -le			Demonstrative Of Distance
M-	1st Person	*ni-*				-
	2nd Person	*u-*				-
	3rd Person	*a-*(exception)	*-le*			*yule*
WA-	1st Person	*tu-*				-
	2nd Person	*m-*				-
	3rd Person	*wa-*	+ *-le*	+	=	*wale*
M-		*u-*	+ *-le*	+	=	*ule*
MI-		*i-*	+ *-le*	+	=	*ile*
JI-		*li-*	+ *-le*	+	=	*lile*
MA-		*ya-*	+ *-le*	+	=	*yale*
KI-		*ki-*	+ *-le*	+	=	*kile*
VI-		*vi-*	+ *-le*	+	=	*vile*
N-		*i-*	+ *-le*	+	=	*ile*
N-		*zi-*	+ *-le*	+	=	*zile*
U-		*u-*	+ *-le*	+	=	*ule*
U-		*zi-*	+ *-le*	+	=	*zile*
PA-		*pa-*	+ *-le*	+	=	*pale*
KU-		*ku-*	+ *-le*	+	=	*kule*
M-		*m(w)-*	+ *-le*		=	*mle*
KU-		*ku-*	+ *-le*	+	=	*kule*

Demonstratives of Distance follow the same word order as Demonstratives of Proximity.

Practice Exercise C

Translate the following sentences into English.

21. *Matufaha kijani yale.*
22. *Vijana warefu wale wanakimbia.*
23. *Jengo lile la zamani lilivunjika.*
24. *Mito mirefu ile ni myembamba.*
25. *Simba kijana mnene yule amelala.*
26. *Mahali pazuri pale ni kasri la rais.*
27. *Kusoma kurefu kule kunapendeza.*
28. *Kuta fupi zile ni nyeusi.*
29. *Vyombo vyetu vile vimetoka Ufaransa.*
30. *Nguo ile ya jirani haitakauka.*

Section D: Demonstrative of Reference for Distance

When the Demonstrative of Distance is used to refer to someone or something that has already been discussed, we use the Demonstrative of Reference for Distance. When using the Demonstrative of Reference for Distance, the demonstrative used is the same as the Demonstrative of Distance. However, unlike the Demonstrative of Distance which comes after the noun, the Demonstrative of Reference for Distance usually comes before the noun.

Here are few examples using the Demonstrative of Reference for Distance:

Lile ua ni zuri. – That (referred to) flower is nice.
Yale maua ni mazuri. – Those (referred to) flowers are nice.
Yule paka alilala. – That (referred to) cat was asleep.
Wale paka walilala. – Those (referred to) cats were asleep.

When the Demonstrative of Reference for Distance is used with an adjective, the Demonstrative of Reference is placed immediately after the noun. For example:

Ua lile jeupe ni zuri. – That (referred to) white flower is nice.
Maua yale meupe ni mazuri. – Those (referred to) white flowers are nice.

When a Demonstrative of Reference for Distance is used with a personal possessive and an adjective, the personal possessive is placed immediately after the noun. The Demonstrative of Reference for Distance follows the personal possessive and finally, the adjective follows the Demonstrative of Reference for Distance.

Ua langu lile jeupe ni zuri. – That (referred to) white flower of mine is nice.

Maua yangu yale meupe ni mazuri. – Those (referred to) white flowers of mine are nice.

Practice Exercise D

Translate the following sentences into English.

31. *Ile miradi ilianza mwaka jana.*
32. *Kiko changu kile kinauma.*
33. *Mahali kule mbali si salama.*
34. *Mablanketi yale mazito ni yao.*
35. *Yule mpanda mlima si busara.*
36. *Mmea ule kijani utaota wiki ijayo.*
37. *Kule kuimba ni kubaya.*
38. *Shule ya sekondari haikununua meza zako zile.*
39. *Zile kweli ni wazi.*
40. *Kile chakula cha jamaa kinanukia.*

New Vocabulary

anza: start, begin
blanketi/ma-: blanket(s)
busara: wise
-eupe: white
-eusi: black
-fupi: short
ijayo: next
jengo/ma-: building(s)
kale: ancient
kasri/ma-: palace(s)
kauka: dry
kiko/vi-: elbow(s)

mpanda/wa- mlima: mountaineer(s)
mradi/mi-: project(s)
mwaka jana: last year
ota: grow, dream
pendeza: beautiful, pleasant, attractive, fancy
tufaha/ma-: apple(s)
Ufaransa: France
uma: bite, hurt
wazi: obvious, self evident
wiki: week(s)
zamani: long ago, old (for non-living things)
-zito: heavy, severe

Key to Exercises

Answers to Practice Exercise A

1. *Matufaha kijani haya.*
2. *Vijana warefu hawa wanakimbia.*
3. *Jengo hili la zamani lilivunjika.*
4. *Mito mirefu hii.*
5. *Simba kijana mnene huyu amelala.*
6. *Mahali pazuri hapa ni kasri la rais.*
7. *Kusoma kurefu huku kunapendeza.*
8. *Kuta fupi hizi ni nyeusi.*
9. *Vyombo vyetu hivi vimetoka Ufaransa.*
10. *Nguo hii ya jirani haitakauka.*

Answers to Practice Exercise B

11. *Hiyo miradi ilianza mwaka jana.*
12. *Kiko changu hicho kinauma.*
13. *Mahali huko karibu si salama.*
14. *Mablanketi hayo mazito ni yao.*
15. *Huyo mpanda mlima si busara.*
16. *Mmea huo kijani utaota wiki ijayo.*
17. *Huko kuimba ni kubaya.*
18. *Shule ya sekondari haikununua meza zako hizo.*
19. *Hizo kweli ni wazi.*
20. *Hicho chakula cha jamaa kinanukia.*

Answers to Practice Exercise C

21. Those green apples.
22. Those tall boys are running.
23. That old building was destroyed.
24. Those long rivers are narrow.
25. That young fat lion has been asleep.
26. That beautiful place is the presidential palace.
27. That/Those long reading(s) is/are lovely.
28. Those short walls are black.
29. Those utensils of ours are from France.
30. That cloth of the neighbour will not dry.

Answers to Practice Exercise D

31. Those (referred to) projects started last year.
32. That (referred to) elbow of mine is hurting.
33. That (referred to) far-away place is not safe.
34. Those (referred to) heavy blankets are theirs.
35. That (referred to) mountaineer is not wise.
36. That (referred to) green plant will grow next week.
37. That (referred to) singing is bad.
38. The (referred to) secondary school did not buy those tables of yours.
39. Those (referred to) truths are self-evident.
40. That (referred to) food of the relative smells good.

Chapter 15

Comparatives and Superlatives

Comparatives and comparative adjectives have the same use in Swahili as in English, to compare two nouns to each other. There are only two main categories of comparatives. The first category is comparatives of equality where two things are compared to show that they have an equal quality to each other. The second category is comparatives of superiority/inferiority where two things are compared to show one as superior or inferior to the other. In addition to comparative adjectives, the Swahili language has superlatives and superlative adjectives which have the same use in Swahili as in English. Superlatives are used to show that something has the maximum degree of a quality compared to anything else in that context or category.

Section A: Comparatives of Equality

In Swahili comparatives of equality can be made in several ways and using many different words. The most common ways involve comparative adjectives or certain verbs which will be shown below:

The word *kama* can be used to make the comparative of equality "as . . . as," for example:

> *Kijana huyu ni shujaa kama mwanajeshi.* – This youth is as brave as a soldier.

The following words can be used with or without *kama*:

> *vilevile* – also
> *sawa* – equal (to/in)
> *sawasawa* – same
> *Sisi tunasoma Kiswahili vilevile.* – We study Swahili also.
> *Mazulia yale ni sawa kwa sifa.* – Those carpets are equal in quality.
> *Televisheni na kompyuta zinatumia kiasi sawasawa cha umeme.* – A television and a computer use the same amount of electricity.

Another way to make a comparative of equality is with *sawa na* which means "equal to."

> *Miwani yangu ya jua ni sawa na yako.* – My sunglasses are the same as yours.

The verb *lingana* meaning "match" or "harmonize" and the verb *fanana* meaning "resemble" can be used with or without *kama*:

> *Urefu wako unalingana na urefu wa mpenzi wako.* – Your height matches with your girlfriend's height.
> *Sura za mapacha hawa zinafanana.* – The faces of these twins resemble (each other).

Practice Exercise A

Translate the following sentences into Swahili.

1. Hindi is as difficult a language as the English language.
2. Her nose resembles my nose.
3. We are writing a Swahili book also.
4. She is as light as a feather.
5. It rained just as strongly (heavily) as yesterday.

Section B: Comparatives of Superiority or Inferiority

In Swahili comparatives of superiority/inferiority can be made in several ways and using many different words. The most common ways involve comparative adjectives or certain verbs which will be shown below:

The word *kuliko* can be used as a comparative of superiority/inferiority and carries the meaning of ". . . than" where the blank spot would be filled by another adjective, for example when using the adjective *hodari* with *kuliko* you get *hodari kuliko* which means "cleverer than" as shown below:

> *Mtoto wangu ni hodari kuliko mtoto wako.* – My child is cleverer than your child.

Note however that *kuliko* can also be used not only as an comparative of superiority/inferiority but as a locative to indicate a place where something exists, for example:

> *Hapa ni mahali kuliko na watu wengi sana.* – This is the place where there are many people.

The word *bora* meaning "better" or "best" must be combined with *kuliko:*

> *Afya ni bora kuliko mali.* – Health is better than wealth.

The words *afadhali* and *heri* must be used at the start of the sentence and are translated as "better" or "it is better" and must have *kuliko* in the sentence to form a comparative of superiority:

> *Heri kununua nyumba kuliko kununua gari.* – Better to buy a house than to buy a car.
> *Afadhali kuchelewa kuliko kukosa.* – Better late than to miss (it).

The adjective *zaidi* can be combined with the *-a* of Association to form *zaidi ya* which is a comparative of superiority meaning "more than." The verb *zidi*, meaning "increased" and/or "more than," which is the root word of *zaidi* can be used instead of *zaidi ya*.

Mfuko wangu ni mpana zaidi ya mfuko wake. – My bag is wider
than his/her bag.
Bei ya chakula imezidi mfumko. – The price of food has increased
more than inflation.

The verbs *shinda* and *pita* can be used in a comparative sense. The
literal translation of *shinda* is "pass, defeat" and the translation of *pita* is
"pass, exceed." When these verbs are used in a comparative sense they
take the meaning of "better than" and are comparatives of superiority.

Timu ya mpira ya Hispania imeshinda timu ya Uholanzi.
Literally: The Spanish soccer team has beaten the Dutch team.
Therefore: The Spanish soccer team is better than the Dutch team.

Unafahamu Kirusi kupita Kiingereza.
Literally: Your understanding of Russian exceeds English.
Therefore: You (sing.) understand Russian better than English.

The adjective *duni* can be combined with the *-a* of Association to
form *duni ya* which is a comparative of inferiority meaning "less than."
The verb *pungua* meaning "become less" can also be used as a comparative of inferiority.

Masanduku ya hati yana uzani duni ya sanduku la betri. – The
boxes of documents weigh less than the box of batteries.
Chakula kimepungua utamu. – The food has become less tasty.

Comparative statements can also be formed by naming two nouns
and making a statement that compares the two nouns. The comparison
can be either a comparison of equality or a comparison of superiority/
inferiority, for example:

Mohammad na Henry, Henry ni mwembamba. – Mohammad and
Henry, Henry is thinner.

In some cases the two nouns being compared can be replaced by the
appropriate demonstratives, for example:

Huyu na yule, yule ni mwembamba. – This (person) and that (person), that is thinner.

Practice Exercise B

Translate the following sentences into English.

6. *Yeye ni mwoga kuliko mtu wa kawaida.*
7. *Damu ni nzito kuliko maji.*
8. *Fedha na dhahabu, dhahabu ni ghali zaidi.*
9. *Sanaa umbuji hii ni muhimu kuliko sanaa ya nchi ile.*
10. *Dunia ni moto duni ya Zuhura.*

Section C: Superlatives

As stated in the introduction, superlatives have the same use in Swahili as in English, to show that something has the maximum degree of a quality compared to anything else in that context. In Swahili superlatives are formed by using one of the words, *-ote* or *-o -ote*, also sometimes *kuliko* can be used, for example:

My dad is better than all dads. (My dad is the best). – *Baba yangu ni bora kuliko baba wote.*

In Swahili superlative adjectives can be made in several ways and using many different words. The most common words will be shown below.

The adjective *zaidi ya* or the verb *zidi* can be used to form a superlative.

Mfuko wangu ni mpana zaidi ya mifuko yote. – My bag is wider than all bags.
Mfuko wangu ni mpana zaidi ya mfuko wo wote. – My bag is wider than any bag.
Bei ya chakula imezidi bei zote. – The price of food has increased more than all prices.
Bei ya chakula imezidi bei yo yote. – The price of food has increased more than any price.

The adjective *duni ya* or the verb *pungua* can be used to form a superlative.

Masanduku ya hati yana uzani duni ya masanduku yote. – The boxes of documents weigh less than all boxes.

Masanduku ya hati yana uzani duni ya sanduku lo lote. – The boxes of documents weigh less than any box.

Chakula kimepungua utamu kuliko vyakula vyote. – The food has become less tasty than all foods.

Chakula kimepungua utamu kuliko chakula cho chote. – The food has become less tasty than any food.

The verbs *shinda* and *pita* can be used to form a superlative.

Timu ya mpira ya Hispania imeshinda timu zote. – The Spanish soccer team has beaten all teams.

Timu ya mpira ya Hispania inaweza kushinda timu yo yote. – The Spanish soccer team is able to beat any team.

Unafahamu Kirusi kupita lugha nyingine zote. – Your understanding of Russian exceeds all other languages.

Unafahamu Kirusi kupita lugha nyingine yo yote. – Your understanding of Russian exceeds any other language.

A statement can be used to form a superlative.

Henry ni mwembamba kuliko watu wote. – Henry is thinner than all people.

Henry ni mwembamba kuliko mtu ye yote. – Henry is thinner than any person.

Practice Exercise C

Translate the following sentences into Swahili.

11. The cobra is a more dangerous snake than any snake.
12. Francis's handwriting is neater than the handwriting of all the students.
13. My car insurance is the largest of all my bills.
14. The environment of Canada is better than the environment of any country.
15. The flowers from Tanzania are more beautiful than all flowers.

New Vocabulary

-a kawaida: usual, average, normal
afadhali: better, it is better
afya: health
bei: price(s)
betri: battery(ies)
bili: bill(s)
bima: insurance
chelewa: be late
damu: blood
dhahabu: gold
duni ya: less than
fanana: resemble
hati: document(s), certificate(s)
heri: better, it is better
Hispania: Spain
jana: yesterday
kama: as, if, like, "as . . . as," about
kiasi/vi-: amount(s), measure(s)
Kirusi: Russian, Russian language
kosa: miss, fail
kuliko: more, . . . than, where something exists
kutoka: from
lingana: match, harmonize
lugha: language(s)
mali: wealth, property(ies), possession(s)
mazingira: environment(s)
mfumko: inflation
miwani: eyeglasses
mpenzi/wa-: dear(s), loved one(s), girlfriend(s)
muhimu: important, urgent
mwanajeshi/wa-: soldier(s)
mwandiko/mi-: handwriting(s)
mwoga/waoga: swimmer(s), coward(s)
nadhifu: clean, neat, tidy
nguvu: strength, power, force
nyesha: rain
pacha/ma-: twin(s)

-pana: wide, flat
pita: pass, exceed
pua: nose(s), nozzle(s)
pungua: reduce, become less
sanaa: art(s), craft(s)
sanaa umbuji: fine art(s)
sawa na: equal to, similar
sawasawa: same, O.K.
shinda: pass, defeat, win
shujaa: brave
sifa: quality(ies), praise(s), characteristic(s)
sura: face(s), appearance(s)
swila: cobra(s)
televisheni: television(s)
timu: team(s)
Uholanzi: The Netherlands, Holland
unyoya/manyoya: feather(s)
utamu: sweetness, tastiness
uzani: weight
vilevile: also, equally
weza: able
zaidi: more
zaidi ya: more than
zidi: increase, more than
Zuhura: Venus
zulia/ma-: carpet(s), rug(s)

Key to Exercises

Answers to Practice Exercise A

1. *Kihindi ni lugha ngumu kama Kiingereza.*
2. *Pua yake inafanana na pua yangu.*
3. *Sisi tunaandika kitabu cha Kiswahili vilevile.*
4. *Yeye ni mwepesi kama unyoya.*
5. *Ilinyesha kwa nguvu sawasawa kama jana.*

Answers to Practice Exercise B

6. He/She is more afraid than the average person.
7. Blood is heavier than water. (Swahili proverb meaning Blood is thicker than water)
8. Silver and gold, gold is more expensive.
9. This fine art is more important than that country's art.
10. The Earth is less hot than Venus.

Answers to Practice Exercise C

11. *Swila ni nyoka hatari zaidi kuliko nyoka ye yote.*
12. *Mwandiko wa Francis ni nadhifu kuliko miandiko ya wanafunzi wote.*
13. *Bima ya gari langu ni kubwa kuliko bili zangu zote.*
14. *Mazingira ya nchi ya Kanada ni bora kuliko mazingira ya nchi yo yote.*
15. *Maua kutoka Tanzania ni mazuri zaidi kuliko maua yote.*

Chapter 16

Question Words, Phrases and Statements

Questions in Swahili are formed from question words, question phrases and by changing statements into questions. Each of these ways is discussed in detail below.

Section A: Question Words

Listed below are nine commonly used question words:

1. *Je?* – Well, how about?
2. *Nani?* – Who?
3. *Nini?* – What?
4. *Lini?* – When?
5. *Wapi?* – Where?
6. *Vipi?* – How?
7. *-pi?* – What?, Which?, or Where?
8. *-ngapi*? – How many?
9. *Gani?* – What?, What kind (of), How? or Which?

Note on word order: As you will see, the majority of question words listed above can appear at the beginning, in the middle or at the end of the sentence. The question word *Gani?* is the only one which appears either in the middle or at the end of the sentence but NEVER at the beginning of the sentence as we shall see in the examples below.

Je? (meaning "Well, How about?")

The question word *Je?* is used in three ways. The first one is when it is used at the beginning of a sentence to alert the listener that a question is about to be asked as shown in the examples below:

Je, mwalimu hajambo? – How is the teacher?
Je, unasema Kiswahili? – Do you speak Swahili?

The second way is when *Je?* is used at the end of the sentence to enquire about someone or something. For example:

Na yule mtoto je? – And what about that child?
Na nyumba ile je? – And what about that house?

The third way of using the question word *Je?* is when it is suffixed to the main verb, no matter where the verb occurs in a sentence. In this context, *Je?* imparts the meaning of "how" something is done. For example:

Kijana aliandikaje barua pepe? – How did the youth write the email?
Mwalimu alifundishaje Kireno? – How did the teacher teach Portuguese?

Practice Exercise A

Translate into English.

1. *Mkulima alilimaje shamba?*
2. *Je, baba yako hajambo?*
3. *Wachezaji walikwendaje Los Angeles?*
4. *Je, wanafunzi hawajambo?*
5. *Tutafanyaje?*

Nani? (meaning "Who?")

The word *Nani?* is used to ask questions about people. For example:

Nani ni Rais wa Marekani? – Who is the President of the United States?
Wewe ni nani? – Who are you?

Ninataka kujua, nani ni daktari? – I want to know, who is the doctor?

Translate into Swahili.

6. Who is studying in Japan?
7. Who speaks Swahili?
8. Who wrote the song?
9. Who bought the oranges?
10. Who are they?

Nini? (meaning "What?")

The word *Nini?* is used to ask questions about things. For example:

Anafanya nini? – What is he/she doing?
Polisi walifanya nini dukani? – What did the police do in the store?
Nini ilianguka? – What fell down?

Translate into Swahili.

11. What is Fatima doing?
12. What is the editor reading?
13. What will he/she do tomorrow?
14. What are you doing?
15. What is uncle reading?

Lini? (meaning "When?")

The word *Lini?* is used to ask questions about when something was done. For example:

Joshua alikwenda lini New York? – When did Joshua go to New York?
Lini utasoma Kifaransa? – When will you study French?
Mgeni alifika lini? – When did the guest arrive?

Translate into English.

16. *Lini atakwenda Ajentina?*
17. *Mwanasiasa atafika lini?*
18. *Lini utanunua Kamusi ya Kiingereza?*

19. *Lini utasoma?*
20. *Lini baba atarudi?*

Wapi? (meaning "Where?")

The word *Wapi?* is used to ask questions about places. For example:

Wapi tutapata maji ya kunywa? – Where shall we get drinking water?
Thomas anasoma wapi? – Where does Thomas study?
Mwalimu alifundisha wapi mwaka jana? – Where did the teacher teach last year?

Translate into English.

21. *Mhandisi anakaa wapi?*
22. *Msichana alinunua wapi kitabu?*
23. *Utakwenda wapi Jumamosi?*
24. *Wapi atanunua diski madhubuti?*
25. *Atafanya kazi wapi baada ya masomo yake?*

Vipi? (meaning "How?")

The word *Vipi?* is used to ask about how something was done. For example:

Vipi alisafiri kwenda London? – How did he/she travel to London?
Waliandika vipi? – How did they write?
Mlisoma vipi vitabu vya Kirusi? – How did you (pl.) read the Russian books?

Note: Questions using the word "How?" can also be asked using the question phrases *Kwa vipi?* (How?) or *Kwa namna gani?* (How?). However, these two question phrases can appear only at the end of a Swahili question sentence. For example:

Alisafiri kwa vipi? – How did he/she travel?
Aliendesha gari namna gani? – How did he/she drive the car?

Translate into Swahili.

26. How did he/she swim?
27. How did they build the house?
28. How did they work?
29. How did the child converse?
30. How did he/she travel?

-pi? (meaning "What?," "Which?" or "Where?")

The Interrogative Suffix *-pi?* can be used to ask questions about people and objects by combining the Interrogative Prefixes with the Interrogative Suffix *-pi?* in both singular and plural forms as shown in Table 16.1

TABLE 16.1
Interrogative Prefixes

Singular/Plural	Noun Class	Interrogative Prefix	Interrogative Suffix
Singular/Plural	M-/WA-	*yu-/we-*	*-pi?*
Singular/Plural	M-/MI-	*u-/i-*	*-pi?*
Singular/Plural	JI-/MA-	*li-/ya-*	*-pi?*
Singular/Plural	KI-/VI-	*ki-/vi-*	*-pi?*
Singular/Plural	N-	*i-/zi-*	*-pi?*
Singular/Plural	U-	*u-/zi-*	*-pi?*
Singular/Plural	PA-	*pa-*	*-pi?*
		ku-	*-pi?*
		m-	*-pi?*
Singular	KU-	*ku-*	*-pi?*

If we want to ask: "Which person?" we combine the Interrogative Prefix *yu-* with the Interrogative Suffix *-pi?* to form *Yupi?* (Which person?) for third person singular. For plural form we combine the Interrogative Prefix *we-* with the Interrogative Suffix *-pi?* to form *Wepi?* (Which people?). Hence we get:

Mtu yupi? – Which person?
Watu wepi? – Which people?

Examples:

> *Mwanajeshi yupi alipata nishani?* – Which soldier received a medal?
> *Mti upi ulianguka?* – Which tree fell?
> *Maneno yapi?* – Which words?

Provide the Interrogative Prefixes by filling the blank spaces before the Interrogative Suffix *-pi?* as shown in the example below.

> Question: *Kitabu ___ -pi?*
> Answer: *Kitabu kipi?*

> 31. *Mtu _____ -pi?*
> 32. *Mwindaji _____ -pi?*
> 33. *Waganga _____ -pi?*
> 34. *Mti _____ -pi?*
> 35. *Miti _____ -pi?*
> 36. *Baiskeli (pl.) _____ -pi?*
> 37. *Vitabu _____ -pi?*
> 38. *Nyumba (pl.) _____ -pi?*
> 39. *Ua _____ -pi?*
> 40. *Mgiriki _____ -pi?*

-ngapi? (meaning "How many?")

The word *-ngapi?* which denotes quantity, is used to ask questions about people or things. This is done by combining the Plural Nominal Prefixes with the Interrogative Suffix *-ngapi?* as seen in Table 16.2

Note: Since the Question Word *-ngapi?* involves quantities of things, the singular nominal prefixes are not used. As well, plural nominal prefixes are not required for nouns in N- and U- noun classes.

Thus if we want to ask questions relating to people or objects, we combine the appropriate Plural Nominal Prefix with the Interrogative Suffix *-ngapi?* (See Table 16.2). For example:

> *Alifundisha wafanyakazi wangapi?* – How many workers did he/
>   she teach?
> *Wangapi watasaidia?* – How many people will help?
> *Ulinunua mito mingapi?* – How many pillows did you buy?
> *Walikaa katika nyumba ngapi?* – How many houses did they live
>   in?

TABLE 16.2
Interrogative Suffix Nominal Prefixes

Singular/Plural	Noun Class	Plural Nominal Prefixes	Interrogative Suffix
Singular/Plural	M-/WA	*wa-*	*-ngapi?*
Singular/Plural	M-/MI-	*mi-*	*-ngapi?*
Singular/Plural	JI-/MA-	*ma-*	*-ngapi?*
Singular/Plural	KI-/VI-	*vi-*	*-ngapi?*
Singular/Plural	N-		*ngapi?*
Singular/Plural	U-		*ngapi?*
Singular/Plural	PA-	*pa-*	*-ngapi?*
Singular/Plural	KU-	*ku-*	*-ngapi?*

> *Baba alinunua baiskeli ngapi mwaka jana?* – How many bicycles did dad buy last year?

Translate into English.

41. *Walikuja watu wangapi?*
42. *Wachezaji walinunua vitabu vingapi?*
43. *Atakaa Ghana siku ngapi?*
44. *Tutasoma Kihindi miezi mingapi?*
45. *Tutanunua meza ngapi?*

Gani? (meaning "What?," "What kind (of)," "How?" or Which?)

The word *Gani?* is used to ask questions about objects. Note on word order: As mentioned above, this question word appears either in the middle or at the end of the sentence but NEVER at the beginning of a sentence. For example:

> *Mary anakaa mtaa gani?* – On which/what street does Mary reside?
> *Mtoto alicheza mchezo gani?* – What type of game did the child play?
> *Mtu gani?* – Which person?

Note: In the last example, the word *mtu* does not refer to a specific person. Instead, it refers to a person as a general object.

Translate into English.

46. *Mshonaji atakuja siku gani?*
47. *Habari gani bwana?*
48. *Wageni gani walifika jana usiku?*
49. *Mkulima gani alipata trekta?*
50. *Babu alipanda ndege gani?*

Section B: Question Phrases

Phrases that are used to ask questions in Swahili include the following:

1. *Kwa nini?* – Why? or By what means (of transport)?
2. *Kwa sababu gani?* – Why? or For what reason?
3. *Kwa nani?* – At whose place?

Note on word order: Question Phrases are divided into two categories. The first category comprises Question Phrases that can appear either at the beginning or at the end of the sentence as shown in the examples below:

Kwa nini alisoma Kiarabu? – Why did he/she study Arabic?
Sarah anakwenda shuleni kwa nini? – By what means does Sarah travel to school?
Kwa sababu gani alikwenda Marekani? – For what reason did he/she go to America?
Waliandika kitabu kwa sababu gani? – For what reason did they write the book?

The second category of Question Phrases is that which is used at the end of the sentence only, NEVER at the beginning as shown in the examples below:

John alikaa kwa nani? – At whose place did John stay?

Practice Exercise B

Translate into Swahili.

51. Why is he/she studying English?
52. At whose place did he/she stay?
53. Why did he/she cry?

Section C: Questions from Statements

Another way of asking questions in Swahili is by making a statement and raising your voice slightly at the end of the sentence for the last two or three syllables and lowering the voice for the final syllable[1] just like in other languages including English.

Examples:

Statement: *Anasoma kitabu cha Kijerumani* – He/She is reading a German book.

Question: *Anasoma kitabu cha Kijerumani?* – He/She is reading a German book?

Practice Exercise C

Translate into Swahili.

54. Is he/she teaching French?
55. Are they reading English books?

New Vocabulary

Ajentina: Argentina
baada ya: after, afterwards
barua pepe: e-mail(s)
diski madhubuti: compact disk(s)
endesha: drive
Japani: Japan
Jumamosi: Saturday
Kijerumani: German, German language
kwa nini?: Why?
lia: cry

lini?: when?
Mgiriki/wa-: Greek(s)
mhandisi/wa-: engineer(s)
mjomba/wa-: maternal uncle(s)
mshonaji/wa-: tailor(s)
namna: type(s), kind(s)
neno/ma-: word(s)
nini?: what?
nishani: ceremonial medal(s)
-pi?: which?
sababu: cause, reason
safari: travel
shamba/ma-: farm(s)
siku: day(s)
trekta/ma-: tractor(s)
usiku: night(s)
vipi?: how?
wimbo/nyimbo: song(s)
zungumza: converse

Key to Exercises

Answers to Practice Exercise A

1. How did the farmer cultivate the farm?
2. How is your father?
3. How did the players travel to Los Angeles?
4. How are the students?
5. How shall we do it?
6. *Nani anasoma Japani?*
7. *Nani anasema Kiswahili?*
8. *Nani aliandika wimbo?*
9. *Nani alinunua machungwa?*
10. *Wao ni nani?*
11. *Fatima anafanya nini?*
12. *Mhariri anasoma nini?*
13. *Atafanya nini kesho?*
14. *Unafanya nini?*

15. *Mjomba anasoma nini?*
16. When will he/she go to Argentina?
17. When will the politician arrive?
18. When will you buy an English Dictionary?
19. When will you study?
20. When will father return?
21. Where does the engineer live?
22. Where did the girl buy the book?
23. Where will you go on Saturday?
24. Where will he/she buy a compact disk?
25. Where will he/she work after his/her studies?
26. *Aliogelea vipi?*
27. *Walijenga vipi nyumba?*
28. *Walifanya kazi vipi?*
29. *Mtoto alizungumza vipi?*
30. *Alisafiri vipi?*
31. *yupi?*
32. *yupi?*
33. *wepi?*
34. *upi?*
35. *ipi?*
36. *zipi?*
37. *vipi?*
38. *zipi?*
39. *lipi?*
40. *yupi?*
41. How many people came?
42. How many books did the players buy?
43. For how many days will he/she stay in Ghana?
44. For how many months shall we study Hindi?
45. How many tables shall we buy?
46. Which day will the tailor come?
47. How are you sir?
48. What kind of guests arrived last night?
49. Which farmer got a tractor?
50. Which airplane did grandpa fly on?

Answers to Practice Exercise B

51. *Kwa nini anasoma Kiingereza?*
52. *Alikaa kwa nani?*
53. *Alilia kwa sababu gani/kwa nini?*

Answers to Practice Exercise C

54. *Anafundisha Kifaransa?*
55. *Wanasoma vitabu vya Kiingereza?*

Note

1. Wilson, 77.

Chapter 17

The Verbs 'To Be,' 'To Have' and 'To Be in a Place'

The verb *kuwa* means "to be" or "to become," the verb *kuwa na* means "to have" or "to be with" and the verb *kuwako* means "to be in a place." All of these verbs are derived from the Monosyllabic verb *wa* which means "be." Since these verbs are derived from a Monosyllabic verb, they follow the rules studied in Chapters 5, 6, 10 for making and negating sentences using Monosyllabic verbs. *Kuwa*, *kuwa na* and *kuwako* can be used with all tenses, however, in the present tense, they take irregular forms. In the present tense, the verb *kuwa* becomes *ni*, the verb *kuwa na* becomes *-na* and the verb *kuwako* becomes *-ko*.

Section A: *Kuwa* (to be or to become)

The verb *kuwa* means "to be" or "to become." As you may recall from our previous Chapters, verbs are used in the following structure in a simple sentence:

Subject prefix + Tense marker + Verb

The following are a few examples of sentences using *kuwa* in the simple past, past perfect and future tenses.

Alikuwa hodari. – He/She was clever.
Wamekuwa matajiri. – They have become wealthy people.
Nitakuwa mwalimu. – I will become a teacher.

The above sentences are negated as follows:

Hakuwa hodari. – He/She was not clever.
Hawajakuwa matajiri. – They have not yet become wealthy people.
Sitakuwa mwalimu. – I will not become a teacher.

When we use *kuwa* in the present tense, the verb *kuwa* is substituted by *ni*. In this context the word *ni* is translated as "am," "is" or "are" and carries the meaning of "be." It should not be confused with the subject prefix *ni-* which translates as "I."

~~Subject prefix~~ + ~~Tense marker~~ + Irregular form of the Verb (*ni*)

The following are a few examples of sentences using *ni*.

Baba yake ni mhasibu. – His/her father is an accountant.
Sahani hizi ni ghali. – These plates are expensive.
Maembe yale ni mabivu. – Those mangoes are ripe.

In order to negate sentences using *ni* in the present tense, the verb *ni* is replaced by its negative form, which is *si* and is translated as "am not," "is not" or "are not" and carries the meaning of "not to be." Therefore, the above sentences are negated as follows:

Baba yake si mhasibu. – His/her father is not an accountant.
Sahani hizi si ghali. – These plates are not expensive.
Maembe yale si mabivu. – Those mangoes are not ripe.

Practice Exercise A

Translate the following sentences into English.

1. *Shangazi alikuwa mgonjwa.*
2. *Wanawake watakuwa maofisa wa kampuni.*
3. *Mpishi amekuwa mmlikaji wa hoteli.*
4. *Mjomba wangu atakuwa mwigizaji.*
5. *Yeye ni nani?*
6. *Kusoma kwake ni kuzuri.*
7. *Mwezi huu si Januari.*

8. *Watakuwa wapeketevu baada ya kupata vyeo vipya.*
9. *Sasa hivi ni baridi nje.*
10. *Mananasi yale hayajakuwa matamu.*
11. *Majani yatakuwa manjano katika majira ya pukutiko la majani.*
12. *Mashua hayakuwa tayari kusafiri.*
13. *Bendera hii haitakuwa chafu.*
14. *Wakati wa majira ya baridi, matunda ni ghali.*
15. *Tembo wako atakuwa mzee baada ya miaka michache.*

Section B: *Kuwa na* (to have or to be with)

The verb *kuwa na* means "to have" or "to be with." As you may recall from our previous Chapters, verbs are used in the following structure in a simple sentence:

Subject prefix + Tense marker + Verb

The following are a few examples of sentences using *kuwa na* in the simple past, past perfect and future tenses.

Nilikuwa na watoto wangu. – I was with my children.
Watakuwa na gari kesho kutwa. – They will have a car the day
    after tomorrow.
Mmekuwa na bahati nzuri. – You (pl.) have had good luck.
Palikuwa na wadudu wengi. – The place (definite) had many
    insects.

The above sentences are negated as follows:

Sikuwa na watoto wangu. – I was not with my children.
Hawatakuwa na gari kesho kutwa. – They will not have a car the
    day after tomorrow.
Hamjakuwa na bahati nzuri. – You (pl.) have not yet had good
    luck.
Hapakuwa na wadudu wengi. – The place (definite) did not have
    many insects.

When we use *kuwa na* in the present tense, the verb *kuwa na* is substituted by *-na*. In this context, the word *-na* still carries the meaning of "have" and it should not be confused with *-na* which is used to construct reciprocal verbs as taught in Chapter 27.

Subject prefix + ~~Tense marker~~ + Irregular form of the Verb (*-na*)

The following are a few examples of sentences using *-na*:

> *Kiti hiki kina rangi nyekundu.* – This chair has a red colour.
>   (This chair is red).
> *Wana mboga za aina nyingi sokoni.* – They have many kinds of
>   vegetables in the market.
> *Seremala ana wateja wapya.* – The carpenter has new customers.

As you can see in the sentences above, the present tense is implied and therefore, the present tense marker *-na-* is omitted.

The above sentences are negated as follows:

> *Kiti hiki hakina rangi nyekundu.* – This chair does not have a red
>   colour. (This chair is not red).
> *Hawana mboga za aina nyingi sokoni.* – They do not have many
>   kinds of vegetables in the market.
> *Seremala hana wateja wapya.* – The carpenter does not have
>   new customers.

Practice Exercise B

Translate the following sentences into Swahili.

16. He/She has a good driver.
17. Their grandmother has a good soul.
18. They have several bags of onions.
19. That village has few inhabitants.
20. I will have a good life.
21. The beggar does not have any food.
22. Do you have a bag?
23. Will he/she not have enough money?
24. The room did not have large windows.
25. He/She has not yet had the opportunity to go to school.

26. Your brother has a good wife.
27. The students will not have an exam at the end of the term.
28. I have not yet had the time to finish my work.
29. We will have a great cook.
30. The author does not have his/her manuscript.

Section C: *Kuwako* (to be in a place)

The verb *kuwako* means "to be in a place." As you may recall from our previous Chapters, verbs are used in the following structure in a simple sentence:

Subject prefix + Tense marker + Verb

The following are a few examples of sentences using *kuwako* in the simple past, past perfect and future tenses. As you may recall about the PA- (Mahali) class taught in Chapter 10, it consists of the locative suffixes -*ko*, -*po* and -*mo* which represent indefinite, definite and inside a place respectively.

Watakuwako barabarani. – They will be on the street.
Ua lilikuwapo bustanini. – The flower was in the garden.
Mchele umekuwamo kabatini. – The uncooked rice has been in the cupboard.

The above sentences are negated as follows:

Hawatakuwako barabarani. – They will not be on the street.
Ua halikuwapo bustanini. – The flower was not in the garden.
Mchele haujakuwamo kabatini. – The uncooked rice has not yet been in the cupboard.

When *kuwako* is used in the present tense, the verb *kuwako* is substituted by -*ko*, -*po* or -*mo* depending on the location.

Subject prefix + ~~Tense marker~~ +
Irregular form of the Verb (-*ko*, -*po*, -*mo*)

The following are a few examples of sentences using *-ko, -po* or *-mo*:

Fatuma yuko shambani. – Fatuma is on the farm.
Wafamasi wapo dukani. – The pharmacists are in the shop.
Vyombo vimo kabatini. – The utensils are in the cupboard.

The above sentences are negated as follows:

Fatuma hayuko shambani. – Fatuma is not on the farm.
Wafamasi hawapo dukani. – The pharmacists are not in the shop.
Vyombo havimo kabatini. – The utensils are not in the cupboard.

Please note when using subject prefixes with locative suffixes *-ko, -po* or *-mo,* the subject prefix for 3rd person singular *a-* changes to *yu-* as you can see from the example above.

In addition to using *kuwako* to indicate "to be in a place," we can also use *kuwa* to indicate location. This can be done in simple past, past perfect and future tenses but cannot be done in present tense. Here are few examples:

Watakuwako barabarani. – They will be on the street.
Watakuwa barabarani. – They will be on the street.

Please note that when we use *kuwa* to indicate "to be in a place," we cannot specify whether it is indefinite, definite or inside a place.

Practice Exercise C

Translate the following sentences into Swahili.

31. *Chui atakuwako zu.*
32. *Nyangumi wamo baharini.*
33. *Jirani hayuko mahakamani.*
34. *Mayai hayamo frijini.*
35. *Kisu kimekuwapo mezani kutwa.*
36. *Mapiramidi yako Misri.*
37. *Maharamia walikuwa hapa mwezi wa Machi.*
38. *Almasi zipo ardhini.*
39. *Ndege mwekundu yupo tawini.*
40. *Mwanafunzi yule hakuwa darasani jana.*

41. *Saa ya ukuta itakuwamo chumba cha kulia.*
42. *Abiria wamo katika basi.*
43. *Tangazo lipo ubaoni.*
44. *Wazo hili halikuwa kichwani mwangu.*
45. *Mchezaji sinema mashuhuri atakuwa katika tamasha la filamu.*

New Vocabulary

abiria: passenger(s)
aina: kind(s), type(s) of
almasi: diamond(s)
ardhi: land(s), ground(s)
bahari: sea(s), ocean(s)
bahati: luck
basi/ma-: bus(es)
bendera: flag(s)
-bivu: ripe
-chache: few
cheo/vy-: position(s), title(s)
chui: leopard(s)
chumba/vy- cha/vya kulia: dining room(s)
embe/ma-: mango(es)
filamu: film(s)
friji: refrigerator(s)
haramia/ma-: bandit(s), pirate(s)
hoteli: hotel(s), restaurant(s)
Januari: January
kadhaa: several
kampuni: company(ies)
kesho kutwa: day after tomorrow
kichwa/vi-: head(s)
kijiji/vi-: village(s)
kitunguu/vi-: onion(s)
kutosha: enough
kutwa: all day
kuwako: to be in a place
Machi: March
mahakama: law court(s)
maisha: life(ves)

majira ya baridi: winter(s)
majira ya pukutiko la majani: autumn(s)
mashua: small boat(s)
mashuhuri: famous, important
mchele: uncooked rice
mfamasi/wa-: pharmacist(s)
mhasibu/wa-: accountant(s)
Misri: Egypt
mkazi/wa-: inhabitant(s), resident(s)
mmilikaji/wa-: owner(s)
mpeketevu/wa-: arrogant person(s)
mswada/mi-: manuscript(s), legislative bill(s)
mteja/wa-: customer(s)
mtunzi/wa-: author(s), composer(s)
muda: period(s), time(s)
muhula/mihula: term(s), period(s)
mwigizaji/wa-: actor(s)
nafasi: space(s), opportunity(ies)
njano: yellow
nje: outside
nyangumi: whale(s)
piramidi/ma-: pyramid(s)
rangi: colour(s)
roho: spirit(s), soul(s)
saa ya/za ukuta: clock(s)
sahani: plate(s)
sasa hivi: right now
seremala/ma-: carpenter(s)
tajiri/ma-: wealthy person(s)
tamasha: festival(s), show(s)
tangazo/ma-: notice(s), advertisement(s)
tembo: elephant(s)
-wa na: be with, have
zu: zoo(s)

Key to Exercises

Answers to Practice Exercise A

1. The aunt was sick.
2. The women will be officers of companies.
3. The cook has become the owner of the hotel/restaurant.
4. My uncle will become an actor.
5. Who is he/she?
6. His/her reading is good.
7. This month is not January.
8. They will become arrogant people after getting new positions.
9. Right now, it is cold outside.
10. Those pineapples have not yet become sweet.
11. The leaves will become yellow in the autumn.
12. The boats were not ready to travel.
13. This flag will not become dirty.
14. In the winter, the fruits are expensive.
15. Your elephant will become old after a few years.

Answers to Practice Exercise B

16. *Ana dereva mzuri.*
17. *Bibi yao ana roho nzuri.*
18. *Wana mifuko kadhaa ya vitunguu.*
19. *Kijiji kile kina wakazi wachache.*
20. *Nitakuwa na maisha mazuri.*
21. *Mwombaji hana chakula cho chote.*
22. *Una mfuko?*
23. *Hatakuwa na pesa za kutosha?*
24. *Chumba hakikuwa na madirisha makubwa.*
25. *Hajakuwa na nafasi ya kwenda shuleni.*
26. *Kaka yako ana mke mwema.*
27. *Wanafunzi hawatakuwa na mtihani mwisho wa muhula.*
28. *Sijakuwa na muda wa kumaliza kazi yangu.*
29. *Tutakuwa na mpishi mzuri.*
30. *Mtunzi hana mswada wake.*

Answers to Practice Exercise C

31. The tiger will be at the zoo.
32. The whales are in the ocean.
33. The neighbor is not at the court.
34. The eggs are not in the fridge.
35. The knife has been on the table all day.
36. The pyramids are in Egypt.
37. The pirates were here in March.
38. The diamonds are in the ground.
39. The red bird is on the branch.
40. That student was not in class yesterday.
41. The clock will be in the dining room.
42. The passengers are in the bus.
43. The notice is on the board.
44. This idea was not in my head.
45. The famous actor will be at the film festival.

Chapter 18

Numbers

In this Chapter we will learn about cardinal numbers, which are used to count in Swahili, numbers that take noun class agreement, and the proper word order when using numbers in a sentence.

Section A: From 0 to 9

Here are the numbers from the "singles column" in Swahili.

0 – *sifuri*
1 – *moja*
2 – *mbili*
3 – *tatu*
4 – *nne*
5 – *tano*
6 – *sita*
7 – *saba*
8 – *nane*
9 – *tisa*

When used to count nouns the numbers 1, 2, 3, 4, 5 and 8 take agreement with the noun they describe. The numbers 6, 7 and 9 do not take noun class agreement. (See Section D)

10 to 90

Here are the numbers from the "tens column" in Swahili.

10 – *kumi*
20 – *ishirini*
30 – *thelathini*
40 – *arobaini*
50 – *hamsini*
60 – *sitini*
70 – *sabini*
80 – *themanini*
90 – *tisini*

Using the numbers from the "tens column" above and the numbers from the "singles column" in Section A, it is possible to construct any number between 11 and 99. This is done by using a special construction known as the *na* (and) construction. For example, the word for "eleven" in Swahili is *kumi na moja*. This word is constructed from *kumi* (ten) and *moja* (one) and uses the word *na* (and) to join them together. Below are more examples of numbers from 11 to 99.

11 – *kumi na moja*
19 – *kumi na tisa*
34 – *thelathini na nne*
66 – *sitini na sita*
97 – *tisini na saba*

Practice Exercise A

Write the following numbers in Swahili.

1. 15
2. 26
3. 29
4. 38
5. 47
6. 55
7. 61
8. 72
9. 88
10. 92

Section B: Higher Numbers

100 – *mia*
1,000 – *elfu*
100,000 – *laki*
1 million – *milioni*
1 billion – *bilioni*

The *na* (and) construction is also used to make higher numbers up to infinity. Here are some examples:

109 – *mia moja na tisa*
851 – *mia nane, hamsini na moja*
3,003 – *elfu tatu na tatu*
75,400 – *elfu sabini na tano, mia nne*

However, not all higher numbers need the *na* (and) construction to form numbers. For example, simple numbers such as 4 000 000 are made by stating the column, in this case *milioni* and then how many millions *nne* to form *milioni nne*. Here are more examples of simple numbers.

3,000 – *elfu tatu*
500 – *mia tano*
8,000,000,000 – *bilioni nane*
100,000 – *laki moja*

Now let us combine all of the rules learned so far and look at numbers consisting of many units.

109,007 – *laki moja, elfu tisa na saba*
2,908,330 – *milioni mbili, laki tisa, elfu nane, mia tatu na thelathini*
8,177,345 – *milioni nane, laki moja, sabini na saba elfu, mia tatu, arobaini na tano*

Note that in the second example the *na* at the end of the sentence is optional.

There is one final thing that the reader should be aware of when dealing with higher numbers in Swahili and that is the potential for confusion. This confusion can occur when dealing with numbers containing "thousands" (*elfu*), "millions" (*milioni*) or "billions" (*bilioni*). Some examples will illustrate the problem.

10,004 – *elfu kumi na nne* – literally – thousands ten and four
14,000 – *elfu kumi na nne* – literally – thousands fourteen

As you can see by the examples above, the words in Swahili referring to the numbers would be written exactly the same. To avoid this confusion many Swahili speakers these days break the normal grammar rule of putting the number of thousands AFTER the word "*elfu*" and INSTEAD put the number of thousands IN FRONT of the word "*elfu*" so 14,000 would be like in English:

kumi na nne elfu – literally – ten and four (fourteen) thousands

This solution is also used for numbers containing millions and billions.

For example, 100 billion would be:

mia moja bilioni – literally – one hundred billion.

Practice Exercise B

Write these numbers in Swahili.

11. 34,899
12. 555,978
13. 8,132
14. 642
15. 9,437,450
16. 67,000
17. 544
18. 1,220
19. 7,795,794
20. 6,885
21. 11,000,004

22. 78,000
23. 3,710,001
24. 360,009
25. 908,695

Section C: Counting Nouns

Numbers in Swahili are considered to be a type of adjective, however, as mentioned at the end of Section A, only the numbers 1, 2, 3, 4, 5, and 8 must agree with the nouns they qualify. This is because these numbers are Bantu numbers, the rest having been borrowed primary from Arabic with a few English words for very large numbers. This noun class agreement is based on the agreement an adjective must take, with a few exceptions. Table 18.1 illustrates the correct agreement (if any) for each noun class.

Please note that when dealing with several of the noun classes, the word for two (*mbili*) changes to the form *-wili* and then has the appropriate prefix attached to it. The number 2 is the only number that changes form before having a prefix attached. The numbers 1, 3, 4, 5 and 8 simply have the prefix attached without any modifications. Here are some more examples using numbers besides 1 and 2.

Magari matano – five cars
Vichwa vitatu – three heads
Wafanyakazi wanane – eight workers
Mahali panne – four places

Noun agreement is applied whenever the numbers 1, 2, 3, 4, 5, and 8 are used in the "single digit column," even if it is part of a larger number. Here are some examples:

Vitabu mia moja na kimoja – one hundred and one books
Magari tisini na manane – Ninety-eight vehicles
Rafiki thelathini na nne – Thirty-four friends

Note that in the final example *nne* does not have a prefix because the word *rafiki* is an N- class noun.

TABLE 18.1
Agreement Prefixes for Numerals 1, 2, 3, 4, 5, and 8

Noun Class	Agreement Prefix	Example	Translation
M-/WA- Singular	*m-*	*mtu mmoja*	one person
Plural	*wa-*	*watu wawili*	two people
M-/MI- Singular	*m-*	*mti mmoja*	one tree
Plural	*mi-*	*miti miwili*	two trees
JI-/MA- Singular	No prefix	*jicho moja*	one eye
Plural	*ma-*	*macho mawili*	two eyes
KI-/VI- Singular	*ki-*	*kiti kimoja*	one chair
Plural	*vi-*	*viti viwili*	two chairs
N- Singular	No prefix	*baiskeli moja*	one bicycle
Plural	No prefix	*baiskeli mbili*	two bicycles
U- Singular	No prefix	*unywele moja*	one hair
Plural	No prefix	*nywele mbili*	two hairs
PA- Singular	*pa-*	*mahali pamoja*	one definite place
Plural	*pa-*	*mahali pawili*	two definite places
	ku-	*mahali kumoja*	one indefinite place
	ku-	*mahali kuwili*	two indefinite places
	m-	*mahali mmoja*	one inside place
	m-	*mahali mwili*	two inside places
KU- Singular	*ku-*	*kusoma kumoja*	one reading
Plural	*ku-*	*kusoma kuwili*	two readings

One final note before we continue to the Practice Exercise. Here again is the proper word order for a Swahili sentence.

Noun, personal possessive, adjective,
quantity, demonstrative and possessive.

Example:

Visu vyangu vikubwa vitano vile vya kale. – Those five big ancient knives of mine.

Practice Exercise C

Write the following sentences in Swahili.

26. Three fruits.
27. One hundred and one people.
28. Those three big clay pots of mine.
29. Your (pl.) six apples.
30. His twenty-eight French students.
31. These twelve very expensive shops.
32. I want five tasty mangoes.
33. Where are our two fancy chairs?
34. Our two fancy chairs are here.
35. He will sell twenty-four fresh eggs at the market.
36. They need to buy one bag of salt.
37. The truck is carrying ninety-four barrels of crude oil.
38. The police confiscated twenty-five cell phones.
39. We have drunk five cups of hot tea.
40. There are one hundred and seventy-three pairs of stylish glasses.
41. My friend's house has two stoves.
42. Every year the world uses 800 billion plastic bags.
43. There are six shirts in the suitcase.
44. The government will construct nine hospitals.

New Vocabulary

-a fahari kupita: stylish
-a moto: hot
-a plastiki: plastic
arobaini: forty
beba: carry
begi/ma-: bag(s)
bilioni: billion
chungu/vy-: pot(s)
elfu: thousand
hamsini: fifty
ishirini: twenty
kumi: ten
kumi na mbili: twelve
kumi na moja: eleven

kumi na nane: eighteen
kumi na nne: fourteen
kumi na saba: seventeen
kumi na sita: sixteen
kumi na tano: fifteen
kumi na tatu: thirteen
kumi na tisa: nineteen
kuna: there is/are
laki: hundred thousand
lori/ma-: truck(s), from the English "lorry"
mafuta ghafi: crude oil
mbili: two
mia: hundred
milioni: million
moja: one
nane: eight
nne: four
nyang'anya: take away (forcefully)
pipa/ma-: barrel(s)
saba: seven
sabini: seventy
sifuri: zero
simu ya/za mkono: cell phone(s) (literally a telephone of the hand)
sita: six
sitini: sixty
tano: five
tatu: three
thelathini: thirty
themanini: eighty
tisa: nine
tisini: ninety
udongo wa kinamu: clay (literally "soil of flexibility")
uza: sell

Key to Exercises

Answers to Practice Exercise A

1. *kumi na tano*
2. *ishirini na sita*
3. *ishirini na tisa*
4. *thelathini na nane*
5. *arobaini na saba*
6. *hamsini na tano*
7. *sitini na moja*
8. *sabini na mbili*
9. *themanini na nane*
10. *tisini na mbili*

Answers to Practice Exercise B

11. *elfu thelathini na nne, mia nane, tisini na tisa*
12. *laki tano, elfu hamsini na tano, mia tisa, sabini na nane*
13. *elfu nane, mia moja, thelathini na mbili*
14. *mia sita, arobaini na mbili*
15. *milioni tisa, laki nne, elfu thelathini na saba, mia nne na hamsini*
16. *elfu sitini na saba*
17. *mia tano, arobaini na nne*
18. *elfu moja, mia mbili na ishirini*
19. *milioni saba, laki saba, elfu tisini na tano, mia saba, tisini na nne*
20. *elfu sita, mia nane, themanini na tano*
21. *kumi na moja milioni na nne*
22. *sabini na nane elfu*
23. *milioni tatu, laki saba, kumi elfu na moja*
24. *laki tatu, sitini elfu na tisa*
25. *laki tisa, elfu nane, mia sita, tisini na tano*

Answers to Practice Exercise C

26. *Matunda matatu.*
27. *Watu mia moja na mmoja.*
28. *Vyungu vyangu vikubwa vitatu vile vya udongo wa kinamu.*

29. *Tufaha zenu sita.*
30. *Wanafunzi wake Wafaransa ishirini na wanane.*
31. *Maduka ghali sana kumi na mawili haya.*
32. *Ninataka maembe matamu matano.*
33. *Viti vyetu viwili vya kupendeza viko wapi?*
34. *Viti vyetu viwili vya kupendeza vipo hapa.*
35. *Atauza mayai mapya ishirini na manne sokoni.*
36. *Wanahitaji kununua mfuko mmoja wa chumvi.*
37. *Lori linabeba mapipa tisini na manne ya mafuta ghafi.*
38. *Polisi walinyang'anya simu za mkono ishirini na tano.*
39. *Tumekunywa vikombe vitano vya chai ya moto.*
40. *Kuna miwani mia moja, sabini na tatu ya fahari kupita.*
41. *Nyumba ya rafiki yangu ina meko mawili.*
42. *Kila mwaka dunia inatumia mabegi ya plastiki mia nane bilioni.*
43. *Kuna mashati sita katika sanduku.*
44. *Serikali itajenga hospitali tisa.*

Chapter 19

More About Swahili Numbers

In this Chapter we will find such concepts as ordinal numbers, weights and measures, fractions, decimals, percentages, temperature and currencies in Swahili.

Section A: Ordinal Numbers

Unlike cardinal numbers, which are used for counting, (as learned in Chapter 18) ordinal numbers are used for placing things in sequential order. All ordinal numbers except for first (*-a kwanza*) and second (*-a pili*) are derived directly from cardinal numbers as shown in the lists below.

Cardinal Number

moja – one
mbili – two
tatu – three
nne – four
tano – five
sita – six
saba – seven
nane – eight
tisa – nine
kumi – ten

Ordinal Number

-a kwanza – first
-a pili – second
-a tatu – third
-a nne – fourth
-a tano – fifth
-a sita – sixth
-a saba – seventh
-a nane – eighth
-a tisa – ninth
-a kumi – tenth

Note that the *-a* of Association must be used in the singular form to construct an ordinal number.

Here are some phrases containing ordinal numbers.

*mwanafunzi wa kwanza*the – first student
kitabu cha pili – the second book
duka la tatu – the third shop
nyumba ya ishirini na moja – the twenty-first house
kisu cha ishirini na mbili – the twenty-second knife
mti wa thelathini na saba – the thirty-seventh tree
gari la mia mbili na mbili – the two hundred and second car

As you can see from the above examples, all numbers above ten follow the same pattern where the *-a* of Association is used with a cardinal number. Also note that higher numbers using the numbers one and two do NOT use *kwanza* or *pili*. They are instead constructed using the cardinal numbers *moja* or *mbili* as shown in the examples above.

Finally, the word *-a mwisho* is used in ordinal numbers to indicate the last position. Here are examples of phrases containing *-a mwisho*:

mwanafunzi wa mwisho – the last student
kitabu cha mwisho – the last book

It should also be noted that an ordinal number is a quantitative adjective hence it should come after descriptive adjectives in a Swahili phrase. For example:

paka mjanja wa tano – the fifth cunning cat
kibiriti ghali cha tatu – the third expensive match box

Unlike cardinal numbers 1, 2, 3, 4, 5 and 8, which take agreement with the noun as learned in Chapter 18, ordinal numbers do not need to take agreement since the *-a* of Association takes agreement with the noun.

Practice Exercise A

Translate these sentences into Swahili.

1. The eighth bicycle.
2. The seventeenth coconut.
3. The sixth guard.
4. The first cheap shirt.
5. The last lion.
6. The second big police officer.
7. The one hundred and first airplane.
8. The fourth dangerous river.
9. The fiftieth President.
10. The tenth telephone.

Section B: Weights and Measures

The Metric System, known as *Mfumo wa Metriki,* is the standard weights and measures system used in the East African Community of Tanzania, Kenya and Uganda. Consequently, the Metric System is more well known there than the U.S. Customary System.

Metric Weights

gramu – gram
kilo – kilogram
tani – tonne

U.S. Weights

aunsi – ounce
ratili or *ratli* – pound
tani – ton

The Swahili word *tani* applies to both a metric "tonne" and a U.S. "ton" which are not the same units of measurement.

Metric Distance Measurements

milimita – millimetre
sentimita – centimetre
mita – metre
kilomita – kilometre

U.S. Distance Measurements

inchi – inch
futi – foot
yadi – yard
maili – mile

Metric Area Measurements

hekta – hectare

U.S. Area Measurements

eka or *ekari* – acre

Distance measurements can be converted into area measurements by using the words *-a mraba*, which means "squared." For example:

kilomita moja ya mraba – one square kilometre
yadi sabini na tatu za mraba – seventy-three square yards

Metric Volume Measurements

mililita – millilitre
lita – litre

U.S. Volume Measurements

painti – pint
galoni – gallon

Distance and volume measurements can be converted into cubic measurements by using the words *-a mchemraba,* which means "cubic." Once converted into a cubic measurement, it can only be used to refer to volume. For example:

sentimita thelathini za mchemraba – thirty cubic centimetres
inchi elfu moja za mchemraba – one thousand cubic inches
lita kumi za mchemraba za maziwa – ten cubic litres of milk

Practice Exercise B

Translate these sentences into Swahili.

11. The government owns ten thousand square kilometres of land near here.
12. The girl is selling two litre jugs of milk.
13. I need sixteen metres of blue cloth.
14. This luggage weighs nineteen kilograms.
15. That firefighter bought ten acres of land.
16. The bottle contains (has) six hundred and fifty millilitres of orange juice.
17. The bag is able to hold one thousand eight hundred cubic centimetres.
18. His apartment is eleven hundred square feet.
19. That weighs only two grams.
20. The country of Tanzania is four thousand seven hundred miles from Britain.

Section C: Fractions

When the fraction is made up of a half, a third, or a quarter, it is expressed using specific words in Swahili, derived from Arabic, which are shown below:

nusu – one half ($1/2$)
theluthi – one third ($1/3$)
robo – one quarter ($1/4$)

Further fractions can be made from *theluthi* and *robo* as shown below.

>   *theluthi mbili* – two thirds ($^2/_3$)
>   *robo tatu* – three quarters ($^3/_4$)

When a fraction does not contain a half, a third, or a quarter the word *sehemu* is used. *Sehemu* means a "part" out of a larger whole, for example:

>   *sehemu moja ya saba* – one "part" of seven ($^1/_7$)
>   *sehemu tisa za kumi na sita* – nine "parts" of sixteen ($^9/_{16}$)
>   *sehemu kumi na tatu za kumi na nane* – thirteen "parts" of eighteen ($^{13}/_{18}$)

Since the *-a* of Association takes agreement with the noun, which is *sehemu* in this case, you will note that the *-a* of Association is *ya* when dealing with one "part" and is *za* when dealing with more than one "part" as is the case with all nouns from the N- class.

Fractions are added to a whole number using the *na* (and) construction.

>   *kumi na nne na nusu* – fourteen and a half (14 $^1/_2$)
>   *ishirini na theluthi mbili* – twenty and two thirds (20 $^2/_3$)
>   *tisini na tisa na sehemu tisa za kumi* – ninety-nine and nine tenths (99 $^9/_{10}$)

As mentioned in Chapter 12, there is a specific word order to be followed in a Swahili sentence as shown below:

>   Noun, personal possessive, adjective,
>   quantity, demonstrative and possessive.

In the list above the position in a sentence devoted to quantity can be filled either by a whole number, a fraction or both.

Practice Exercise C

Translate these sentences into English.

>   21. *Nusu yangu ya tufaha ni tamu.*
>   22. *Mimi ninataka robo ratili ya sukari.*

23. *Themanini na nane na sehemu moja ya nane.*
24. *Sehemu mbili za ishirini na moja.*
25. *Gari langu lina theluthi mbili za tangi la petroli.*

Translate these sentences into Swahili.

26. My quarter of the business.
27. Forty-one and a quarter inches.
28. Do you have half a bag of flour?
29. Fifty and one sixth.
30. Two thirds of a cup.

Section D: Decimals

The word for "decimal" or "point" is *nukta*, however the word *pointi* from the English word "point" is widely used these days. In Swahili, numbers after the word *pointi* or *nukta* are read out individually as in English.1 For example:

ishirini na saba pointi tatu, moja, nne, tano – 27.3145
sifuri nukta saba, sita, moja, moja, tatu – 0.76113

Practice Exercise D

Translate into Swahili.

31. 2.456
32. 1002.77
33. 0.952

Translate into English

34. *Mia nane na themanini nukta tisa.*
35. *Tatu pointi moja, nne, saba, tisa, tano.*
36. *Sifuri nukta moja moja sifuri sita.*

Section E: Percentages

Asilimia is the most common and direct way to express percentages in Swahili. *Asilimia* is made up of two words, *asili* which means "origin" and *mia* which means "hundred." When the words are combined it means "originating from a hundred" or in other words "percent." For example:

Asilimia sitini na nane – 68 percent
Asilimia elfu moja – 1000 percent

Note that the word order in the above examples is the reverse of how percentages are expressed in English.

The other way to express percentages in Swahili is to use the phrase "*kwa mia*." Unlike when using the word *asilimia,* the phrase "*kwa mia*" comes after the numeral. For example:

sabini kwa mia – 70 percent
moja kwa mia – 1 percent
mia moja na moja kwa mia – 101 percent

Practice Exercise E

Translate into Swahili using *asilimia.*

37. My mother paid 50 percent of my school fees.
38. 321 percent.
39. My share of the profit is 88 percent.

Translate into Swahili using *kwa mia.*

40. His bank pays 11 percent interest.
41. The company's expenses are 72 percent of its revenues.
42. 1000 percent

Section F: Temperature

Temperature in Swahili (*halijoto*) can be expressed, as in English, either by Celsius (*Selsiasi*) or in Fahrenheit (*Farenihaiti*). For example:

Digrii ishirini na mbili za Selsiasi – Twenty-two degrees Celsius
Digrii tisini na tano za Farenihaiti – Ninety-five degrees Fahrenheit

Practice Exercise F

Translate into Swahili.

43. Thirty-three degrees Celsius
44. Sixty-four degrees Fahrenheit
45. One hundred degrees Celsius

Section G: Currencies

The three countries of the East African community, Kenya, Tanzania and Uganda have named their currencies after the British Shilling. Each currency is different and has its own value. The word for "shilling" in Swahili is *shilingi* so the currencies are named as follows:

Shilingi ya Kenya – Kenyan Shilling
Shilingi ya Tanzania – Tanzanian Shilling
Shilingi ya Uganda – Ugandan Shilling

Other important currencies would be:

Dola moja ya Marekani – One American dollar
Pauni moja ya Uingereza – One British Pound
Randi moja ya Afrika Kusini – One South African Rand
Rupia moja ya Uhindi – One Indian Rupee
Yuro moja ya Ulaya – One Euro

Practice Exercise G

Translate into English.

46. *Je umepoteza Yuro za Ulaya ishirini?*
47. *Tutabadilisha pesa zetu kwa Rupia za Uhindi.*
48. *Pauni ya Uingereza ina thamani zaidi kuliko Dola ya Marekani.*
49. *Walitumia Randi zao za Afrika Kusini kununua viatu.*
50. *Hoteli hii haipokei Yuro za Ulaya.*

New Vocabulary

-a kwanza: first
-a mwisho: last
-a pili: second
asili: origin
asilimia: percent, originating out of a hundred
aunsi: ounce(s) (U.S. unit of weight)
badilisha: exchange, change
benki/ma-: bank(s)
biashara: business(es), commerce

buluu: blue
digrii: degree(s)
Dola: Dollar(s)
eka/ekari: acre(s) (U.S. unit of measurement)
faida: profit(s)
Farenihaiti: Fahrenheit
fleti: apartment(s), flat(s)
futi: foot (feet) (U.S. unit of measurement)
galoni: gallon(s) (U.S. unit of volume)
gharama: expense(s)
gramu: gram(s) (Metric unit of weight)
halijoto: temperature(s)
hekta: hectare(s) (Metric unit of measurement)
hisa: stock(s), share(s)
jagi/ma-: jug(s)
karo: fee(s)
kilo: kilogram(s) (Metric unit of weight)
kilomita: kilometre(s) (Metric unit of measurement)
kwa mia: from/out of a hundred
lipa: pay
lita: litre(s) (Metric unit of volume)
maili: mile(s) (U.S. unit of measurement)
maji ya machungwa: orange juice
mchemraba/mi-: cube(s)
Mfumo wa Metriki: Metric System
miliki: own
mililita: millilitre(s) (Metric unit of volume)
milimita: millimetre(s) (Metric unit of measurement)
mita: metre(s) (Metric unit of measurement)
mjanja: cunning, sly
mlinzi/wa-: guard(s)
mraba/mi-: square(s)
mzimamoto/wa-: firefighter(s)
nazi: coconut(s)
nukta: point(s), decimal(s), dot(s), period(s)
nusu: half(ves) (as a fraction)
painti: pint(s) (U.S unit of volume)
pato/ma-: revenue(s)
Pauni: Pound(s) (British currency)

pointi: point(s), decimal(s)
pokea: accept, receive
poteza: lose, waste
Randi: South African Rand
ratili/ratli: pound(s) (U.S. unit of weight)
riba: interest (financial)
robo: quarter(s)(as a fraction)
Rupia: Indian Rupee
S*elsiasi*: Celsius
sentimita: centimetre(s) (Metric unit of measurement)
shika: catch, hold
Shilingi: Shilling(s) (name of currencies used by Kenya, Tanzania and Uganda)
sukari: sugar
tangi/ma-: tank(s), reservoir(s)
tani: tonne(s) (Metric unit of weight) also a "ton(s)" as U.S. unit of weight
theluthi: third(s) (as a fraction)
tu: only
unga: flour
uzito: weight(s)
yadi: yard(s) (U.S. of measurement)
Yuro: Euro currency

Key to Exercises

Answers to Practice Exercise A

1. *Baisikeli ya nane.*
2. *Nazi ya kumi na saba.*
3. *Mlinzi wa sita.*
4. *Shati rahisi la kwanza.*
5. *Simba wa mwisho.*
6. *Polisi mkubwa wa pili.*
7. *Ndege ya mia moja na moja.*
8. *Mto wa hatari wa nne.*
9. *Rais wa hamsini.*
10. *Simu ya kumi.*

Answers to Practice Exercise B

11. *Serikali inamiliki kilomita elfu kumi za mraba za ardhi karibu na hapa.*
12. *Msichana anauza majagi ya lita mbili za maziwa.*
13. *Ninahitaji nguo ya buluu ya mita kumi na sita.*
14. *Mzigo huu una uzito wa kilo kumi na tisa.*
15. *Mzimamoto yule alinunua eka kumi za ardhi.*
16. *Chupa ina mililita mia sita na hamsini za maji ya machungwa.*
17. *Mfuko unaweza kushika sentimita elfu moja mia nane za mchemraba.*
18. *Fleti yake ni futi elfu moja mia moja za mraba.*
19. *Ile ina uzito wa gramu mbili tu.*
20. *Nchi ya Tanzania ni maili elfu nne mia saba kutoka Uingereza.*

Answers to Practice Exercise C

21 My half of the apple is tasty.
22. I want a quarter pound of sugar.
23. Eighty-eight and one eighth.
24. Two/twenty-firsts.
25. My car has two thirds of a tank of gas.
26. *Robo yangu ya biashara.*
27. *Inchi arobaini na moja na robo.*
28. *Je una nusu ya mfuko wa unga?*
29. *Hamsini na sehemu moja ya sita.*
30. *Theluthi mbili za kikombe.*

Answers to Practice Exercise D

31. *Mbili nukta* (or *pointi*) *nne, tano, sita.*
32. *Elfu moja na mbili nukta* (or *pointi*) *saba, saba.*
33. *Sifuri nukta* (or *pointi*) *tisa, tano, mbili.*
34. 880.9
35. 3.14795
36. 0.1106

Answers to Practice Exercise E

37. *Mama yangu alilipa asilimia hamsini ya karo yangu ya shule.*
38. *Asilimia mia tatu ishirini na moja.*
39. *Hisa ya faida yangu ni asilimia themanini na nane.*
40. *Benki yake inalipa riba ya kumi na moja kwa mia.*
41. *Gharama za kampuni ni sabini na mbili kwa mia ya mapato yake.*
42. *Elfu moja kwa mia.*

Answers to Practice Exercise F

43. *Digrii thelathini na tatu za Selsiasi.*
44. *Digrii sitini na nne za Farenihaiti.*
45. *Digrii mia moja za Selsiasi.*

Answers to Practice Exercise G

46. Have you lost twenty Euros?
47. We will exchange our money for Indian Rupees.
48. The British Pound is worth more than the American Dollar.
49. They used their South African Rand to buy shoes.
50. This hotel does not accept Euros.

Note

1. Wilson, 103.

Chapter 20

Telling the Time in Swahili

In this chapter, we will learn about the basics of telling the time in Swahili and other important vocabulary related to telling the time.

Section A: The Basics of Telling the Time in Swahili

In order to learn how to tell the time in Swahili it is important to know a little about the geography of Swahili speaking East Africa which lies close to the Equator. There is very little variation throughout the year in the time that the sun rises and sets.

The sun rises between 6 a.m. to 7 a.m. and sets between 6 p.m. to 7 p.m. This naturally divides a 24 hour day into two equal 12 hour segments, day and night. This division of a 24 hour day into two halves is the key to telling time in Swahili. 7 a.m. is considered by the Swahili people to be the start of the first full hour of daylight, and so it is called *saa moja*, literally "hour one." The Swahili people count forward starting from *saa moja* (7 a.m.) until *saa kumi na mbili* (6 p.m.) literally "hour twelve." After 6 p.m. darkness starts to set in and so the Swahili people consider 7 p.m. as the start of the first hour of darkness and so they begin counting again starting with *saa moja* until *saa kumi na mbili* (6 a.m.).

Below are the times in Swahili and its equivalent in English. Note that the word *saa* must always be used when telling the time in Swahili.

saa moja – 7 o'clock
saa mbili – 8 o'clock
saa tatu – 9 o'clock
saa nne – 10 o'clock
saa tano – 11 o'clock
saa sita – 12 o'clock
saa saba – 1 o'clock
saa nane – 2 o'clock
saa tisa – 3 o'clock
saa kumi – 4 o'clock
saa kumi na moja – 5 o'clock
saa kumi na mbili – 6 o'clock

As you can see from above, the difference between the Swahili time and the English time is exactly 6 hours. As stated above, the Swahili people use *saa moja* to mean either 7 a.m. if it is daytime or 7 p.m. if it is nighttime. Since the words *saa moja* could mean either 7 a.m. or 7 p.m., it is necessary to use additional words for clarification. English uses the convention of a.m. or p.m. to clarify what "7 o'clock" is being spoken about, but Swahili instead uses specific adverbs of time that describe the time of day. Below are the most important examples.

asubuhi – morning – 6:00 a.m. to 11:59 a.m.
mchana – daytime – 12:00 p.m. to 4:59 p.m.
jioni – evening – 5:00 p.m. to 6:59 p.m.
usiku – night – 7:00 p.m. to 5:59 a.m.

One of the above adverbs of time must be combined with a specific time in order to give the proper time in Swahili. For example, if the time was 8 a.m. one would say *saa mbili asubuhi.*

More Examples:

11:00 a.m. – *Saa tano asubuhi.*
2:00 p.m. – *Saa nane mchana.*
5:00 p.m. – *Saa kumi na moja jioni.*
8:00 p.m. – *Saa mbili usiku.*

Certain periods of day and night are denoted by special words that are derived from the Islamic prayer times. They begin with the phrase *wakati wa* which means "time of." These periods are:

wakati wa alfajiri – dawn prayer time – between 5:45 a.m. to 6:30 a.m.
wakati wa adhuhuri – noon prayer time – between 12:00 p.m. to 12:45 p.m.
wakati wa alasiri – late afternoon prayer time – between 4:00 p.m. to 4:45 p.m.
wakati wa magharibi – late evening prayer time – between 6:30 p.m. to 7:15 p.m.

The above phrases cannot be used in combination with *saa moja, saa mbili* etc. as learned previously. These phrases represent a certain time of day and are sufficient by themselves to indicate the approximate time.

Also, there is a certain period of night that is denoted by special word:

usiku wa manane – late at night – between 12 a.m. to 4:00 a.m. (figuratively "dead of night")

FIGURE 20.1
Swahili Clocks

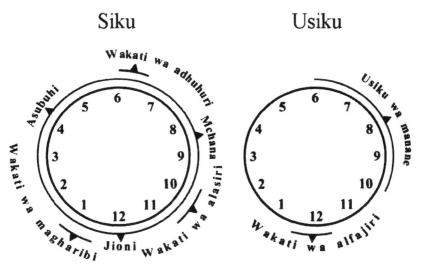

Practice Exercise A

Translate these times into Swahili.

1. 6:00 a.m.
2. 12:00 p.m.
3. 4:00 p.m.
4. 10:00 p.m.
5. 1:00 a.m.

Section B: Minutes, Quarters and Half Hours when Telling the Time

In Section A, we were able to tell time in Swahili to the nearest hour. Now we will learn to tell time in Swahili to the nearest quarter or minute. The words for minute, quarter and half hour are listed below.

dakika – minute
robo – quarter (of an hour in this case)
nusu – half (of an hour in this case)

Minutes, quarters and half hours can be either added to the hour or subtracted from the following hour using the words below:

na – and (used to add minutes, quarters and half hours to a whole
    hour)
kasoro – less (used to subtract minutes and quarters from a whole
    hour)

Note that when *kasoro* (less) is used with the word *robo* (quarter), it can be contracted into the single word *kasorobo* (less a quarter).

With the terms you have just learned in Section B, you can now tell the time in hours and minutes as shown below.

Examples:

3:15 p.m. – *Saa tisa na robo mchana.*
9:55 a.m. – *Saa nne kasoro dakika tano asubuhi.* OR
Saa tatu na dakika hamsini na tano asubuhi.
12:21 a.m. – *Saa sita na dakika ishirini na moja usiku.*

11:45 p.m. – *Saa sita kasorobo usiku.* OR *Saa tano na dakika arobaini na tano usiku.*

Practice Exercise B

Translate the following into Swahili.

6. 7:45 a.m.
7. 2:11 p.m.
8. 6:30 p.m.
9. 10:49 a.m.
10. 5:05 p.m.
11. 3:12 p.m.
12. 1:01 a.m.
13. 4:40 a.m.
14. 9:58 p.m.
15. 8:35 a.m.

Section C: Other Important Vocabulary

The following words are used in connection with telling the time in Swahili.

Saa ngapi? – What time is it?
Saa ngapi sasa hivi? – What time is it right now?
kamili – exactly
kama – about
mpaka – until
tangu – since, from
karibu – near
baada ya – after

For example:

Saa kumi kamili mchana. – Exactly 4 p.m.
Ni kama saa kumi na mbili jioni. – It is about 6:00 p.m.
Alipika mpaka saa nane mchana. – He/She cooked until 2:00 p.m.
Alingoja tangu wakati wa adhuhuri. – He/She waited since the time of noon prayers.
Ni karibu saa mbili asubuhi. – It is near (almost) 8:00 a.m.
Ni baada ya saa moja na nusu usiku. – It is after 7:30 p.m.

Practice Exercise C

Translate the following sentences into Swahili.

16. Mohammad will dig a trench from exactly 1:00 p.m. until about 5:30 p.m.
17. The engineer finished the model at about 2:15 p.m.
18. The manager surfed the Internet after 7:50 a.m.
19. What time will the technician fix the railroad crossing?
20. What time will the sailors visit the nightclub?

When measuring a period of time, as opposed to telling the time, the phrase *"muda wa"* meaning "a period of" must always be used to avoid confusion. For example:

Lima shamba kwa muda wa saa tatu. – Cultivate the farm for a period of three hours.
Lima shamba saa tatu. – Cultivate the farm at nine o'clock.

When using quarters and half hours with the phrase *"muda wa,"* the word order is reversed so that the word *saa* comes after the word *robo* or *nusu*. For example:

Muda wa robo saa. – A period of a quarter of an hour.
Muda wa nusu saa. – A period of half an hour.
Muda wa robo tatu ya saa. – A period of three quarters of an hour.

Other examples:

Muda wa dakika saba. – A period of seven minutes.
Muda wa saa nne na dakika ishirini. – A period of four hours and twenty minutes.

Finally, if telling the time down to the nearest second is required, the word *sekunde* (second) is used:

Dakika tano na sekunde ishirini na tano. – Five minutes and twenty-five seconds.

Practice Exercise D

Translate the following sentences into English.

21. *Juliet alisoma shajara kwa muda wa saa saba.*
22. *Sherehe iliendelea kwa muda wa saa tatu.*
23. *Ataanza kutoa hotuba saa saba mchana.*
24. *Kijana alifanya mazoezi ya viungo kwa muda wa robo tatu ya saa.*
25. *Mwogeleaji yule anaweza kuzuia pumzi katika maji kwa dakika tano na sekunde kumi.*
26. *Mkutubi alitumia kikompyuta kwa muda wa saa mbili na robo.*
27. *Walifunga bwawa la kuogelea kwa muda wa siku mbili.*
28. *Sala ziliendelea kwa muda wa dakika ishirini.*
29. *Ametajirika kwa sababu aliweka akiba ya pesa kwa muda wa miaka mingi.*
30. *Mbwa alibweka kwa muda wa dakika kumi.*

Section E: Dialogue Practice

Mama: Habari za asubuhi?

Baba: Nzuri sana.

Mama: Unatarajia kwenda kazini saa ngapi?

Baba: Nitaondoka saa mbili kamili asubuhi. Je, watoto waliondoka kwenda shuleni saa ngapi?

Mama: Waliondoka saa moja na robo asubuhi.

Baba: Je, utapika chakula gani leo jioni?

Mama: Nitapika ugali na mchuzi wa kamba.

Baba: Chakula kitakuwa tayari saa ngapi?

Mama: Inategemea, utarudi saa ngapi?

Baba: Nitarudi baada ya saa kumi na moja na robo jioni.

Mama: Sasa hivi ni saa mbili na dakika mbili. Basi fanya haraka usije ukachelewa kazini.

Baba: Kwa heri mpenzi. Tutaonana jioni.

Practice Exercise E

Answer the following questions in English.

31. What time did the father say he would leave for work?
32. Did the children leave before the father left?
33. What time did the children leave?
34. What did the mother say she would cook for dinner?
35. What time did the father say he would return?

New Vocabulary

adhuhuri: noon(s), midday(s)
akiba: saving(s), deposit(s)
alasiri: late afternoon(s)
alfajiri: dawn(s)
ambaa: surf
baharia/ma-: sailor(s)
basi: enough, stop, well, then, so
bwawa/ma-: pool(s), swamp(s)
bweka: bark
chimba: dig
fundisanifu/ma-: technician(s)
funga: close, lock
handaki/ma-: trench(es), tunnel(s)
haraka: quick, quickly, rush
hotuba: speech(es)
jioni: evening(s)
kamba: prawn(s), rope(s)
kamili: exactly
kasoro: less, lack
kasorobo: less a quarter
kikompyuta/vi-: laptop computer(s)
klabu: club(s)
magharibi: late evening(s)
mchana: daytime(s), afternoon(s)
mchuzi/mi-: curry(ies), sauce(s)
meneja/ma-: manager(s)
mfano/mi-: model(s), example(s)
mkutubi/wa-: librarian(s)

mpaka: until, as far as, up to
mtandao: the internet
mwogeleaji/wa-: swimmer(s)
ngoja: wait
ondoka: leave, depart
panda: crossing(s), fork(s)
pumzi: breath(s)
reli: rail(s), railway(s)
saa: time(s), hour(s), clock(s)
saa ngapi?: What time is it?
sala: prayer(s)
sekunde: second(s) (unit of time)
shajara: diary(ies)
sherehe: celebration(s), party(ies)
tajirika: become rich
tangu: since, from
tarajia: expect to
tegemea: depend, rely on, expect
tengeneza: fix, repair, manufacture
toa: give, deliver, remove
usiku wa manane: late at night, dead of night
weka: keep, save, set aside
zoezi/ma- la/ya viungo: physical exercise(s)
zuia: hold, stop, prevent

Key to Exercises

Answers to Practice Exercise A

1. *Saa kumi na mbili asubuhi.*
2. *Saa sita mchana.*
3. *Saa kumi mchana.*
4. *Saa nne usiku.*
5. *Saa saba usiku.*

Answers to Practice Exercise B

6. *Saa mbili kasorobo asubuhi. OR Saa moja na dakika arobaini na tano asubuhi.*
7. *Saa nane na dakika kumi na moja mchana.*

8. *Saa kumi na mbili na nusu jioni.*
9. *Saa tano kasoro dakika kumi na moja asubuhi.* OR *Saa nne na dakika arobaini na tisa asubuhi.*
10. *Saa kumi na moja na dakika tano jioni.*
11. *Saa tisa na dakika kumi na mbili mchana.*
12. *Saa saba na dakika moja usiku.*
13. *Saa kumi na moja kasoro dakika ishirini usiku.* OR *Saa kumi na dakika arobaini usiku.*
14. *Saa nne kasoro dakika mbili usiku.* OR *Saa tatu na dakika hamsini na nane usiku.*
15. *Saa tatu kasoro dakika ishirini na tano asubuhi.* OR *Saa mbili na dakika thelathini na tano asubuhi.*

Answers to Practice Exercise C

16. *Mohammad atachimba handaki tangu saa saba kamili mchana mpaka kama saa kumi na moja na nusu jioni.*
17. *Mhandisi alimaliza mfano kama saa nane na robo mchana.*
18. *Meneja aliambaa kwenye mtandao baada ya saa mbili kasoro dakika kumi asubuhi*
    OR *saa moja na dakika hamsini asubuhi.*
19. *Saa ngapi fundisanifu atatengeneza njia panda ya reli?*
20. *Saa ngapi mabaharia watatembelea klabu ya usiku?*

Answers to Practice Exercise D

21. Juliet read the diary for a period of seven hours.
22. The celebration lasted for a period of three hours.
23. He/She will begin to give a speech at 1:00 p.m.
24. The youth did physical exercises for a period of three quarters of an hour.
25. That swimmer can hold his/her breath underwater for five minutes and ten seconds.
26. The librarian used the laptop for a period of two hours and fifteen minutes.
27. They closed the swimming pool for two days.
28. The prayers continued for a period of twenty minutes.
29. He/She became rich because he/she saved money for a period of many years.
30. The dog barked for a period of ten minutes.

Answers to Practice Exercise E

31. The father said that he would leave at exactly 8:00 a.m.
32. Yes.
33. The children left at 7:15 a.m.
34. She said she would cook ugali (corn meal) and shrimp curry.
35. The father said he would return after 5:15 p.m.

Chapter 21

Days, Months, and Dates in Swahili

This chapter will focus on how the Swahili people name the days of the week, months of the year and form dates in Swahili.

Section A: Days of the Week (*Siku za wiki*)

In Swahili culture the first day of the week is Saturday, which is translated as *Jumamosi,* literally meaning "first day of the week." As you can see from the chart below, most days of the week follow the same pattern except Thursday and Friday, which are of Arabic origin. In Swahili, Thursday is translated as *Alhamisi.* The Arabic translation of *Alhamisi* is "The fifth" (day), however it is actually the sixth day of the Swahili week. It is followed by Friday (*Ijumaa*), which is the seventh day of the week. *Ijumaa* literally means "prayer day."

English – Swahili – Abbreviation
Saturday – *Jumamosi* – J1.
Sunday –*Jumapili* – J2.
Monday – *Jumatatu* – J3.
Tuesday –*Jumanne* – J4.
Wednesday – *Jumatano* – J5.
Thursday – *Alhamisi* – Al.
Friday – *Ijumaa* – Ij.

In Kenya, Tanzania and Uganda the "weekend" (*wikiendi*) consists of Saturday and Sunday as in the Western world, although many Muslims on the coasts of Kenya and Tanzania consider Friday as a day of rest and prayer also.

When using Swahili days of the week in a sentence, the day of the week is placed in the same way as in English, either directly before the subject or at the end of the sentence, for example:

> *Ijumaa Aziza atarudi London.* – On Friday Aziza will return from London.
> *Aziza atarudi London Ijumaa.* – Aziza will return from London on Friday.

As you can see from the sentences above the word *Ijumaa* does not take a preposition to become "on Friday." However, days of the week can take demonstratives, and are N- class nouns. Therefore the examples above could be modified to the following:

> *Ijumaa hii Aziza atarudi London.* – This Friday Aziza will return from London.
> *Aziza atarudi London Ijumaa hii.* – Aziza will return from London this Friday.

Days of the week can also be referred to by using adverbs of time. Below is a list of examples:

> *zamani* – long ago, in ancient times
> *juzijuzi* – the other day
> *juzi* – the day before yesterday
> *jana* – yesterday
> *leo* – today
> *kesho* – tomorrow
> *kesho kutwa* – the day after tomorrow
> *mtondo* – three days from now
> *mtondogoo* – four days from now

Examples:

> *Kesho atarudi kutoka London.* – Tomorrow he/she will return from London.
> *Atarudi London kesho.* – He/She will return to London tomorrow.

Atarudi kutoka London kesho. – He/She will return from London
tomorrow.

As you can see from the above examples, adverbs of time also do not
take prepositions.

Practice Exercise A

Translate the following sentences into Swahili.

1. That Monday I went to the post office before closing time.
2. The other day a rhinoceros was seen near that old village.
3. Four days from now they will have an important meeting for all the managers.
4. On Sunday several rivers near the mountains overflowed their banks.
5. Long ago the Arabs built a fort with a mosque here.
6. These three Wednesdays will be quiet.
7. Yesterday we waited until after 11:15 a.m.
8. Tomorrow I will buy your airline ticket.
9. The lawyer will go to the town council on Tuesday.
10. These days you (pl.) are always busy.

Section B: Months

The names of the months in Swahili are taken directly from English.
Here are the Swahili months of the year:

Januari – January
Februari – February
Machi – March
Aprili – April
Mei – May
Juni – June
Julai – July
Agosti – August
Septemba – September
Oktoba – October
Novemba – November
Desemba – December

As with all Swahili words, the pronunciation stress continues to fall on the second last syllable. When speaking about a particular month the names of the months can be used on their own or they can be preceded by the words *mwezi* meaning "month..." or *mwezi wa* meaning "month of..." For example:

Aprili niliogelea. – In April I went swimming.
Katika mwezi Aprili niliogelea. – In the month of April I went swimming.
Katika mwezi wa Aprili niliogelea. – In the month of April I went swimming.

Although it is perfectly acceptable to use the "names" of the months as they are, some Swahili people prefer the easier way of counting the months "first month, second month, etc." as shown below:

Mwezi wa kwanza – January
Mwezi wa pili – February
Mwezi wa tatu – March
Mwezi wa nne – April
Mwezi wa tano – May
Mwezi wa sita – June
Mwezi wa saba – July
Mwezi wa nane – August
Mwezi wa tisa – September
Mwezi wa kumi – October
Mwezi wa kumi na moja – November
Mwezi wa kumi na mbili – December

For example:

Katika mwezi wa nne niliogelea. – In the fourth month (April) I went swimming.

As with the days of the week, when using months in a sentence the month is placed in the same way as in English, either directly before the subject or at the end of the sentence. So the preceding examples in this section could haven been written as:

Niliogelea Aprili. – I went swimming in April.

Niliogelea katika mwezi Aprili. – I went swimming in the month
of April.

Niliogelea katika mwezi wa Aprili. – I went swimming in the
month of April.

Niliogelea katika mwezi wa nne. – I went swimming in the fourth
month. (April)

When naming the months directly, the months are N- class nouns,
however if the word *mwezi* is used before the name of the month then
noun class agreement must be with *mwezi* which is in the M-/MI- noun
class.

Practice Exercise B

Translate the following sentences into Swahili.

11. After June, the government will close the airport for repairs.
12. The writer was on vacation for the whole month of September.
13. I am leaving this May to travel to Mozambique.
14. He/She advertised that job in December.
15. My child returned from Russia in October.

Section C: Dates in Swahili

When saying the date in Swahili, two different formats can be used.
Either the word *tarehe*, which means "date" is said followed by a cardinal number or *tarehe ya ...* meaning "date of . . ." is used followed by an
ordinal number. For example:

Tarehe moja or *Tarehe ya kwanza* – The First (of the month)
Tarehe mbili or *Tarehe ya pili* – The Second (of the month)

Therefore "the 5th of July" could be said as either:

Tarehe tano Julai. Or *Tarehe ya tano Julai.*

When saying the number "one" (*moja*) sometimes one will hear the
word *mosi* used instead when saying the date. The word *mosi* is an old
form of the word *moja*.

When saying the year in Swahili the words *mwaka*, which means "year" or *mwaka wa . . .* meaning "year of . . ." is used followed by a cardinal number.

The year 1981

Mwaka elfu moja, mia tisa, themanini na moja or
Mwaka wa elfu moja, mia tisa, themanini na moja

Finally, when saying the full date in Swahili the format day, month and then year is usually followed, although it is also possible to use the format month, day and then year. For example:

The 18th of October 2002.

Tarehe kumi na nane, mwezi wa Oktoba, mwaka wa elfu mbili na mbili.

Practice Exercise C

Translate the following sentences into Swahili.

16. The 24th of August 1972 is my best friend's birthday.
17. Kenyan Independence Day is the 12th of December 1963.
18. The mayor retired July 31st 1999.
19. The trade talks will start January 1st 2014.
20. The Second World War ended on the 15th of August 1945.
21. Tanzanian Independence Day is December 9th 1961.
22. My child was born March 13th 2001.
23. He built that building on the 5th of May 1821.
24. The government will make a decision by September 17th 2026.
25. Ugandan Independence Day is October 9th 1962.

New Vocabulary

Agosti: August
Alhamisi: Thursday
Aprili: April
boma/ma-: fort(s), compound(s)
daima: always
Desemba: December
Februari: February
furika: overflow, flood
halmashauri ya/za mji/miji: town council(s)
Ijumaa: Friday
Januari: January
Julai: July
Jumamosi: Saturday
Jumanne: Tuesday
Jumapili: Sunday
Jumatano: Wednesday
Jumatatu: Monday
Juni: June
juzi: the day before yesterday
juzijuzi: the other day
kabla: before
kwa ajili: for, because
likizo: holiday(s), vacation(s)
Machi: March
matengenezo: repair(s)
Mei: May
meya: mayor(s)
mkutano/mi-: meeting(s)
msikiti/mi-: mosque(s)
Msumbiji: Mozambique
mtondo: three days from now
mtondogoo: four days from now
mwanasheria/wa-: lawyer(s)
Novemba: November
Oktoba: October
onekana: be seen, appear
posta: post, post office(s)

Septemba: September
shughuli: business(es), activity(ies)
siku ya/za kuzaliwa: birthday(s)
Siku ya Uhuru: Independence Day
staafu: retire
tangaza: advertise, announce
tarehe: date(s)
tiketi: ticket(s)
tulivu: quiet
uwanja/nyanja wa/za ndege: airport(s)
Vita vya Pili vya Dunia: The Second World War
wikiendi: weekend(s)
zaliwa: born

Key to Exercises

Answers to Practice Exercise A

1. *Jumatatu ile nilikwenda posta kabla ya wakati wa kufunga.*
2. *Juzijuzi kifaru alionekana karibu na kijiji kile cha zamani.*
3. *Mtondogoo watakuwa na mkutano muhimu kwa ajili ya mameneja wote.*
4. *Jumapili mito kadhaa karibu na milima ilifurika kingo zao.*
5. *Zamani Waarabu walijenga boma lenye msikiti hapa.*
6. *Jumatano tatu hizi zitakuwa tulivu.*
7. *Jana tulingoja mpaka baada ya saa tano na robo asubuhi.*
8. *Kesho nitanunua tiketi yako ya ndege.*
9. *Mwanasheria atakwenda halmashauri ya mji Jumanne.*
10. *Siku hizi daima mna shughuli.*

Answers to Practice Exercise B

11. *Baada ya Juni serikali itafunga uwanja wa ndege kwa ajili ya matengenezo.*
12. *Mwandishi alikuwa katika likizo kwa mwezi wote wa Septemba.*
13. *Ninaondoka mwezi huu wa tano kusafiri Msumbiji.*
14. *Alitangaza kazi ile Desemba.*
15. *Mtoto wangu alirudi kutoka Urusi mwezi wa kumi.*

Answers to Practice Exercise C

16. *Tarehe ishirini na nne, mwezi wa Agosti, mwaka wa elfu moja, mia tisa, sabini na mbili ni siku ya kuzaliwa ya rafiki yangu mpenzi.*

17. *Siku ya Uhuru wa Kenya ni tarehe ya kumi na mbili, mwezi Desemba, mwaka elfu moja, mia tisa, sitini na tatu.*

18. *Meya alistaafu tarehe thelathini na moja, mwezi wa saba, mwaka wa elfu moja, mia tisa, tisini na tisa.*

19. *Mazungumzo ya biashara yataanza tarehe ya kwanza, Januari, mwaka elfu mbili, kumi na nne.*

20. *Vita vya Pili vya Dunia ilimalizika tarehe ya kumi na tano, mwezi Agosti, mwaka wa elfu moja, mia tisa, arobaini na tano.*

21. *Siku ya Uhuru wa Tanzania ni tarehe ya tisa, mwezi wa Desemba, mwaka wa elfu moja, mia tisa, sitini na moja.*

22. *Mtoto wangu alizaliwa tarehe kumi na tatu, mwezi wa tatu, mwaka wa elfu mbili na moja.*

23. *Yeye alijenga jengo lile tarehe ya tano, Mei, mwaka wa elfu moja, mia nane, ishirini na moja.*

24. *Serikali itafanya uamuzi kabla ya tarehe kumi na saba, mwezi wa Septemba, mwaka elfu mbili, ishirini na sita.*

25. *Siku ya Uhuru wa Uganda ni tarehe tisa, mwezi wa kumi, mwaka elfu moja, mia tisa, sitini na mbili.*

Chapter 22

Adverbs

An adverb is commonly used to modify a verb, but it can also modify an adjective, another adverb or a phrase in a sentence. An adverb shows how, when or where a person or an object does an action. There are five main types of adverbs: Adverbs of Manner, Place, Time, Frequency and Degree. In this chapter, we will discuss the different kinds of Adverbs and how they are formed.

Section A: Adverbs of Manner

An Adverb of Manner is used to show how an action took place, is taking place or will take place. It can be formed in one of the following ways: Single words, *ki-* or *vi-* prefixes, *u-* or *w-* prefixes, duplicative adverbs, using *kwa* and lastly, imitative adverbs.

1. Single words

There are some common adverbs which exist in Swahili.

ghafla – suddenly
haraka – quickly
kabisa – completely, thoroughly
hasa – especially
pamoja – together
taratibu – slowly
peke – -self, alone

Examples:

Simba alikufa ghafla. – The lion died suddenly.
Wataimba pamoja. – They will sing together.

2. By using *ki-* or *vi-* prefixes attached to adjectives or nouns. The choice of attaching a *ki-* or *vi-* prefix was arbitrarily chosen by Swahili people, depending on what sounded better to them. These prefixes have no differences in meaning.

kitoto – like a child
kizungu – like a European
kipumbavu – like an idiot
kiaskari – like a soldier
kiume – like a man
kikondoo – like a sheep
kizee – like an old man
vizuri – nicely
vibaya – badly
vigumu – difficult
vingine – in another way

Examples:

Ameandika vibaya. – He/She wrote badly.
Nitatengeneza pesa vingine. – I will make money in another way.
Ninapenda kula kizungu. – I like to eat in European style (with knife and fork).
Alijibu maswali kipumbavu. – He/She answered questions like an idiot.

3. By using *u-* or sometimes *w-* prefix attached to adjectives or nouns to form adverbs.

upesi – fast
upande – sideways
upya – new
wima – upright

Examples:

Simama wima. – Stand upright.
Gari lile limekwenda upande. – That car has gone sideways.

4. By duplicative adverbs.

polepole – slowly
sawasawa – same
vilevile – equally
mojamoja – one by one
mbalimbali – different, differently
kisirisiri – secretly
kizunguzungu – dizzy
katakata – completely
nyatunyatu – stealthily

Examples:

Mlitembea polepole. – You (pl.) walked slowly.
Nilimwambia kisirisiri. – I told him/her secretly.

5. By using words such as *kwa*.

kwa ghafla – suddenly
kwa haraka – with speed
kwa kusudi – intentionally
kwa kifupi – in short
kwa bahati – with luck
kwa sauti – loudly
kwa siri – secretly
kwa ndege – by air
kwa shida – with difficulty
kwa nguvu – with force

Examples:

Amepika kwa haraka. – He/She has cooked fast.
Kwa bahati, nilifaulu. – Luckily, I passed.
Nilimwoa kwa siri. – I married her secretly.

6. By imitative adverbs which represents an idea in sound.

pumzika fofofo – resting soundly
nuka fee – smell badly
anguka pu – fall on the sand
kufa fofofo – stone dead

Examples:

Yaya atapumzika fofofo. – The nanny will rest soundly.
Nyati wa kufugwa alinuka fee. – The water buffalo smelled badly.

Practice Exercise A

Translate into Swahili

1. They walked like a soldier.
2. The villagers travelled on foot.
3. Melissa lives by herself.

Section B: Adverbs of Place

An Adverb of Place is used to show where an action took place, is taking place or will take place. It can be formed in two ways: Single words or with "mahali" class markers *p*, *k* or *m*.

1. Single words

There are some common adverbs which exist in Swahili.

ndani – inside
mbali – far, far away
karibu – near, near by
nje – outside
chini – below
mbele – front, in front
juu – above
nyuma – behind
katikati – among, middle

Examples:

Kimondo kilianguka katikati ya ziwa. – The meteor fell in the middle of a lake.
Unyang'anyi utatokea mbali. – The robbery will happen far away.

2. Using "mahali" class markers *p*, *k* or *m*

These markers can be used in a variety of ways such as demonstratives, adjectives, possessives, and -*a* of Association.

hapa – here (definite)
kule – there (indefinite)
mwenye – having (inside)
pengine – another place (definite)
kwao – their place (indefinite)
pangu – my place (definite)
kwa mwalimu – at teacher's place (indefinite)

Examples:

Alinunua mahali pote. – He/She bought the whole place (definite).
esoma kwa Ali. – He/She has studied at Ali's place (indefinite).
Mle kuna kioski. – Inside there, there is a kiosk.

Note that sometimes it is possible to add the locative suffix -*ni* to nouns denoting places to form an Adverb of Place. For example:

Nyumbani humo mna nyoka. – Inside this house, there are snakes.

Practice Exercise B

Translate into English

4. *Nilimwalika kwangu kwa ajili ya sikukuu.*
5 *Tafadhali njoo hapa.*
6. *Viatu havimo ndani ya kabati.*

Section C: Adverbs of Time

An Adverb of Time is used to show when an action took place, is taking place or will take place. It can be formed in two ways: Single words or compound words, or with "mahali" class markers *p*, *k* or *m*. The single or compound words may be specific to a particular time, such as a day, month or time of the year or they may not refer to any particular time.

1. Single or compound words

There are some common adverbs which exist in Swahili.

> *Jumamosi* – Saturday
> *Mwaka wa 2010* – The Year of 2010
> *saa mbili asubuhi* – 8 am
> *jioni* – evening
> *mwaka jana* – last year
> *baadaye* – after
> *zamani* – long ago
> *sasa* – now

Examples:

> *Zamani palinyesha.* – Long ago, it rained here (definite place).
> *Uchaguzi utakuwa saa tatu asubuhi.* – The election will be at 9 am.

2. Using "mahali" class markers *p*, *k* or *m*

Unlike in the Adverbs of Place, these markers can only be used in a limited number of ways as Adverbs of Time and do not refer to any particular time.

> *huku* – while, meanwhile
> *mara pale pale* – just then
> *mnamo* – about

Examples:

> *Alisoma gazeti huku anakula.* – He/She was reading the newspaper while eating.
> *Mara pale pale, alizimia.* – Just then, he/she fainted.
> *Tunatarajia kurudi mnamo saa moja .* – We expect to return at about seven o'clock.

Practice Exercise C

Translate into Swahili

7. The rooster crows every dawn.
8. The mailman will come at 4 pm.
9. We will cook while listening to music.

Section D: Adverbs of Frequency

An Adverb of Frequency is used to show how often an action took place, is taking place or will take place. It can be formed using single or compound words.

1. Single or Compound words

There are some common adverbs which exist in Swahili.

mara moja – once
mara tatu – thrice
mara ya kwanza – first time
mara ya mwisho – last time
mara chache – few times
mara nyingi – many times
tena – again

Examples:

Nilitoa sadaka mara chache mwaka uliopita. – I gave charity a few times last year.
Tunasafiri mara ya kwanza kwa ndege. – We are travelling for the first time by air.
Aliiba tena. – He/She stole again.

Practice Exercise D

Translate into English

10. *Mara nyingi, kompyuta haifanyi kazi.*
11. *Nilikwenda duka la maua lile mara moja tu.*
12. *Hii ni mara ya mwisho utapata bonasi.*

Section E: Adverbs of Degree

An Adverb of Degree shows the degree or intensity of something.

zaidi – more
mno – a lot, very
kiasi – a bit
sana – very, a lot
kabisa – completely
kwa kweli – really, truly

Examples:

Kahawa ilikuwa moto mno. – The coffee was very hot.
Alikuwa na akili sana. – He/She has a lot of intelligence.

Please note that there are a few single words that exist as more than one type of adverb. For example, *kabisa* can be used as an Adverb of Manner as well as an Adverb of Degree.

Adverb of Manner
Nimewahi kabisa. – I arrived completely on time.

Adverb of Degree
Mteja hakuwa na sababu kabisa. – The customer is completely
    unreasonable.

Practice Exercise E

Translate into Swahili

13. The kite flew up a bit.
14. Really, you bought seven shirts?
15. They got a lot of praise for their discovery.

New Vocabulary

akili: intelligence
alika: invite
anguka pu: fall on the sand
baadaye: after
bonasi: bonus(es)
chini: below, under
faulu: be successful, pass (a test)
ghafla: suddenly
hasa: especially
huku: while, meanwhile
jogoo/ma-: rooster(s)
juu: up, above, on top
kabisa: completely, thoroughly
katakata: completely
katikati: among, middle
kiasi: a bit
kiaskari: like a soldier
kikondoo: like a sheep
kimondo/vi-: meteor(s)
kioski: kiosk(s)
kipumbavu: like an idiot
kisirisiri: secretly
kitoto: like a child
kiume: like a man
kizee: like an old man
kizungu: like a European
kizunguzungu: dizzy
kufa fofofo: stone dead
kwa kifupi: in short
kwa kusudi: intentionally
kwa kweli: really, truly
kwa sauti: loudly
mara: time(s), occasion(s)
mara pale pale: just then
mbalimbali: different, differently
mbele: front, in front
mnamo: about

mno: a lot

mojamoja: one by one

mtu/wa- anayeleta/wa- barua: mailman/mailmen

muziki: music

mwanakijiji/wa-: villager(s)

ndani: inside

njoo: come

nuka fee: smell badly

nyati wa kufugwa: water buffalo(es)

nyatunyatu: stealthily

nyuma: behind

oa: marry (for men only)

pamoja: together

peke: -self, alone

polepole: slowly

pumzika fofofo: resting soundly

sadaka: charity(ies)

sasa: now

shida: trouble(s), difficulty(ies), hardship(s)

sikukuu: holiday(s)

tafadhali: please

taratibu: slowly

tembea: walk

tiara: kite(s)

tokea: happen, come out

uchaguzi: election(s)

ugunduzi: discovery(ies)

unyang'anyi: robbery(ies)

upande: sideways

upesi: fast

upya: new

vibaya: badly

vigumu: difficult

vingine: in another way

vizuri: nicely, well

wahi: be on time

wika: crow

wima: upright

yaya/ma-: nanny(ies)

zimia: faint
ziwa/ma-: lake(s), pond(s)

Key to Exercises

Answers to Practice Exercise A

1. *Walitembea kiaskari.*
2. *Wanakijiji walisafiri kwa miguu.*
3. *Melissa anaishi peke yake.*

Answers to Practice Exercise B

4. I invited him/her to my place because of the holiday(s).
5. Please come here.
6. The shoes are not inside the locker.

Answer to Practice Exercise C

7. *Jogoo anawika kila alfajiri.*
8. *Mtu anayeleta barua atakuja saa kumi jioni.*
9. *Tutapika huku tunasikia muziki.*

Answer to Practice Exercise D

10. Many times, the computer does not work.
11. I went to that flower store once only.
12. This is the last time you will get a bonus.

Answer to Practice Exercise E

13. *Tiara iliruka kwenda juu kiasi.*
14. *Kwa kweli, ulinunua mashati saba?*
15. *Wao walipata sifa nyingi kwa ajili ya ugunduzi wao.*

Chapter 23

Passive Form of the Verb

This Chapter explains how Passive Verbs (*Vabo ya Kutendewa*) are formed in Swahili using verbs of Bantu origin, verbs of Arabic origin and Monosyllabic verbs. It should be pointed out from the outset that the object of an active sentence becomes the subject of the passive sentence. Also, in passive verbs, actions done by animates are followed by the conjunction *na* meaning "by" while actions done by inanimates are followed by conjunction *kwa* meaning "with" and conveys the idea of using a tool.

Section A: Verbs of Bantu Origin

Verbs of Bantu origin are made passive by the insertion of the infix *-w-* before the final vowel *-a* if the verb ends with a single vowel. Examples:

Active Form
> *lima* – cultivate
> *Shangazi yangu alilima shamba.* – My aunt cultivated the farm.

Passive Form
> *limwa* – be cultivated
> *Shamba lililimwa na shangazi yangu.* – The farm was cultivated by my aunt.

Active Form

   soma – read
   Gavana alisoma hotuba Bungeni. – The Governor read the speech
      in Parliament.

Passive Form

   somwa – be read
   Hotuba ilisomwa Bungeni na Gavana. – The speech was read in
      Parliament by the Governor.

Bantu verbs which end with double vowels *-aa,- ia* or *-ua* have *-liw-*
inserted between the two vowels. Examples:

Active Form

   kaa – sit
   Mike alikaa juu ya kochi. – Mike sat on the couch.

Passive Form

   kaliwa – be sat on
   Kochi lilikaliwa na Mike. – The couch was sat on by Mike.

Active Form

   tia – put
   Mimi nilitia pilipili katika mboga. – I put pepper on the vegetables.

Passive Form

   tiliwa – put on
   Pilipili ilitiliwa katika mboga na mimi. – The pepper was put on
      the vegetables by me.

Active Form

   pakua – unload
   Wafanyakazi walipakua mizigo. – The workers unloaded the lug-
      gage.

Passive Form

   pakuliwa – unloaded
   Mizigo ilipakuliwa na wafanyakazi. – The luggage was unloaded
      by the workers.

Bantu verbs which end with double vowel *-ea* or *-oa* have *-lew-* inserted between the two vowels. Examples:

Active Form

lea – bring up or raise
Bibi yule alilea mtoto wangu. – That lady raised my child.

Passive Form

lelewa – be raised
Mtoto wangu alilelewa na bibi yule. – My child was raised by
    that lady.

Active Form

toa – remove
Mohamed alitoa takataka. – Mohamed removed the garbage.

Passive Form

tolewa – be removed
Takataka zilitolewa na Mohamed. – The garbage was removed
    by Mohamed.

Bantu verbs ending with *-wa* are made passive by inserting the infix *-iw-* between the original *w* and the final *a*.

Active Form

nawa – wash
Tulinawa maji. – We washed (with) water.

Passive Form

nawiwa – washed with
Maji yalinawiwa na sisi. – The water was used for washing by us.

Active Form

gawa – distribute
Magaidi waligawa silaha. – The terrorists distributed weapons.

Passive Form

gawiwa – be distributed
Silaha ziligawiwa na magaidi. – The weapons were distributed
    by terrorists.

Note in the example above, the active verb ends with -*wa*. In other words, not all verbs ending with the suffix -*wa* are automatically passive verbs.

The verb *ua* (kill) has the irregular passive form *uawa* (be killed).

Active Form
> *Wanakijiji walimwua simba.* – The villagers killed the lion.

Passive Form
> *Simba aliuawa na wanakijiji.* – The lion was killed by the villagers.

Practice Exercise A

Change the following sentences into Passive.

1. *Mkulima alikata miti kwa shoka.*
2. *Seremala alitengeneza mlango mkubwa sana.*
3. *Vijana walileta maji ya kunywa.*
4. *Opereta wa simu alikaa katika kiti.*
5. *Kaka yangu alilipa deni.*
6. *Wezi walichukua kila kitu.*
7. *John alimwoa msichana mzuri sana.*
8. *Wazimamoto waliwaokoa akina mama na watoto.*
9. *Walilea watoto wetu.*
10. *Kabla ya kwenda shuleni watoto walinawa maji.*

Section B: Verbs of Arabic Origin

Verbs of Arabic origin which end with the vowel -*i* or -*u* are made passive by changing the final vowel to -*iwa*. Examples:

Active Form
> *jadili* – discuss
> *Wazee walijadili jambo hili.* – The elders discussed this matter.

Passive Form
> *jadiliwa* – be discussed
> *Jambo hili lilijadiliwa na wazee.* – This matter was discussed by
> the elders.

Active Form

    jibu – answer
    Jaji alijibu swali lake. – The judge answered his/her question.

Passive Form

    jibiwa – be answered
    Swali lake lilijibiwa na jaji. – His/her question was answered by
        the judge.

Arabic verbs ending with the vowel *-e* are made passive by changing the final vowel to
-ewa. Example:

Active Form

    samehe – forgive
    Mama alimsamehe mtoto. – The mother forgave her child.

Passive Form

    samehewa – be forgiven
    Mtoto alisamehewa na mama. – The child was forgiven by his/
        her mother.

Arabic verbs ending with the vowels *-au* are made passive by the addition of the suffix
-liwa. Example:

Active Form

    dharau – despise
    Mke atamdharau mume wake. – The wife will despise her husband.

Passive Form

    dharauliwa – be despised
    Mume atadharauliwa na mke wake. – The husband will be de-
        spised by his wife.

Practice Exercise B

Change the following Passive sentences into Active.

11. *Mtihani ulirudiwa kuandikwa na wanafunzi.*
12. *Wafungwa wote walisamehewa makosa yao na Waziri Mkuu.*
13. *Maswali yetu yote yalijibiwa na viongozi.*
14. *Jambo hili lilifikiriwa na mimi kwa muda mrefu sana.*
15. *Vijana wale walihitajiwa mahakamani na polisi.*
16. *Maombi yetu hayakukubaliwa na Chuo Kikuu cha Minesota, Marekani.*
17. *Kazi ile ngumu haikujaribiwa na wafanyakazi.*
18. *Serikali ilishukuriwa na wananchi kwa msaada wake.*
19. *Baridi kutoka dirishani ilihisiwa na mgonjwa.*
20. *Vyombo vilisahauliwa kuoshwa na mimi.*

Section C: Monosyllabic Verbs

Each Monosyllabic verb has its own passive form as shown below. Examples:

Active Form
 la – eat
 Wanamuziki wamekula chakula chote. – Musicians have eaten all the food.

Passive Form
 liwa – be eaten
 Chakula chote kimeliwa na wanamuziki. – All the food has been eaten by musicians.

Active Form
 nywa – drink
 Mgonjwa alikunywa maji mengi sana. – The sick person drank a lot of water.

Passive Form
 nywewa – be drunk
 Maji mengi sana yalinywewa na mgonjwa. – A lot of water was drunk by the sick person.

Active Form
  ja – come
  Watalii walikuja Serengeti. – The tourists came to Serengeti.

Passive Form
  jiwa – come for
  Serengeti ilijiwa na watalii. – Serengeti was visited by the tourists.

Active Form
  pa – give
  Nilimpa mtoto pesa. – I gave the child some money.

Passive Form
  pewa – be given
  Mtoto alipewa pesa na mimi. – The child was given some money
     by me.

Active Form
  fa – die
  Mke wa jirani yetu alikufa. – The wife of our neighbour died.

Passive Form
  fiwa – be bereaved
  Jirani yetu alifiwa na mke wake. – Our neighbour lost his wife.
     (i.e. she has died)

Note that the passive verb *fiwa* can only be used when a person has lost his/her friends or family.

Practice Exercise C

Translate into English.

21. *Watu wote walipewa fidia na serikali.*
22. *Tulijiwa na wageni usiku wa manane.*
23. *Matunda mengi yaliliwa na wagonjwa.*
24. *Maji yote yalinywewa.*
25. *Rafiki yangu alifiwa na binamu yake.*

Practice Exercise D

Translate the following sentences into Swahili.

26. The cloth was stitched by mom with a needle and thread.
27. All the juice was drunk by the children.
28. The work was not done properly.
29. The rope was cut into two pieces.
30. The seeds were planted in November.
31. The vegetables were cooked by my brother.
32. Our project did not start because the director did not return.
33. Salaries were increased by ten percent.
34. Our house was rented by embassy officials.
35. The Bill was read in Parliament.
36. He was remembered by his children.
37. The floor was cleaned by the nanny.
38. If she is married, I will be happy.
39. Elephants are hunted every day.
40. Guests were forbidden to smoke in my parent's house.
41. The water was drunk by the nomads.
42. All the food was not eaten.
43. The best worker was given a car by the company.
44. Mt. Kilimanjaro is climbed by people of many nationalities.

Provide the correct passive form of the verb in bracket as shown in the example below using the simple past tense. Example:

Kitoto (tafuta). – Kilitafutwa.

45. *Redio kubwa zile mbili (funga).*
46. *Vinanda vyake vyote saba (nunua).*
47. *Barua zetu (chukua).*
48. *Aina hii ya vyakula (la) sana na watu kutoka Mexico.*
49. *Wanasemina (fundisha) jinsi ya kutumia teknolojia ya kisasa.*
50. *Amanda (fikiri) kupandishwa cheo.*
51. *Mameneja wote wa Ushuru wa Forodha (fukuza) kazi.*
52. *Je, nyumba yake (uza)?*
53. *Lango la jumba lile (fungua).*
54. *Vijiko vyote (safisha) baada ya kutumiwa.*
55. *Kijiti (kata) kwa kisu leo asubuhi.*

56. *Kiswahili (fundisha) katika Chuo Kikuu cha Toronto.*
57. *Zawadi (pl.) (pokea) na wote.*
58. *Wazee (amkia) kwa heshima.*
59. *Ukuta mchafu ule (paka) rangi nyeupe.*
60. *Barua pepe (sing.) (andika) kwenda kwa kila mwananchi.*
61. *Roketi (pl.) (rusha) kwenda kwenye sayari ya Mars.*
62. *Magari (endesha) ovyo barabarani na kusababisha ajali nyingi sana.*

New Vocabulary

afisa/ma-: officer(s), official(s)
ajali: accident(s)
akina mama: women folk
amkia: greet
bunge/ma-: parliament(s)
deni/ma-: debt(s)
fidia: compensation(s)
fukuza: chase, terminate (from work)
furahi: be happy
gaidi/ma-: terrorist(s)
gavana/ma-: governor(s)
gawa: distribute, divide
heshima: honour(s), respect(s)
hisi: feel
jadili: discuss
jaji/ma-: judge(s)
jaribu: try
jinsi: the way that, how
juisi: juice(s)
jumba/ma-: mansion(s)
kataza: forbid, prohibit
kijiti/vi-: twig(s), stick(s), small tree(s)
kinanda/vi-: piano(s)
kiongozi/vi-: guide(s), leader(s)
kitoto/vi-: infant(s)
kochi/ma-: couch(es)
kodi: hire, rent
kosa/ma-: mistake(s), fault(s), offence(s)

kumbuka: remember
lango/ma-: gate(s)
lea: raise, bring up
leta: bring
mbegu: seed(s)
mfungwa/wa-: prisoner(s)
mhamahamaji/wa-: nomad(s)
mkurugenzi/wa-: director(s)
msaada/mi-: assistance
mshahara/mi-: salary(ies)
mtalii/wa-: tourist(s)
mume/waume: husband(s)
mwanamuziki/wa-: musician(s)
mwananchi/wa-: citizen(s)
mwanasemina/wa-: seminar participant(s)
mzazi/wa-: parent(s)
nawa: wash
okoa: rescue
ombi/ma-: request(s), application(s)
ongeza: increase
opereta/ma-: operator(s)
osha: wash
ovyo: carelessly
paka rangi: apply colour(s) (paint)
pakua: serve, unload
pandisha: promote
pilipili: pepper(s)
redio: radio(s)
roketi: rocket(s)
rusha: fly
sababisha: cause
safisha: clean
sahau: forget
sakafu: floor(s)
sayari: planet(s)
shoka: axe(s)
shona: stitch, sew
silaha: weapon(s)

sindano: needle(s)
tafuta: look for, search
taifa/ma-: nation(s)
teknolojia: technology(ies)
tia: put
ubalozi: embassy(ies)
Ushuru wa Forodha: Duties and Customs Department
vuta: pull, smoke
waziri/ma- mkuu/wa-: prime minister(s)
winda: hunt

Key to Exercises

Answers to Practice Exercise A

1. *Miti ilikatwa na mkulima kwa shoka.*
2. *Mlango mkubwa sana ulitengenezwa na seremala.*
3. *Maji ya kunywa yaliletwa na vijana.*
4. *Kiti kilikaliwa na opereta wa simu.*
5. *Deni lililipwa na kaka yangu.*
6. *Kila kitu kilichukuliwa na wezi.*
7. *Msichana mzuri sana aliolewa na John.*
8. *Akina mama na watoto waliokolewa na wazimamoto.*
9. *Watoto wetu walilelewa na wao.*
10. *Maji yalinawiwa na watoto kabla ya kwenda shuleni.*

Answers to Practice Exercise B

11. *Wanafunzi walirudia kuandika mtihani.*
12. *Waziri Mkuu aliwasamehe wafungwa wote makosa yao.*
13. *Viongozi walijibu maswali yetu yote.*
14. *Mimi nililifikiria jambo hili kwa muda mrefu sana.*
15. *Polisi waliwahitaji vijana wale mahakamani.*
16. *Chuo Kikuu cha Minesota, Marekani hakikuyakubali maombi yetu.*
17. *Wafanyakazi hawakuijaribu kazi ile ngumu.*
18. *Wananchi waliishukuru serekali kwa msaada wake.*
19. *Mgonjwa alihisi baridi kutoka dirishani.*
20. *Mimi nilisahau kuosha vyombo.*

Answers to Practice Exercise C

21. All the people were given compensation by the government.
22. We were visited by guests late in the night.
23. Many fruits were eaten by the sick people.
24. All the water was drunk.
25. My friend lost his/her cousin (the cousin has died).

Answers to Practice Exercise D

26. *Nguo ilishonwa na mama kwa sindano na uzi.*
27. *Juisi yote ilinywewa na watoto.*
28. *Kazi haikufanywa vizuri.*
29. *Kamba ilikatwa vipande viwili.*
30. *Mbegu zilipandwa mwezi wa Novemba.*
31. *Mboga zilipikwa na kaka yangu.*
32. *Mradi wetu haukuanzwa kwa sababu mkurugenzi hakurudi.*
33. *Mishahara iliongezwa kwa asilimia kumi.*
34. *Nyumba yetu ilikodiwa na maafisa wa ubalozi.*
35. *Mswada ulisomwa Bungeni.*
36. *Alikumbukwa na watoto wake.*
37. *Sakafu ilisafishwa na yaya.*
38. *Akiolewa nitafurahi.*
39. *Tembo wanawindwa kila siku.*
40. *Wageni walikatazwa kuvuta sigara katika nyumba ya wazazi wangu.*
41. *Maji yalinywewa na wahamahamaji.*
42. *Chakula chote hakikuliwa.*
43. *Mfanyakazi bora alipewa gari na kampuni.*
44. *Mlima wa Kilimanjaro unapandwa na watu kutoka mataifa mbalimbali.*
45. *zilifungwa*
46. *vilinunuliwa*
47. *zilichukuliwa*
48. *viliiwa*
49. *walifundishwa*
50. *alifikiriwa*
51. *walifukuzwa*
52. *iliuzwa*

53. *lilifunguliwa.*
54. *vilisafishwa*
55. *kilikatwa*
56. *kilifundishwa*
57. *zilipokelewa*
58. *waliamkiwa*
59. *ulipakwa*
60. *iliandikwa*
61. *zilirushwa*
62. *yaliendeshwa*

Chapter 24

Stative Form of the Verb

Stative verbs express a current condition of the subject or the potential of entering that condition. Stative verbs that express a current state of the subject use the past perfect tense marker *-me-*, while stative verbs that express the potential of entering that condition generally use the present tense marker *-na-* but can use other tenses. Stative verbs can be used in both affirmative and negative sentences, and follow the rules learnt in previous chapters. Unlike passive verbs, stative verbs do not indicate who performed the action. Most stative verbs are derived from other verbs; however a few are formed from nouns and adjectives. In addition, some causative verbs can be changed to stative. Stative verbs are formed from the following categories:

1. Bantu verbs where the 2nd last syllable contains A, I, or U
2. Bantu verbs where the 2nd last syllable contains E or O
3. Bantu verbs which end with double vowels
4. Arabic verbs
5. Verbs which already exist in the Stative form
6. Stative verbs derived from nouns and adjectives
7. Exception verbs

Section A: Bantu Verbs with a Previous Stem Vowel A, I, or U

Bantu verbs where the 2nd last syllable contains A, I, or U are made stative by inserting *-ik-* before the last vowel. Monosyllabic verbs also fall in this category.

panda – climb = *pandika* – climbable
Ukuta wa mawe unapandika. – The rock wall is climbable.
lima – cultivate = *limika* – cultivatable
Shamba hili linalimika. – This farm is cultivatable.
vunja – break = *vunjika* – broken
Kiti kimevunjika. – The chair is broken.

Practice Exercise A

Translate into Swahili.

1. Those mirrors are broken.
2. The apprentice is teachable.
3. These fruits will be edible.
4. The road is passable during the dry season only.
5. Their cart was pushable.
6. This hurdle was not jumpable.
7. The water pipe is bent.
8. Those doors are not closable.
9. Can this fine be payable?
10. The lottery is winnable.

Section B: Bantu Verbs with a Previous Stem Vowel E or O

Bantu verbs where the 2nd last syllable contains E or O are made stative by inserting *-ek-* before the last vowel. For example:

penda – love = *pendeka* – lovable
Mji huu unapendeka. – This city is lovable.
soma – read = *someka* – readable
Kitabu chake kinasomeka. – His/Her book is readable.

Practice Exercise B

Translate into English.

11. *Nyama ya mbuzi imechomeka.*
12. *Mchezo huu mpya unachezeka.*
13. *Shati langu limeshoneka.*

14. *Nyumba ile imejengeka.*
15. *Barua yake yote haikusomeka.*
16. *Barua hizi zinapelekeka.*
17. *Maswali yako hayaeleweki.*
18. *Nguo za mabinti zinashoneka.*
19. *Viazi vinapondeka.*
20. *Barabara imenyosheka.*

Section C: Bantu Verbs which End with Double Vowels

Bantu verbs ending with double vowel *-aa* are made stative by inserting *-lik-* before the last vowel.

> *kaa* – stay = *kalika* – habitable
> *Mahali hapa panakalika.* – This place is habitable.
> *hadaa* – deceive = *hadalika* – deceivable
> *Mfanyakazi wa huduma za jamii anahadalika.* – The social worker
>   is deceivable.

Bantu verbs ending with double vowels and the second last vowel is I or U are made stative by inserting *-k-* or *-lik-* before the last vowel.

> *fungua* – open = *funguka* – openable
> *Kopo la samaki limefunguka.* – The can of fish is open.
> *sikia* – hear = *sikika* (or *sikilika*) – audible
> *Sauti yake inasikika mpaka hapa.* – His/Her voice is audible up
>   to here.

Bantu verbs ending with double vowels and the second last vowel is E or O are made stative by inserting *-lek-* before the last vowel.

> *lea* – raise = *leleka* – raisable
> *Mtoto wake haleleki.* – His/Her child is not raisable. (difficult to
>   raise)
> *ondoa* – remove = *ondoleka* – removable
> *Theluji hii haiondoleki.* – This snow is not removable.

Practice Exercise C

Translate into Swahili.

> 21. The window of our house was open.
> 22. His/Her good car is bought.
> 23. The runway is wide.
> 24. The Boston marathon is runnable.
> 25. My tooth is not extractable.

Section D: Arabic Verbs

Arabic verbs ending with E or I are made stative by adding *-ka* as a suffix.

> *samehe* – forgive = *sameheka* – forgivable
> *Kosa la mfungwa linasameheka.* – The offence of the prisoner is
>   forgivable.
> *fikiri* – think = *fikirika* – be thinkable
> *Jambo hili halifikiriki.* – This matter is not thinkable.

Arabic verbs ending with U are made stative by changing the last vowel to *i* and adding *-ka* as a suffix.

> *jibu* – answer = *jibika* – be answerable
> *Swali hili linajibika.* – This question is answerable.

Arabic verbs ending with double vowels are made stative by adding *-lika* as a suffix.

> *sahau* – forget = *sahaulika* – forgettable
> *Wimbo wenu unasahaulika.* – Your (pl.) song is forgettable.

Practice Exercise D

Translate into English.

> 26. *Kamera hii hairudishiki.*
> 27. *Makosa yake yote yanasameheka.*
> 28. *Hali ya hewa inabadilika.*
> 29. *Jambo hili limesahaulika.*

30. *Kampuni ya kifedha inadirikika.*
31. *Matokeo ya tatizo lile yamefahamika.*
32. *Ninafikiri kwamba meneja wangu atasema kwamba mkataba huu unakubalika.*
33. *Haiba yake inadharaulika.*
34. *Maelezo ya mkimbizi hayaaminiki.*
35. *Jiwe la madini lile linathaminika.*

Section E: Verbs Which Already Exist in the Stative Form

Some verbs are inherently in the stative form and do not need to take *-ka* to make them stative as shown in the examples below:

lewa – be drunk
Yule kijana amelewa. – That youth is drunk.
shiba – be full
Baba ameshiba. – My father is full.
anguka – be in fallen state
Nyumba imeanguka. – The house has fallen.

Practice Exercise E

Translate into Swahili.

36. It is not good to be late to work.
37. The crocodiles will go to sleep because they are full.
38. The ostrich is asleep.
39. The socks will not be dry in an hour.
40. The customs officer was angry.

Section F: Stative Verbs Derived from Nouns and Adjectives

Only some nouns and adjectives can be used to form stative verbs as shown below.

shughuli – business = *shughulika* – be busy
Walishughulika kupiga chapa usiku kucha. – They were busy printing all night.

bahati – luck = *bahatika* – be lucky
Walibahatika kupata mtoto. – They were lucky to have a child.
-erevu – clever = *erevuka* – be clever
John ameerevuka siku hizi. – John has become clever these days.
-pevu – ripe = *pevuka* – ripened
Mananasi yamepevuka. – The pineapples have ripened.
bora – better = *boreka* – become better
Polepole, Kiswahili chake kimeboreka. – Slowly, his/her Swahili
    has become better.

As you can see from the examples above, the majority of stative verbs formed from nouns and adjectives are made by attaching *-ka* to the end of the word. However, some nouns and adjectives have their final vowel changed before attaching *-ka* to make them stative.

Practice Exercise F

Translate into English.

41. *Mawasiliano yamerahisika kwa sababu ya teknolojia ya kisasa.*
42. *Ziwa limesafika kwa sababu ya ukosefu wa **kuvuja** kwa **mafuta.***
43. *Urafiki wao umeimarika baada ya wiki chache tu.*
44. *Wananchi wametaabika kwa ajili ya kushuka kwa uchumi.*
45. *Madaladala matatu yale yamezeeka.*

Section G: Exception Verbs

Some verbs, nouns, and adjectives do not follow any particular rules when they become stative verbs as shown below.

nusa – smell, sniff = *nuka* – to smell bad
Maduriani yale yananuka. – Those Durian fruits smell bad.
hasira – anger = *kasirika* – be angry
Mkutubi amekasirika sana. – The librarian is very angry.

Practice Exercise G

Translate the following passage into Swahili.

The tickets to travel to Arusha to climb Mount Kilimanjaro are bought at the bus station at 8 am. The fare can be paid in Tanzanian Shilling or

US Dollars. The tourists already had their breakfast before boarding the bus. The stewardess distributed interesting and readable magazines in order to entertain the tourists. At 1 pm, the bus stopped at a local restaurant for a break. Many tourists were busy eating local food such as skewered meat, cassava chips and roasted fish. The skewered meats were very nicely roasted and the cassava chips were fresh. After a period of five hours, the bus arrived in Arusha. However, because the sun had set, Mount Kilimanjaro was not climbable and the tourists were angry. The second day, the tourists were lucky to climb Mount Kilimanjaro.

New Vocabulary

amini: believe
au: or
badili: change
bahati nasibu: lottery(ies)
barabara ya/za ndege: runway(s)
binti/ma-: daughter(s)
bomba/ma-: pipe(s)
burudisha: entertain, refresh
chamshakinywa/vy-: breakfast(s)
chipsi: chip(s), French fries
daladala/ma-: minibus(es)
diriki: manage
duriani/ma-: Durian fruit(s)
elewa: understand
elezo/ma-: explanation(s)
-erevu: clever
faini: fine(s)
forodha: customs, customs duty(ies)
freshi: fresh
hadaa: deceive
haiba: personality(ies), appearance(s)
hali ya hewa: weather
hasira: anger
hata hivyo: even though, however
ili: so that, in order that
kama vile: such as
kamera: camera(s)

kasirika: get angry
kiangazi/vi-: dry season(s)
kifedha: financial
kiunzi/vi-: hurdle(s)
kopo/ma-: can(s)
kwamba: if, whether, that
lewa: to be intoxicated
madini: mineral(s)
mamba: crocodile(s)
marathoni: marathon(s)
mawasiliano: communication(s)
mbuni: ostrich(es)
mbuzi: goat(s)
mfanyakazi/wa- wa huduma za jamii: social worker(s)
mkataba/mi-: contract(s)
mkimbizi/wa-: refugee(s)
mkokoteni/mi-: cart(s)
mshikaki/mi-: skewered meat(s)
muhogo/mi-: cassava root(s)
mwanagenzi/wa-: apprentice(s)
nauli: fare(s)
ng'oa: extract
nusa: smell
nyosha: straighten
ondoa: remove
panua: widen
peleka: send
-pevu: ripe
piga chapa: type, print
pinda: bend
pitia: pass through, transit through
ponda: crush
pumziko/ma-: break(s), rest period(s)
sauti: voice(s), sound(s)
shiba: be full
shuka: descend
soksi: sock(s)
taabu: troubled, distressed

thamini: value, appraise
theluji: snow(s)
tokeo/ma-: consequence(s)
uchumi: economy(ies)
urafiki: friendship(s)
usiku kucha: all night
vuja: leak, spill out
vutia: attract, interest
zeeka: old, worn out

Key to Exercises

Answers to Practice Exercise A

1. *Vioo vile vimevunjika.*
2. *Mwanagenzi anafundishika.*
3. *Matunda haya yatalika.*
4. *Barabara inapitika wakati wa kiangazi tu.*
5. *Mkokoteni wao ulisukumika.*
6. *Kiunzi hiki hakikurukika.*
7. *Bomba la maji limepindika.*
8. *Milango ile haifungiki.*
9. *Je, faini hii inalipika?*
10. *Bahati nasibu inashindika.*

Answers to Practice Exercise B

11. The goat's meat is roasted.
12. This new game is playable.
13. My shirt is sewn.
14. That house is built.
15. All of his/her letter was not readable.
16. These letters are sendable.
17. Your questions are not understandable.
18. The daughters' clothes are sewable.
19. The potatoes are crushable.
20. The road is straight.

Answers to Practice Exercise C

21. *Dirisha la nyumba yetu limefunguka.*
22. *Gari lake zuri limenunulika.*
23. *Barabara ya ndege imepanuka.*
24. *Marathoni ya Boston inakimbilika.*
25. *Jino langu haling'oleki.*

Answers to Practice Exercise D

26. This camera is not returnable.
27. All his/her faults are pardonable.
28. The weather is changeable.
29. This matter is forgotten.
30. The financial company is manageable.
31. The consequences of that problem are understood.
32. I think that my manager will say that this contract is agreeable.
33. His/Her personality is despisable.
34. The explanations of the refugee are not believable.
35. That mineral stone is valuable.

Answers to Practice Exercise E

36. *Si vizuri kuchelewa kazini.*
37. *Mamba watakwenda kulala kwa sababu wameshiba.*
38. *Mbuni amelala.*
39. *Soksi hazitakauka katika muda wa saa moja.*
40. *Ofisa wa forodha alikasirika.*

Answers to Practice Exercise F

41. Communication has become easy because of new technology.
42. The lake has become clean because of the absence of oil spills.
43. Their friendship has become firm after only a few weeks.
44. The citizens are troubled by the economic recession.
45. Those three mini-buses are old.

Answers to Practice Exercise G

Tiketi za kusafiri kwenda Arusha kupanda Mlima Kilimanjaro zinanunulika katika kituo cha basi saa mbili asubuhi. Nauli inalipika katika Shilingi za Kitanzania au Dola za Kimarekani. Watalii wameshakula chamshakinywa kabla ya kupanda basi. Mtumishi aligawa magezeti ya kuvutia na kusomeka ili kuwaburudisha watalii. Saa saba mchana, basi lilisimama kwenye hoteli ya mahali kwa ajili ya mapumziko. Watalii wengi walishughulika kula chakula cha mahali kama vile mishikaki, chipsi za muhogo, na samaki wa kuchoma. Mishikaki ilichomeka vizuri sana, na chipsi za muhogo zilikuwa freshi. Baada ya muda wa saa tano, basi lilifika Arusha. Hata hivyo, kwa sababu jua limekuchwa, Mlima Kilimanjaro haukupandika na watalii walikasirika. Siku ya pili, watalii walibahatika kupanda Mlima Kilimanjaro.

Chapter 25

Causative Form of the Verb

Most causative verbs express the meaning of "to make something happen" or "to cause an action to take place," however, some convey a somewhat different meaning from the original verb. Causative verbs are derived from nouns, adjectives, adverbs and conjunctions; can be used with any tense, and are negated in the same way as regular verbs. There are four categories of causative verbs which will be taught in this chapter, namely:

1. Causative verbs formed with the suffix *-esha* or *-eza*.
2. Causative verbs formed with the suffix *-isha* or *-iza*.
3. Causative verbs formed with the infix *-z-*, *-lish-* or *-liz-*.
4. Causative verbs that do not fit into any of the above categories.

Section A: Causative verbs which end with either *-esha* or *-eza*

Verbs where the 2nd last syllable contains O or E are made causative by the suffix *-esha* or *-eza* as shown in the examples below:

cheka – laugh = *chekesha* – cause to laugh
Mchekeshaji aliwachekesha wasikilizaji. – The comedian made the audience laugh.
oga – bathe = *ogesha* – bathe someone
Mama wanawaogesha watoto wao. – Mothers bathe their children.
penda – love = *pendeza* – please

Tabia yake haikutupendeza. – His/Her behaviour did not please us.
tokea – come out = *tokeza* – cause to come out
Roshani ilitokeza juu ya mlango wa mbele. – The balcony stuck out above the front door.

Practice Exercise A

Translate into English.

1. *Madereva wanatakiwa kuendesha magari yao kwa uangalifu.*
2. *Benki ilimkopesha mfanyabiashara dola milioni mbili.*
3. *Huu ni wakati wa kuorodhesha wapiga kura.*
4. *Mfalme hakuwasomesha watoto wake.*
5. *Ninatumaini hawatatusemesha kwa sababu tuna shughuli.*
6. *Kazi ile iliwachokesha sana.*
7. *Dada yangu hakuotesha mimea.*
8. *Wapigamuziki hawakupoteza vifaa vyao.*
9. *Mazingira ya hapa yanapendeza sana.*
10. *Kamanda alichelewesha gwaride.*

Section B: Causative verbs
which end with *-isha* or *-iza*

Verbs where the 2nd last syllable contains A, I or U are made causative by the suffix *-isha* or *-iza* as shown in the examples below:

hama – relocate = *hamisha* – transfer
Seremala alihamisha vyombo vyake. – The carpenter moved his/her tools.
rudi – return = *rudisha* – send back
Kampuni chache zimerudisha magari. – Few companies have re-called the vehicles.
fahamu – understand = *fahamisha* – inform
Madaktari walitufahamisha kuhusu ukimwi. – The doctors informed us about AIDS.
iga – imitate = *igiza* – act
Tuliigiza mchezo wa Shakespeare. – We acted a Shakespeare play.

Practice Exercise B

Translate into Swahili.

11. He made his sister rich by investing her money.
12. The President cut short her visit after the floods.
13. The courier did not deliver all the parcels.
14. The tour guides simplified our safari.
15. The citizenship judge made the new immigrants take an oath.
16. John taught us how to drive a car.
17. We softened the soil before planting the seeds.
18. Mother fed the baby with porridge.
19. We did not make them pay for their mistakes.
20. The earthquake did not relocate many people.
21. The police and firefighters staged the accident.
22. The tourists fulfilled their goal of climbing Mount Kilimanjaro.

Section C: Causative verbs which end with *-z-*, *-lish-* or *-liz-*

Verbs which end in double vowels are made causative by either inserting *-z-*, *-lish-* or *-liz-* between the two vowels as shown in the examples below:

umia – get hurt = *umiza* – cause pain
Magaidi waliwaumiza watu wengi sana. – The terrorists hurt many people.
ingia – enter = *ingiza* – let in
Mchungaji aliingiza mifugo yake yote. – The herder let in all his/her livestock.
kaa – sit = *kalisha* – cause to sit
Kiongozi aliwakalisha chini watu wake. – The leader sat down his/her people.
sikia – hear = *sikiliza* – listen
Waandishi wa habari hawakumsikiliza mhariri. – The reporters did not listen to the editor.

Practice Exercise C

Write the verbs from which the following causative verbs have been derived.

23. *visha*
24. *tembeza*
25. *punguza*
26. *poteza*
27. *oza*
28. *poza*
29. *jaza*
30. *paza*
31. *zoeza*
32. *pokeza*
33. *tokeza*
34. *kataza*
35. *kimbiza*
36. *kuza*
37. *liza*
38. *chomoza*
39. *zalisha*
40. *uguza*

Section D: Causative verbs which do not fit into any of the above categories

1. Some verbs ending with *-ka* and *-ta* are made causative by replacing these suffixes with *-sha* as shown in the examples below:

chemka – boil = *chemsha* – cause to boil
Shangazi alichemsha maji ya kuoga. – The aunt boiled water for the bath.
pata – get = *pasha* – inform
Walitupasha habari za safari yao. – They informed us about their safari.

2. Some verbs ending with -*na* are made causative by replacing the -*na* suffix with

-*nya* as shown below:

ona – see = *onya* – warn
Hatukumwonya juu ya ugonjwa huu. – We did not warn him/her about this disease.
pona – heal = *ponya* – cause to be healed
Daktari aliponya wagonjwa wengi wa malaria. – The doctor healed many malaria patients.

3. Some verbs can be changed into two different causative verbs which convey two different meanings as shown in the examples below:

pita – pass = *pisha* – allow to pass
Mlinzi alitupisha kuingia Ikulu. – The guard allowed us to enter the State House.
pita – pass = *pitisha* – approve
Bosi wake alipitisha maombi yake. – His/Her boss approved his/her requests.

4. Some verbs are causative in their original form as shown below:

fundisha – teach or cause to learn
Kocha aliwafundisha wachezaji njia bora ya kufunga magoli. – The coach taught the players a better way to score goals.

5. Some verbs do not follow any rules when made into their causative form

sawa – equal = *sawazisha* – equalize
Serikali haikusawazisha mishahara ya wafanyakazi wote. – The government did not equalize the salaries of all the workers.

Also note that after being changed into causative verbs, some causative verbs can also be made passive. For example:

soma – read – *somesha* – educate – *someshwa* – educated by
Mwanafunzi alisomeshwa na mwalimu. – The student was educated by the teacher.

Practice Exercise D

Write the verbs from which the following causative verbs have been derived.

41. *washa*
42. *fanya, fanyiza*
43. *kanya*
44. *laza*
45. *shusha*

Translate into Swahili.

46. The food was prepared by a very famous chef.
47. The child was put to sleep by his father.
48. The envelope will be returned by the post man.
49. The buckets of water were filled by the villagers.
50. I was forced to clean my room.

New Vocabulary

apa: swear (the truth)
bahasha: envelope(s)
bosi/ma-: boss(es)
chelewesha: delay
chemka: boil
choka: tired
chomoa: extract
fahamisha: inform
fana: succeed, prosper
fikisha: deliver
funga goli/ma-: score goal(s)
gwaride: parade(s)
hama: relocate, migrate
iga: imitate
igiza: act, stage
Ikulu: State House in Dar-es-Salaam
ingia: enter
jaji/ma- wa uraia: citizenship judge(s)

kamanda/ma-: commander(s)
kana: refuse, reject, deny
kataa: refuse, reject, deny
kifaa/vi-: equipment, instrument(s), supply(ies), material(s)
kifurushi/vi-: parcel(s)
kiongozi/vi- wa watalii: tour guide(s)
kocha/ma-: coach(es)
kopa: borrow
kopesha: lend
kua: grow
kuhusu: concerning, about
laini: soft
lazima: obligation
lazimisha: order, force
lengo/ma-: goal(s)
limbika: set aside, invest
maarufu: famous
mchekeshaji/wa-: comedian(s)
mchungaji/wa-: priest(s), shepherd(s)
mfalme/wa-: king(s)
mfanyabiashara/wa-: businessperson(s)
mfugo/mi-: farm animal(s)
mhamiaji/wa-: immigrant(s)
mpiga/wa- kura: voter(s)
mpigamuziki/wa-: musician(s)
msafirishaji/wa-: courier(s)
msikilizaji/wa-: listener(s)
mtu/wa- wa posta: postal worker(s)
mwandishi/wa- wa habari: reporter(s)
oga: bathe, wash
onya: warn
orodha: list(s)
orodhesha: register
paa: raise, fly
pasha: inform
pitisha: approve
roshani: balcony(ies)
tabia: behaviour(s)

takiwa: require, need
tetemeko/ma- la/ya ardhi: earthquake(s)
timia: complete
tumaini/ma-: hope(s)
uangilifu: care
ugonjwa/magonjwa: disease(s)
ugua: feel sick
uji: porridge
umia: get hurt
waka: burn, shine, light
zaa: bear, produce
ziara: visit(s)
zoea: be used to

Key to Exercises

Answers to Practice Exercise A

1. Drivers are required to drive their cars carefully.
2. The bank lent the businessperson two million dollars.
3. This is the time to register voters.
4. The king did not educate his children.
5. I hope they will not make us speak because we are busy.
6. That work made them very tired.
7. My sister did not grow plants.
8. The musicians did not lose their equipment.
9. The environment of this place is very pleasant.
10. The commander delayed the parade.

Answers to Practice Exercises B

11. *Alimtajirisha dada yake kwa kulimbikiza pesa zake.*
12. *Rais alifupisha ziara yake baada ya mafuriko.*
13. *Msafirishaji hakufikisha vifurushi vyote.*
14. *Viongozi wa watalii walirahisisha safari yetu.*
15. *Jaji wa uraia aliwaapisha wahamiaji wapya.*
16. *John alitufundisha jinsi ya kuendesha gari.*
17. *Tulilainisha udongo kabla ya kupanda mbegu.*
18. *Mama alimlisha mtoto uji.*
19. *Hatukuwalipiza kwa ajili ya makosa yao.*

20. *Tetemeko la ardhi halikuwahamisha watu wengi.*
21. *Polisi na wazimamoto waliigiza ajali.*
22. *Watalii walitimiza lengo lao la kupanda Mlima Kilimanjaro.*

Answers to Practice Exercise C

23. *vaa*
24. *tembea*
25. *pungua*
26. *potea*
27. *oa*
28. *poa*
29. *jaa*
30. *paa*
31. *zoea*
32. *pokea*
33. *tokea*
34. *kataa*
35. *kimbia*
36. *kua*
37. *lia*
38. *chomoa*
39. *zaa*
40. *ugua*

Answers to Practice Exercise D

41. *waka*
42. *fana*
43. *kana*
44. *lala*
45. *shuka*
46. *Chakula kilitayarishwa na mpishi maarufu sana.*
47. *Mtoto alilazwa na baba yake.*
48. *Bahasha itarudishwa na mtu wa posta.*
49. *Ndoo za maji zilijazwa na wanakijiji.*
50. *Mimi nililazimishwa kusafisha chumba changu.*

Chapter 26

Prepositional Form of the Verb

Unlike in English, some Swahili verbs can be made into prepositional forms, the preposition is implied in the meaning of the verb. When the prepositional form of the verb is used, it eliminates the use of the preposition. Prepositional verbs convey a range of meanings depending on the context. They can convey the meaning of doing something to, for, or on behalf of someone. It can also be used to express motion towards or away from something or someone. Most prepositional verbs end with *-ia, -ea, -lia* or *-lea* as will be taught below.

Section A: Prepositional verbs ending with *-ia*

Bantu verbs, including Monosyllabic verbs, where the 2nd last syllable contains A, I or U, are made prepositional by inserting *-i-* before the final vowel as shown in the examples below:

>*lala* – sleep = *lalia* – sleep on
>*Ofisa tawala alinunua mkeka wa kulalia.* – The Administrative Officer bought a mat to sleep on.
>*pika* – cook = *pikia* – cook for/with
>*Utawapikia wakalimani?* – Will you cook for the interpreters?
>*la* – eat = *lia* – eat with
>*Alikulia uma.* – He/She ate with a fork.

Bantu verbs ending in double vowels *-aa* or *-ia* or *-ua* are made prepositional by inserting *-li-* between the two vowels as shown in the examples below:

kaa – sit = *kalia* – sit with/for/on
Godoro la kukalia limechanika. – The mattress for sitting on is torn.
ingia – enter = *ingilia* – enter with/for
Mlango wa kuingilia ulifungwa. – The door for entering was closed.
chukua – take = *chukulia* – take with/for
Hatukumchukulia baiskeli yake. – We did not take the person's bi-
    cycle for him/her.

Arabic verbs ending with *-i* are made prepositional by suffixing it with -
a as a final vowel as shown in the example below:

rudi – return = *rudia* – return to/for
Mohamed alirudia mwavuli wake. – Mohamed returned for his um-
    brella.

Arabic verbs ending with *-u* are made prepositional by dropping their
final vowel and replacing it *-ia* as shown in the example below:

jibu – answer = *jibia* – reply to/for
Mama alinijibia barua pepe zangu. – Mother responded to my emails
    for me.

Note: Not all verbs which end with *-ia* convey a prepositional meaning.
For example, the verb *fagia* simply means "sweep."

Practice Exercise A

Translate into English.

1. *Tulifikiria sana jambo hili kabla ya kufanya uamuzi.*
2. *Shangazi aliuza ngazi yake ya kupandia.*
3. *Sikumlipia mdhamini wangu deni lake.*
4. *Alifikia Hoteli ya Intercontinental katika mwezi wa Januari.*
5. *Mwiko wa kupakulia chakula umeungua.*
6. *Mke wake alimzalia watoto wa kike wazuri watatu.*
7. *Tumebadilisha ufunguo wa kufungulia mlango.*
8. *Walimkaribia adui kufyatua risasi.*
9. *Atamchukulia sindano ya kufumia sweta.*
10. *Nyanya hakumpakulia mtoto chakula cha mchana.*

11. *Utanunua viatu vya kukimbilia?*
12. *Mpokezi wangu alininunulia zawadi nzuri sana.*
13. *Simon alirudia darasa moja kwa sababu alikuwa mgonjwa.*
14. *Utafagilia ufagio upi?*
15. *Mohammed atatulindia nyumba yetu.*

Section B: Prepositional verbs ending with *–ea*

Bantu verbs where the 2nd last syllable contains E, O or Y or Monosyllabic verbs containing Y are made prepositional by inserting -*e*- before the final vowel as shown in the examples below:

soma – read = *somea* – read for
Unasomea nini? – What are you (sing.) reading for?
leta – bring = *letea* – bring for/use to bring
Tutawaletea stempu kutoka Uchina. – We will bring you (pl.) stamps
   from China.
nywa – drink = *nywea* – drink with
Walinywea kikombe. – They drank with a cup.

Bantu verbs ending in double vowels -*ea* or -*oa* are made prepositional by inserting -*le*- between the two vowels as shown in the examples below:

pokea – receive = *pokelea* – receive for
Mfuko wa kupokelea pesa. – A bag for receiving money.
zoa – pick up = *zolea* – pick up with
Alizolea takataka na chombo ghali. – He/She picked up the garbage
   with an expensive pan.

Arabic verbs ending with -*e* are made prepositional by suffixing them with -*a* as shown in the example below:

samehe – forgive = *samehea* – forgive for
Hana huruma ya kuwasamehea makosa yao. – He/She has no compassion for forgiving their mistakes.

Note: Not all verbs which end with -*ea* convey a prepositional meaning. For example, the verb *lea* simply means "bring up or raise a child."

Practice Exercise B

Translate into Swahili.

16. My brother has read a poem of hope for the disabled children.
17. He visited Dubai last year.
18. They removed for us our luggage from the custom's booth.
19. The cook brought for us tea with milk.
20. Where do those youths come from?
21. We did not study with diligence for this job.
22. He went to receive the parcel for them from the post office.
23. The clerk favoured his neighbour's application.
24. He cooled off the porridge for the old man.
25. The judge stared at the accused.
26. They bought a tool for pruning fruit trees.
27. A helicopter for rescuing people has crashed.
28. They sent for him his cheque from the lottery office.
29. The sick person was given a container for keeping medicine.
30. I prayed for his success.

Section C: Other types of Prepositional Verbs

Some prepositional verbs do not fall into the two categories presented above.

1. Some verbs are prepositional in their basic form.

uliza – ask
Mgeni aliniuliza njia ya kwenda sokoni. – The guest asked me the
    road to the market.
tafuta – look for
Mabaharia waliitafuta meli jana. – The sailors searched for the ship
    yesterday.

Note: When the verb *tafuta* is changed to *tafutia*, it translates as "looking for something on behalf of someone." For example:

Mabaharia waliitafutia serikali meli jana. – The sailors searched for
    the ship yesterday on behalf of the government.

2. Some verbs convey special meanings in their prepositional forms.

amka – wake up = *amkia* – greet
Nilimwamkia mzee kwa kusema "shikamoo." – I greeted the elder by
    saying *"shikamoo."*
nuka – stink = *nukia* – smell(s) good
Waridi linanukia. – The rose smells good.

Practice Exercise C

Translate the following sentences into Swahili.

31. The lawyer asked the client questions in the court.
32. The host has treated his dignitaries well.
33. The shopkeeper used trickery to win.
34. The dog owner will give his dog a bone.
35. He did not reach the fruits because he is short.

Section D: Other verb typologies derived from Prepositional verbs

Prepositional verbs can be changed into other verb typologies as shown
below:

Prepositional Passive verb:

The prepositional passive verb is formed by inserting -*w*- before the final
vowel of the prepositional verb. For example:

Prepositional form: *andikia* – write with/for/to
Dada yangu aliwaandikia barua wazazi wetu. – My sister wrote a
    letter to our parents.

Passive form: *andikwa* – written by
Barua iliandikwa kwa wazazi wetu na dada yangu. – A letter was
    written to our parents by my sister.

Prepositional Passive form: *andikiwa* – written for
Wazazi wetu waliandikiwa barua na dada yangu. – Our parents were
    written a letter by my sister.

In Swahili, only the direct object (in this case *barua*) can act as the subject of a passive sentence. This is in contrast to English where either a direct or indirect object can act as the subject of a passive sentence. If you wish the indirect object (in this case *wazazi*) to act as the subject of a passive sentence, you must use a prepositional passive form of the verb.

Prepositional Reciprocal verb:

The prepositional reciprocal verb is formed by suffixing *-na* to the prepositional verb. For example:

Prepositional Reciprocal form: *andikiana* – write to each other
Bondia na refa waliandikiana barua. – The boxer and the referee wrote each other (a) letter(s).

Note: Reciprocal verb typology will be covered in the following chapter.

Practice Exercise D

Change the following prepositional sentence into prepositional passive.

36. *Mwindaji aliwachomea mahindi wahifadhi wa wanyama.*
37. *Jamaa yake kutoka Ulaya alimpigia simu jirani.*
38. *Fundi bomba alitumia spana kupindia bomba.*
39. *Nilimpandia maua mwenyenyumba.*
40. *Mashine ilimkamulia taulo mwanamichezo.*

New Vocabulary

adui/ma-: enemy(ies)
bidii: effort(s), diligence
bondia/ma-: boxer(s)
chakula/vy- cha/vya mchana: lunch(es)
chana: tear
fagia: sweep
fikia: stay at, reach
fuma: weave, knit
fundi/ma- bomba: plumber(s)
fyatua risasi: fire a bullet

godoro/ma-: mattress(es)
hindi/ma-: grain(s) of maize/corn
hundi/ma-: cheque(s)
huruma: compassion
kamua: squeeze, wring
karani/ma-: clerk(s)
kibanda/vi-: booth(s)
kodoa macho: stare
komboa: rescue
linda: guard
mafanikio: success(es)
mashine: machine(s)
mdhamini/wa-: sponsor(s)
meli: ship(s)
mfupa/mi-: bone(s)
mhifadhi/wa- wa wanyama: game keeper(s)
mkalimani/wa-: interpreter(s)
mkeka/mi-: mat(s)
 mlemavu/wa-: disabled person(s)
mpokezi/wa-: receptionist(s)
mshitakiwa/wa-: accused person(s)
mtukufu/wa-: dignitary(ies)
mwanamichezo/wa-: athlete(s)
mwavuli/mi-: umbrella(s)
mwenyembwa/wenyembwa: dog owner(s)
mwenyenyumba/wenyenyumba: houseowner(s)
mwiko/mi-: serving spoon(s)
ngazi: ladder(s), stair(s)
ofisa/ma- tawala: administrative officer(s)
ofisi: office(s)
omba: ask, beg
pendelea: favour
piga: hit, kick, play (music)
pogoa: prune
refa: referee(s)
shairi/ma-: poem(s)
spana: spanner(s), wrench(es)
stempu: stamp(s)
sweta: sweater(s)

taulo: towel(s)
tenda: do, treat
udanganyifu: trickery
ungua: burn
waridi/ma-: rose(s)
zoa: pick up

Key to Exercises

Answers to Practice Exercise A

1. We thought a lot about this matter before making a decision.
2. Aunt sold her ladder for climbing.
3. I did not pay for my sponsor's debt.
4. He/She stayed at the Intercontinental Hotel in January.
5. The spoon for serving has been burned.
6. His wife bore him three beautiful daughters.
7. We have changed the key for opening the door.
8. They approached the enemy to open fire.
9. He/She will take for him/her the needle for weaving a sweater.
10. The grandmother did not serve lunch to the child.
11. Will you buy shoes for running?
12. My receptionist bought me a very good present.
13. Simon repeated one grade because he was sick.
14. Which broom will you use for sweeping?
15. Mohammed will guard our house for us.

Answers to Practice Exercise B

16. *Kaka yangu amewasomea shairi la matumaini watoto walemavu.*
17. *Alitembelea Dubai mwaka jana.*
18. *Wametuondolea mizigo yetu kutoka kibanda cha forodha.*
19. *Mpishi alituletea chai ya maziwa.*
20. *Vijana wale wametokea wapi?*
21. *Hatukusomea kwa bidii kazi hii.*
22. *Alikwenda kuwapokelea kifurushi chao kutoka posta.*
23. *Karani alilipendelea ombi la jirani yake.*
24. *Alimpozea mzee uji.*
25. *Jaji alimkodolea macho mshitakiwa.*
26. *Walinunua chombo cha kupogolea miti ya matunda.*

27. *Helikopta ya kukombolea watu imeanguka.*
28. *Walimpelekea hundi yake kutoka ofisi ya bahati nasibu.*
29. *Mgonjwa alipewa chombo cha kuwekea dawa.*
30. *Nilimwombea mafanikio.*

Answers to Practice Exercise C

31. *Mwanasheria alimwuliza mteja maswali mahakamani.*
32. *Mwenyeji amewatendea watukufu vizuri.*
33. *Mwenye duka alitumia udanganyifu kushinda.*
34. *Mwenyembwa atampa mbwa wake mfupa.*
35. *Hakufikia matunda kwa sababu ni mfupi.*

Answers to Practice Exercise D

36. *Wahifadhi wa wanyama walichomewa mahindi na mwindaji.*
37. *Jirani alipigiwa simu na jamaa yake kutoka Ulaya.*
38. *Bomba lilipindiwa kutumia spana na fundi bomba.*
39. *Mwenyenyumba alipandiwa maua na mimi.*
40. *Mwanamichezo alikamuliwa taulo kwa mashine.*

Chapter 27

Reciprocal Form of the Verb

Reciprocal verbs in Swahili convey the meaning of "doing something to, with or against each other." A reciprocal verb can take either a singular or plural Subject Prefix. When a singular Subject Prefix is used it is implied that the object of the sentence is also reciprocating the action. This category of verbs ends with the suffix -na. The three main categories of Reciprocal verbs are:

1. Reciprocal verbs formed from verb stems ending with -a
2. Prepositional-Reciprocal verbs
3. Reciprocal verbs which acquire different meanings from original verbs

Section A: Reciprocal verbs formed from verbs stems ending with –a

Most Bantu verbs ending with -a are made reciprocal by attaching the suffix -na to the verb stem as shown in the examples below:

oa – marry = *oana* – marry each other
Christina na Mohamed walioana leo. – Christina and Mohamed married each other today.
penda – love = *pendana* – love one another
Rafiki wale wanapendana sana. – Those friends love each other a lot.

Note that Bantu verbs which are prepositional in their basic form are also made reciprocal by attaching the suffix *-na* to the verb stem.

> *tafuta* – look for = *tafutana* – search for one another
> *Mabaharia walitafutana jana.* – The sailors searched for each other yesterday.

Practice Exercise A

Translate into Swahili.

1. We knew each other since December.
2. The Swahili people greeted each other yesterday.
3. The workers divided the company's shares.
4. The residents called each other in times of emergency.
5. Those children like to pull each other's ears.
6. It is not good to argue with one another if you have anger.
7. Athletes competed with each other during the games.
8. They did not seek each other to go to the movie.
9. They met in North America.
10. During the soccer game, spectators pushed one another to get into the stadium.

Section B: Prepositional-Reciprocal verbs

Arabic verbs and some Bantu verbs must be changed into Prepositional form (See Chapter 26) before they are made reciprocal. However, if the Bantu verbs in this category are not changed into prepositional form first, but are directly made reciprocal, they have a negative meaning.

1. Bantu verbs:

> *andika – andikia – andikiana*
> write – write with or to – write to each other
> *Raia na wanajeshi wanaandikiana.* – Citizens and soldiers are writing to each other.

> *andika – andikana*
> write – report each other
> *Raia na wanajeshi wanaandikana.* – Citizens and soldiers are reporting each other.

soma – somea – someana
read – study for – read to each other
Tulisomeana katika shule ya sekondari. – We read to each other in
    secondary school.

soma – somana
read – spy on each other
Tulisomana katika shule ya sekondari. – We spied on each other in
    secondary school.

2. Arabic verbs:

samehe – samehea – sameheana
forgive – forgive for – forgive each other.
Wale ndugu hawakusameheana makosa yao.
Those relatives did not forgive each other their mistakes.

rudi – rudia – rudiana
return – return for – return to each other
Mke na mume wamerudiana.
The husband and wife have returned to each other.

bjibu – jibia – jibiana
answer – answer for or with – answer each other
Mwendesha mashtaka na wakili mtetezi walijibiana mahakamani.
The prosecutor and the defence counsel answered each other in court.

Practice Exercises B

Translate into English.

11. *Tumefahamiana tangu mwaka wa elfu mbili na mbili.*
12. *Waliandikiana kuhusu mauaji ya Rwanda.*
13. *Wakati wa shida, watu walileteana vifaa vya tiba.*
14. *Ndugu walikutana na kukimbiliana.*
15. *Kwa sababu ya ukosefu wa nafasi walilaliana wakati wa safari.*
16. *Wanakwaya walishirikiana vizuri sana wakati wa kuimba.*
17. *Walikimbiana kwa sababu si rafiki tena.*
18. *Tutafikiriana kila siku.*
19. *Watapikiana kwa sababu wanapendana sana.*
20. *Walifurahiana sana baada ya kuonana.*

21. *Kuimbiana ni kitu kizuri sana.*
22. *Miaka mingi imepita na hawajasameheana makosa yao.*
23. *Je, walipatiana anwani zao?*
24. *Menejimenti na wafanyakazi walikubaliana kuhusu kutokuwa na migomo kazini.*
25. *Hawakungojeana baada ya kuangalia sinema.*

Section C: Reciprocal verbs which acquire different meanings than the original verbs

Some verbs acquire different meanings when changed into reciprocal verbs as shown below:

ona – see = *onana* – meet each another
Hawataonana wakati wa mwezi wa Ramadhani. – They will not meet one another during the month of Ramadan.
kosa – miss, fail = *kosana* – quarrelling and not wanting to see each other again
Si vizuri kwa rafiki kukosana. – It is not good for friends to quarrel and not want to see one another.

Practice Exercise C

Translate the following sentences containing reciprocal verbs and provide the meanings of the original verb stems.

26. *Alipatana na mama yake wa kambo.*
27. *Mabondia kutoka Brazili na Bangladeshi watapigana kesho.*
28. *Wapenzi wa miaka mingi wamekimbiana.*
29. *Timu mbili za mpira wa miguu zitachekana.*
30. *Mjukuu na bibi walichekeana.*

Note that the Reciprocal verb of the Monosyllabic verb *pa* (give) is *peana* (give to each other). Also when a Reciprocal verb is used in a sentence with an object, the preposition *na* must be used. For example: *Walifukuzana na mwizi* (They chased after the thief).

Fill in the blanks with the appropriate Reciprocal verb and Subject Prefixes using the simple past tense only.

31. *Wageni na mwenyeji wao _____(salimu).*
32. *Nilisikia kelele kwa sababu vijana _____(piga).*
33. *Mimi na wewe _____(ona) mwaka jana.*
34. *Wapokezi wa simu _____(fuata) na meneja wao kwenda Ujerumani.*
35. *Timu mbili za wachezaji ngoma _____(shinda) katika mashindano ya mkoa.*
36. *Wabunge _____(kubali) kuhusu uchaguzi mkuu.*
37. *Wakimbizi _____(sukuma) kupata chakula.*
38. *Je, wauguzi hawa _____(shiriki) vizuri mwaka juzi?*
39. *Polisi (pl.) _____(fukuza) na wezi.*
40. *Kaka wawili _____(gomba) kwa sababu pesa zao ziliibiwa.*
41. *Chris_____(ona) na yeye kabla ya miaka kumi.*
42. *Baada ya kukutana dada na shangazi ____(andama) kwenda kuona mchezo wa kikapu.*
43. *Peter _____(oa) na Mariam Jumamosi.*
44. *Mwanamuziki _____(ahidi) na watazamaji kwamba atawatumbuiza.*
45. *Watu wengi nchini Rwanda _____(ua) wenyewe kwa wenyewe.*

New Vocabulary

ahidi: promise
Amerika: America
andama: follow
andikana: report each other
anwani: address(es)
Bangladeshi: Bangladesh
bisha: argue
Brazili: Brazil
chekeana: smile at each other
dharura: emergency(ies)
fuata: follow
gomba: quarrel
Kaskazini: North
kelele/ma-: noise(s)

kosana: quarrel, disagree
mama wa kambo: stepmother(s)
mauaji: massacre(s)
mbunge/wa-: member(s) of Parliament
mchezo/mi- wa kikapu: basketball
menejimenti: management
mgomo/mi-: strike(s)
mjukuu/wa-: grandchild(ren)
mkazi/wa-: resident(s)
mkoa/mi-: region(s)
mpira wa miguu: soccer
Mswahili/wa-: Swahili person(s)
mtazamaji/wa-: spectator(s), viewer(s)
mwanakwaya/wa-: choir member(s)
mwendesha/wa- mashtaka: prosecutor(s)
mwuguzi/wa-: nurse(s)
ngoma: dance(s), drum(s)
onana: meet/see each other
raia: citizen(s)
Ramadhani: Ramadan
Rwanda: Rwanda
salimu: greet
shindana: compete
shindano/ma-: competition(s)
shiriki: share, participate
shirikiana: co-operate
somana: spy on each other
tiba: treatment(s), cure(s), medicine(s)
tumbuiza: entertain
uchaguzi mkuu: general election(s)
wakili/ma- mtetezi/wa-: defence counsellor(s)
wenyewe kwa wenyewe: each other

Key to Exercises

Answers to Practice Exercise A

1. *Tulijuana tangu mwezi wa Desemba.*
2. *Waswahili waliamkiana jana.*
3. *Wafanyakazi waligawana hisa za kampuni.*
4. *Wakazi waliitana nyakati za dharura.*
5. *Watoto wale wanapenda kuvutana masikio.*
6. *Si vizuri kubishana kama una hasira.*
7. *Wanamichezo walishindana wakati wa michezo.*
8. *Hawakutafutana kwenda sinema.*
9. *Walikutana Amerika ya Kaskazini.*
10. *Wakati wa mchezo wa mpira wa miguu, watazamaji walisukumana kuingia uwanjani.*

Answers to Practice Exercises B

11. We have known each other since 2002.
12. They wrote each other about the Rwandan massacres.
13. During hardships, the people brought each other medical supplies.
14. The relatives met and ran towards each other.
15. Due to the lack of space, they slept on top of each other during the trip.
16. Choir members co-operated very well with each other while singing.
17. They ran away from each other because they are no longer friends.
18. We will think about each other every day.
19. They will cook for each other because they love one another very much.
20. They were happy with each other after seeing each other.
21. Singing to each other is a very good thing.
22. Many years have passed and they have not yet forgiven each other for their mistakes.
23. Did they give each other their addresses?
24. The management and workers agreed on not having strikes at the work place.
25. They did not wait for each other after watching a movie.

Answers to Practice Exercise C

26. He/She got along with his/her step mother.
    Original verb stem: *pata* – get
27. The boxers from Brazil and Bangladesh will fight tomorrow.
    Original verb stem: *piga* – hit
28. The lovers of many years have run away from each other.
    Original verb stem: *kimbia* – run
29. The two soccer teams will laugh (mockingly) at each other.
    Original verb stem: *cheka* – laugh
30. The grandchild and grandmother smiled at each other.
    Original verb stem: *cheka* – laugh
31. *Wageni na mwenyeji wao walisalimiana.*
32. *Nilisikia kelele kwa sababu vijana walipigana.*
33. *Mimi na wewe tulionana mwaka jana.*
34. *Wapokezi wa simu walifuatana na meneja wao kwenda Ujerumani.*
35. *Timu mbili za wachezaji ngoma zilishindana katika mashindano ya mkoa.*
36. *Wabunge walikubaliana kuhusu uchaguzi mkuu.*
37. *Wakimbizi walisukumana kupata chakula.*
38. *Je, wauguzi hawa walishirikiana vizuri mwaka juzi?*
39. *Polisi walifukuzana na wezi.*
40. *Kaka wawili waligombana kwa sababu pesa zao ziliibiwa.*
41. *Chris alionana na yeye kabla ya miaka kumi.*
42. *Baada ya kukutana dada na shangazi waliandamana kwenda kuona mchezo wa kikapu.*
43. *Peter alioana na Mariam Jumamosi.*
44. *Mwanamuziki aliahidiana na watazamaji kwamba atawatumbuiza.*
45. *Watu wengi nchini Rwanda waliuana wenyewe kwa wenyewe.*

Chapter 28

Relatives - The *amba*- Relative, Relative Infixes and General Relative

In this chapter, we will teach three different types of relatives, which are as follows:

1. The *amba*- Relative
2. Relative Infixes
3. The General Relative

Each type of relative has one specific way by which it can be used to form a sentence containing a relative pronoun. A relative pronoun is used to refer back to a noun, which in English would be translated as "who," "whom" or "which." Relative pronouns must be constructed using the relative particles from the appropriate noun class as shown in Table 28.1

Section A: The *amba*- Relative

The *amba*- Relative can be used with any verb and with any tense. A sentence using the *amba*- Relative must start with a noun, pronoun or a demonstrative used as a noun, followed by the word *amba*-, which must have the relative particle, attached as a suffix. For example, if we want to use the *amba*- Relative with a noun in the M-/WA- noun class in the singular, we must combine *amba*- with the relative particle *-ye* from Table 28.1 to form *ambaye*, which would mean "who" or "whom." If we want to use the *amba*- Relative with a noun in the M-/WA- noun class in the plural, we must combine *amba-* with *-o* to form *ambao*, which would also mean "who" or "whom."

TABLE 28.1
Relative Particles Chart

Noun Class	Relative Particles (Singular)	Relative Particles (Plural)
M-/WA-	*ye*	*o*
M-/MI-	*o*	*yo*
JI-/MA-	*lo*	*yo*
KI-/VI-	*cho*	*vyo*
N-	*yo*	*zo*
U-	*o*	*zo*
PA-	*po, ko, mo*	*po, ko, mo*
KU-	*ko*	*ko*

Examples:
> *Yule ambaye atanunua kompyuta.* – That person who will buy a computer.
> *Kiti ambacho kilivunjika.* – The chair which was broken.
> *Mnyama ambaye tumemwona.* – An animal which we have seen.
> *Jua ambalo linawaka.* – The Sun which is shining.
> *Sisi ambao tulifika salama.* – We who arrived safe.

Sentences using the *amba-* Relative are negated by replacing the affirmative Subject Prefix with the negative Subject Prefix, negating the tense marker and followed by the verb. The *amba-* Relative remains unchanged as shown in the examples below:

> *Yule ambaye hatanunua kompyuta.* – That person who will not buy a computer.
> *Kiti ambacho hakikuvunjika.* – The chair which was not broken.
> *Mnyama ambaye hatujamwona.* – An animal which we have not yet seen.

Jua ambalo haliwaki. – The Sun which is not shining.
Sisi ambao hatukufika salama. – We who did not arrive safe.

Practice Exercise A

Translate the following sentences into Swahili using the *amba-* Relative.

1. The tooth which has been extracted.
2. The walls which have not been painted.
3. The houses which are being built in the city.
4. The place which was sold yesterday.
5. The reading which was good.
6. The student who studies at university.
7. The table which will be sold tomorrow.
8. The doctor who did not treat people with AIDS.
9. The woman who was not married last year.
10. The youth who did not get a present at school.
11. The tractor which was not damaged.
12. The train which is travelling fast.
13. The vehicle which killed the dog.
14. The window which was broken.
15. The floor which was not cleaned.
16. The guests who arrived today.
17. The plane which caught fire.
18. The road which will be repaired.
19. The bed which has not been sold.
20. The women who won.

Section B: Relative Infixes

Unlike the *amba-* Relative, Relative Infixes can only be used with the present, simple past and future tenses. When it is used with the future tense, the syllable *-ka-* is attached to the tense marker *-ta-* to form *taka-*. Relative Infixes are NEVER used with the past perfect tense.

Just like sentences using the *amba-* Relative, sentences using a Relative Infix must also start with a noun, pronoun or a demonstrative used as a noun. This is followed by subject prefix, tense marker, relative particle from Table 28.1 used as an infix, and finally the verb. For example, if we want to make the sentence "The girls who will receive presents," we would have:

Wasichana watakaopata zawadi. – The girls who will receive presents.

Other examples:
Watoto wanaocheka sana. – Children who laugh a lot.
Fedha zilizoibiwa kutoka benki. – Money which was stolen from the bank.
Mashine ya ATM iliyowekwa katika baa. – The ATM machine which was installed in the bar.

Sentences using Relative Infixes are negated depending on the tense marker. If the sentence uses the present tense, it is negated in one of two ways. The first way is by replacing the present tense marker -*na*- with -*si*- as shown in the example below:

Watoto wanaocheka sana. – *Watoto wasiocheka sana.*
Children who laugh a lot. – Children who do not laugh a lot.

Note that the subject prefix, relative particle and the verb remains unchanged.

The second way is by replacing the affirmative Subject Prefix with the negative Subject Prefix, negating the tense marker and verb and finally removing the Relative Infix and attach it to the *amba*- Relative as a suffix as shown in the example below:

Watoto wanaocheka sana. – *Watoto ambao hawacheki sana.*
Children who laugh a lot. – Children who do not laugh a lot.

Sentences using the simple past or future tense are negated in only one way. They are negated by replacing the affirmative Subject Prefix with the negative Subject Prefix, negating the tense marker and finally removing the Relative Infix and attach it to the *amba*- Relative as a suffix as shown in the examples below:

Wasichana watakaopata zawadi. – *Wasichana ambao hawatapata zawadi.*
The girls who will receive presents. – The girls who will not receive presents.

Fedha zilizoibiwa kutoka benki. – Fedha ambazo hazikuibiwa kutoka benki.

The money which was stolen from the bank. – The money which was not stolen from the bank.

Practice Exercise B

Translate into English.

21. *Makarani wasiosoma Kiingereza.*
22. *Matofali yaliyotumika kujenga nyumba.*
23. *Vijana waliofika asubuhi wameondoka.*
24. *Hii ni milango iliyoharibika.*
25. *Mwizi aliyekamatwa amefungwa.*
26. *Dereva aliyepinduka amefariki.*
27. *Moto ambao haukuunguza nyumba.*
28. *Huyu ni meneja atakayefukuzwa kazi.*
29. *Nani atakayekulipia ada?*
30. *Watu waliofungwa wameachiliwa.*
31. *Maduka ambayo hayana faida.*
32. *Mafundi wanaofanya kazi vizuri.*
33. *Jambazi linalowatishia watu.*
34. *Milango isiyofungwa.*
35. *Hoteli zinazojaa watalii.*
36. *Mwezi ambao haukuwa na joto sana.*
37. *Vyuo vikuu vilivyofungwa.*
38. *Mitihani ambayo haikufanyika.*
39. *Watu wasiopendwa.*
40. *Nyumba zilizojengwa kwa mbao.*

Section C: General Relative

Unlike the other two relatives we have discussed thus far, the General Relative is only used with the present tense to denote indefinite present tense. However, note that the present tense marker itself (-*na*-) does not appear with the verb in the sentence. A sentence using a General Relative must also start with a noun, pronoun or a demonstrative used as a noun. This is followed by the Subject Prefix followed immediately by the verb and finally the relative particle is attached as a suffix to the verb.

For example, if we want to make the sentence "A woman who climbs mountains" we would have:

Mwanamke apandaye milima. – A woman who climbs mountains.

More examples:
Miti iotayo porini. – Trees which grow in the wild.
Maua yanunuliwayo sokoni. – Flowers which are bought at the market.
Mahali panukiapo vizuri. – A place which smells good.
Wanyama walao nyasi. – Animals which feed on grass.

Also note that in the last example, the *-ku-* infinitive is not attached to the Monosyllabic verb in the affirmative form.

Sentences using General Relatives are negated by inserting *-si-* between the subject prefix and the verb. In addition, the relative particle changes from being a suffix to an infix as shown in the examples below:

Mwanamke asiyepanda milima. – A woman who does not climbs mountains.
Miti isiyoota porini. – Trees which do not grow in the wild.
Maua yasiyonunuliwa sokoni. – Flowers which are not bought at the market.
Mahali pasiponukia vizuri. – A place which does not smell good.
Wanyama wasiokula nyasi. – Animals which do not eat grass.

Please note that *-si-* is inserted in the same position as the omitted present tense marker. Also note that the *-ku-* infinitive is attached to the Monosyllabic verb in the negated form.

Practice Exercise C

Translate into Swahili using the General Relative.

41. The engineer who builds houses.
42. The child who cries at night.
43. The people who vote.
44. Timber which is bought.
45. Children who do not play Nintendo.
46. The door which is locked.
47. The author who visits schools.

48. The police officer who arrests criminals.
49. The store which sells products.
50. The guard who does not work at night.
51. The father who works two jobs.
52. The person who travels to Brazil.
53. The nation which cares about its people.
54. The carpenter who does not work very hard.
55. The artist who sells expensive pictures.
56. The child who saves money.
57. The dog which guards the house.
58. A city which cleans its streets.
59. The animals that are in the zoo.
60. The cat that catches mice.

New Vocabulary

achia: release
ada: fee(s)
baa/ma-: bar(s)
fundi/ma-: craftsperson(s)
jali: care
joto: hot, heat
kamata: arrest, catch
kasi: fast
kura: vote(s)
mashine ya/za ATM: ATM machine(s)
mbao: wood, timber
mhalifu/wa-: criminal(s)
nyasi/ma-: grass(es)
picha: picture(s)
piga kura: cast a vote
pinduka: overturn
pori: wilderness
tibu: treat, cure
tisha: scare, threaten
tofali/ma-: brick(s)
treni: train(s)
wekwa: put in, install

Key to Exercises

Answers to Practice Exercise A

1. *Jino ambalo limeng'olewa.*
2. *Kuta ambazo hazijapakwa rangi.*
3. *Nyumba ambazo zinajengwa mjini.*
4. *Mahali ambapo paliuzwa jana.*
5. *Kusoma ambako kulikuwa kuzuri.*
6. *Mwanafunzi ambaye anasoma chuo kikuu.*
7. *Meza ambayo itauzwa kesho.*
8. *Daktari ambaye hakuwatibu watu waliokuwa na Ukimwi.*
9. *Mwanamke ambaye hakuolewa mwaka jana.*
10. *Kijana ambaye hakupata zawadi shuleni.*
11. *Trekta ambalo halikuharibika.*
12. *Treni ambalo linasafiri kwa kasi.*
13. *Gari ambalo lilimwua mbwa.*
14. *Dirisha ambalo lilivunjika.*
15. *Sakafu ambayo haikusafishwa.*
16. *Wageni ambao walifika leo.*
17. *Ndege ambayo ilishika moto.*
18. *Barabara ambayo itatengenezwa.*
19. *Kitanda ambacho hakijauzwa.*
20. *Wanawake ambao wameshinda.*

Answers to Practice Exercise B

21. The clerks who are not studying English.
22. The bricks which were used to build a house(s).
23. The youths who arrived in the morning have left.
24. These are the doors which were destroyed.
25. The thief who was arrested has been jailed.
26. The driver who overturned has died.
27. The fire which did not burn down the house
28. This is the manager who will be sacked.
29. Who will pay the fees for you?
30. The people who were jailed have been released.
31. The shops which are not profitable.
32. The craftsmen who do a good job.
33. The gangster who threatens people.

34. The doors which are not locked.
35. The hotels which are full of tourists.
36. The month which was not very hot.
37. The universities which were closed.
38. The exams which were not held.
39. The people who are not liked.
40. The houses which were built of timber.

Answers to Practice Exercise C

41. *Mhandisi ajengaye nyumba.*
42. *Mtoto aliaye usiku.*
43. *Watu wapigao kura.*
44. *Mbao zinunuliwazo.*
45. *Watoto wasiocheza Nintendo.*
46. *Mlango ufungwao.*
47. *Mwandishi atembeleaye shule.*
48. *Polisi akamataye wahalifu.*
49. *Duka liuzalo bidhaa.*
50. *Mlinzi asiyefanya kazi usiku.*
51. *Baba afanyaye kazi mbili.*
52. *Mtu asafiriye kwenda Brazili.*
53. *Taifa lijalilo watu wake.*
54. *Seremala asiyefanya kazi sana.*
55. *Mchoraji auzaye picha kwa bei ghali.*
56. *Mtoto awekaye pesa akiba.*
57. *Mbwa alindaye nyumba.*
58. *Mji usafishao mitaa yake.*
59. *Wanyama walio katika zu.*
60. *Paka akamataye panya.*

Chapter 29

Relatives—Manner, Time and Place

Chapter 28 presented the *amba-* Relative, Relative Infixes and the General Relative. This Chapter presents the remaining three types of relatives, namely:

1. The Relative of Manner
2. The Relative of Time
3. The Relative of Place

Each of the three types of relatives mentioned above have the following common characteristics:

1. They are all used with the present, simple past and future tenses but NEVER with the past perfect tense.
2. The particles *-vyo-* for Relative of Manner, *-po-* for Relative of Time and *-po-, -ko-* and *-mo-* for Relative of Place, can be used as infixes in the present, simple past and future tenses. However, in the present tense, these relative particles can also be used as suffixes.
3. When the relative particles listed in number 2 above are used in the present tense as a suffix, the present tense marker "*-na-*" is dropped.
4. When the relative particle is used as an infix with the future tense, an additional syllable "*-ka-*" is added to the tense marker "*-ta-*" to form "*-taka-*" (See Chapter 28).

Section A: The Relative of Manner

The Relative of Manner is expressed by the particle *-vyo-* either as an infix or suffix in the present tense but only as an infix in the simple past and future tenses. The particle *-vyo-* conveys the meaning of "as," "like," "as far as" etc. The following words can be used in conjunction with the Relative of Manner:

> *jinsi* conveys the meaning of "how, the manner in which."
> *kadiri* conveys the meaning of "as far as, to the limit of ability," etc.
> *kama* conveys the meaning of "as, like."

Examples:

> *Ninasoma kama asomavyo.* – I am reading the way he/she is reading.
> *Waliruka kadiri alivyoruka.* – They jumped as far as he/she jumped.
> *Ataimba kama tutakavyoimba.* – He/She will sing as we will sing.
> *Atafanya jinsi atakavyoelekezwa.* – He/She will do as he/she will be directed.

Sentences using the Relative of Manner are negated as follows:

> *Sisomi kama asomavyo.* – I am not reading the way he/she is reading.
> *Hawakuruka kadiri alivyoruka.* – They did not jump as far as he/she jumped.
> *Hataimba kama tutakavyoimba.* – He/She will not sing as we will sing.
> *Hatafanya jinsi atakavyoelekezwa.* – He/She will not do as he/she will be directed.

Please note that in the negated examples above, the part of the sentence containing the relative particle of manner is not negated. Instead, the verb, which does not contain the relative particle of manner, is negated.

Another way to form the Relative of Manner is by combining *amba-* and the particle *-vyo* to form *ambavyo* which means "as." Here are some examples below:

> *Alipiga mpira jinsi ambavyo Mohamed anapiga.*
> He/She kicked the ball as Mohamed does.
> *Tutafanya kazi jinsi ambavyo wenzetu wanafanya.*
> We will work as our colleagues work.

Ninafunga mlango jinsi ambavyo mama anafunga.
I close the door as mother does.

Sentences using the Relative of Manner *ambavyo* are negated as follows:

Hakupiga mpira jinsi ambavyo Mohamed anapiga.
He/She did not kick the ball as Mohamed does.
Hatutafanya kazi jinsi ambavyo wenzetu wanafanya.
We will not work as our colleagues work.
Sifungi mlango jinsi ambavyo mama anafunga.
I do not close the door as mother does.

Please note that in the negated examples above, the Relative of Manner is not negated.

Practice Exercise A

Negate the following sentences.

1. *Alifundisha jinsi ambavyo kocha alifundisha.*
2. *Anafagia kama baba anavyofagia.*
3. *Watasoma kama tutakavyosoma.*
4. *Alikimbia jinsi ambavyo Mariam anakimbia.*
5. *Walipanda mlima kama walivyopanga.*
6. *Atamsamehe mwizi kama alivyosema.*
7. *Barabara itajengwa kama ilivyotangazwa.*
8. *Watalima kama tunavyolima.*
9. *Tutabeba mizigo kadiri tutakavyoweza.*
10. *Walijaribu kadiri mwezavyo.*
11. *Wanafuta barua pepe kama tulivyokubiliana.*
12. *Walifikiri jinsi ambavyo tunafikiri.*
13. *Tunaendesha gari atakavyoendesha.*
14. *Wanazungumza Kiswahili kama anavyozungumza.*
15. *Nilishika ndizi jinsi ambavyo nyani anashika.*
16. *Vijana walicheka jinsi walivyotaka.*
17. *Wachezaji walicheza kadiri walivyotegemea.*
18. *Kama tunavyojua mtoto atazaliwa mwaka huu.*
19. *Kadiri wanavyokwenda watafika mbali sana.*
20. *Fundi alipaka rangi nyumba kama alivyoelekezwa.*

Section B: The Relative of Time

The Relative of Time is expressed by the particle *-po-* either as an infix or suffix in the present tense but only as an infix in the simple past and future tenses. The relative particle *-po-* conveys the meaning of "when." When the word *kila* is used with the Relative of Time, it conveys the meaning of "whenever." Examples:

> *Kila unapocheka unapendeza.* – Whenever you (sing.) laugh, you (sing.) look beautiful.
>
> *Wageni walipofika tuliwasalimu.* – When the guests arrived, we greeted them.
>
> *Ufanyikapo uchaguzi, uchumi unastawi.* – When there is an election, the economy prospers.
>
> *Pumzika utakapomaliza kazi.* – Rest when you finish work.
>
> *Meneja atakapofika nitampa barua hii.* - When the manager arrives, I will give him/her this letter.

Please note that in the sentences above you can negate the verb containing the Relative of Time (*-po-*) or the "regular" verb or both. Regular verbs are negated as taught in Chapters 5 and 6. For example:

> *Kila unapocheka hupendezi.* – Whenever you (sing.) laugh, you (sing.) do not look beautiful.

Verbs containing the Relative of Time are negated in the following ways.

Present tense:

In the present tense, when the relative particle of time *-po-* is used as an infix or as a suffix, it is negated by using *-sipo-* which must always be used as an infix . For example:

> *Kila unapocheka unapendeza.* – Whenever you laugh, you look beautiful.
>
> *Kila usipocheka unapendeza.* – Whenever you do not laugh, you look beautiful.
>
> *Ufanyikapo uchaguzi, uchumi unastawi.* – When there is an election, the economy prospers.

Usipofanyika uchaguzi, uchumi unastawi. – When there is not an election, the economy prospers.

Simple Past and Future tenses:

In both simple past and future tenses, the relative particle of time *-po-* is negated using the *amba-* Relative as seen in Chapter 28. The *amba-*Relative is always preceded by the word *wakati* meaning "at the time."

Kila ulipocheka ulipendeza. – Whenever you laughed, you looked beautiful.

Kila wakati ambapo hukucheka ulipendeza. – Whenever you did not laugh, you looked beautiful.

Practice Exercise B

Translate into English.

21. *Nitaazima kitabu maktaba itakapofunguliwa.*
22. *Tutakapomwona tutamwuliza jina lake.*
23. *Tutahamia Paris tutakapouza nyumba.*
24. *Madawati kila yanapovunjika tengeneza.*
25. *Alioga maji ya moto alipoona baridi.*
26. *Mtoto asipolala utamwimbia wimbo.*
27. *Wakati ambapo mgonjwa hakulalamika hakupewa dawa.*
28. *Usipomsikia mkuu, utavunjika mguu.*
29. *Watoto wanapokuwa na njaa utawapa keki.*
30. *Kitabu kipoteapo utakitafuta.*
31. *Hawakumwamkia mgeni walipomwona.*
32. *Wakati ambapo hataolewa atakuwa na masikitiko.*
33. *Wakati ambapo watafiti hawatagundua teknolojia mpya maisha hayatakuwa bora.*
34. *Mchezo utakapoanza nitawasha televisheni.*
35. *Sikuwasha redio watoto walipolala.*
36. *King'ora cha moto kinapolia kila mtu atatoka nje.*
37. *Mvua isiponyesha inafaa kukaa nje.*
38. *Haifai kuzurura ovyo inapokuwa giza.*
39. *Ulikuwa wapi Mandela alipokuja Kanada?*
40. *Wakati ambapo umeme ulikatika tulitumia tochi.*

Section C: The Relative of Place

The Relative of Place is expressed by the relative particles *-po-, -ko-* or *-mo-* depending on whether it is a specific place, indefinite place or inside place respectively (See Chapter 10). The relative particles can be used either as an infix or suffix in the present tense but only as an infix in the simple past and future tenses. These relative particles convey the meaning of "where." For example:

> *Inaponyesha mvua, watu wanaishi.* – Where it rains, the people live.
> *Polisi wanajua alikokwenda.* – The police know where he/she has gone.
> *Atakamoingia mwizi ni humu.* – There is where the thief will enter.

Please note that in the sentences above you can negate the verb containing the Relative of Place (*-po-, -ko-* or *-mo-*) or the "regular" verb or both. Regular verbs are negated as taught in Chapter 5 and 6. For example:

> Inaponyesha mvua, watu wanaishi. – Inaponyesha mvua, watu hawaishi.
> Where it rains, the people live. – Where it rains, the people do not live.
> *Polisi wanajua alikokwenda.* – *Polisi hawajui alikokwenda.*
> The police know where he/she has gone. – The police do not know where he/she has gone.
> *Atakamoingia mwizi ni humu.* – *Atakamoingia mwizi si humu.*
> Here is where the thief will enter. – Here is where the thief will not enter.

In all tenses, the simple past, present and future, the relative particles of place are negated using the *amba-* Relative as seen in Chapter 28. The *amba-* relative is always preceded by the word *mahali* meaning "the place."

> *Inaponyesha mvua, watu wanaishi.* – *Mahali ambapo hainyeshi mvua, watu wanaishi.*

Where it rains, people live. – The place where it does not rain, people live.

Polisi wanajua alikokwenda. – Polisi wanajua mahali ambako hakwenda.

The police know where he/she has gone. – The police know where he has not gone.

Atakamoingia mwizi ni humu. – Mahali ambamo hataingia mwizi ni humu.

Here is where the thief will enter. – Here is not where the thief will enter.

Practice Exercise C

Translate into Swahili.

41. Do you know where they live?
42. We know where he/she works.
43. Where they will look, there will be snow.
44. Where they live there is very little water.
45. He/She ran to a place where it is not safe.
46. This is where they looked for the child.
47. I know where mother does not sleep at night.
48. This is where dad rests.
49. Is this where they built the house?
50. She showed me where you saw my pencil.
51. This is not the place where the money was found.
52. Heather knows where Amina lives.
53. John was in the classroom reading.
54. The place where he/she did not go is very far.
55. There were mosquitoes where he/she slept.
56. That place there is where he/she saw the soldiers.
57. We don't know where Khamis plays music.
58. She showed me where he/she hid the treasure.
59. This is not where they planted the tree.
60. They saw the place (inside) where he/she was killed.

New Vocabulary

azima: borrow
dawati/ma-: desk(s)
-dogo: little, small
elekeza: direct, instruct
faa: suitable, useful
ficha: hide
futa: delete, erase
giza: dark, darkness
gundua: discover
hamia: immigrate to, move to
hazina: treasure(s)
kadiri: as far as, to the limit of one's ability
keki: cake(s)
king'ora/vi-: alarm(s)
lalamika: complain
Mandela: Nelson Mandela
mkuu/wa-: elder(s)
mtafiti/wa-: researcher(s)
mvua: rain(s)
nyani: baboon(s)
onyesha: show, demonstrate
penseli: pencil(s)
pumzika: rest
sikitiko/ma-: regret(s)
stawi: prosper
tazama: look at, watch, stare
tochi: flashlight(s)
toka nje: go outside
washa: switch on
zurura: wander around aimlessly

Key to Exercises

Answers to Practice Exercise A

1. *Hakufundisha jinsi ambavyo kocha alifundisha.*
2. *Hafagii kama baba anavyofagia.*
3. *Hawatasoma kama tutakavyosoma.*
4. *Hakukimbia jinsi ambavyo Mariam anakimbia.*
5. *Hawakupanda mlima kama walivyopanga.*
6. *Hatamsamehe mwizi kama alivyosema.*
7. *Barabara haitajengwa kama ilivyotangazwa.*
8. *Hawatalima kama tunavyolima.*
9. *Hatutabeba mizigo kadiri tutakavyoweza.*
10. *Hawakujaribu kadiri mwezavyo*
11. *Hawafuti barua pepe kama tulivyokubaliana.*
12. *Hawakufikiri jinsi ambavyo tunafikiri.*
13. *Hatuendeshi gari atakavyoendesha.*
14. *Hawazungumzi Kiswahili kama anavyozungumza.*
15. *Sikushika ndizi jinsi ambavyo nyani anashika.*
16. *Vijana hawakucheka jinsi walivyotaka.*
17. *Wachezaji hawakucheza kadiri walivyotegemea.*
18. *Kama tunavyojua mtoto hatazaliwa mwaka huu.*
19. *Kadiri wanavyokwenda hawatafika mbali sana.*
20. *Fundi hakupaka rangi nyumba kama alivyoelekezwa.*

Answers to Practice Exercise B

21. I will borrow a book when the library opens.
22. When we see the person, we shall ask for his/her name.
23. We shall move to Paris, when we sell the house.
24. Whenever desks are broken, repair them.
25. He/She took a hot bath when he/she felt cold.
26. When the child is not sleeping, you (sing.) will sing him/her a song.
27. When the sick person did not complain, he/she was not given medicine.
28. When you do not listen to your elder, you will break your leg. (meaning "you will have problems")
29. When children are hungry, you (sing.) will give them cake.
30. When the book is lost, you (sing.) will look for it.

31. They did not greet the guest when they saw him/her.
32. When she does not get married, she will have regrets.
33. When the researchers do not discover new technology, life will not become better.
34. When the game starts, I will switch on the television.
35. I did not switch on the radio when the children were asleep.
36. When the fire alarm goes off, everyone will go outside.
37. When it does not rain, it is suitable to be outside.
38. It is not appropriate to wander aimlessly when it is dark.
39. Where were you when Mandela visited Canada?
40. When the electricity was cut off, we used a flashlight.

Answers to Practice Exercise C

41. *Unajua wanapokaa?*
42. *Tunajua mahali anapofanya kazi.*
43. *Watakapotazama patakuwa na theluji.*
44. *Wanakokaa kuna maji kidogo sana.*
45. *Alikimbilia mahali ambapo si salama.*
46. *Walipomtafuta mtoto ni hapa.*
47. *Ninajua mahali ambapo mama halali usiku.*
48. *Apumzikapo baba ni hapa.*
49. *Walipojenga nyumba ni hapa?*
50. *Alinionyesha mahali ulipoiona penseli yangu.*
51. *Hapa si mahali ambapo zilionekana pesa.*
52. *Heather anajua anapokaa Amina.*
53. *John alikuwamo darasani anasoma.*
54. *Mahali ambako hakwenda ni mbali sana.*
55. *Palikuwa na mbu alipolala.*
56. *Alipowaona wanajeshi ni pale.*
57. *Hatujui mahali Khamis anapopiga muziki.*
58. *Alinionyesha mahali alipoficha hazina.*
59. *Mahali ambapo hawakupanda mti ni hapa.*
60. *Walipaona mahali alimouawa.*

Chapter 30

Imperative Verbs and Their Negations

Imperative verbs are of two kinds: abrupt imperatives and polite imperatives. An abrupt imperative is known as a command while a polite imperative is known as a request. While the subject of an imperative sentence is always the 2nd person singular or plural, the subject is not expressed but rather implied in the sentence. In many cultures, a command seems blunt or even rude, so it is often used with caution. Swahili people never use commands when addressing one's elders but instead they use requests. When speaking to one's equals and subordinates, either a command or a request is acceptable. In English, we can add the word "please" to a command and soften our tone of voice to make it a request. However in Swahili command and requests are differentiated by their prefixes and suffixes. In this chapter, we will learn how to make singular and plural imperative sentences and their negations.

Section A: Singular and Plural Commands

Singular Commands

Many languages, including English, use a verb for a command. In Swahili, the same is done for Bantu and Arabic verbs. Here are some examples:

Bantu verbs:
    Fanya! – Do! (sing.)
    Kata! – Cut! (sing.)
    Ngoja! – Wait! (sing.)

Nunua! – Buy! (sing.)
Safisha! – Clean! (sing.)
Tafuta! – Search! (sing.)

Arabic verbs:
Samehe! – Forgive! (sing.)
Fikiri! – Think! (sing.)
Jaribu! – Try! (sing.)
Jibu! – Answer! (sing.)

For Monosyllabic verbs, the *ku-* infinitive is prefixed to the verb to make it a command. Here are some examples:

Kula! – Eat! (sing.)
Kunywa! – Drink! (sing.)

Plural Commands

While the verb conjugation does not change when giving a command to one person or a group of people in English, a singular and a plural command is differentiated by their suffixes in Swahili. For Bantu verbs, we change the last vowel of the verb (which is always an *a*, see Chapter 5) to the letter *e* followed by the suffix *-ni* to make it a plural command. Here are some examples:

Bantu verbs:
Fanyeni! – Do! (pl.)
Kateni! – Cut! (pl.)
Ngojeni! – Wait! (pl.)
Nunueni! – Buy! (pl.)
Safisheni! – Clean! (pl.)
Tafuteni! – Search! (pl.)

For Arabic verbs, we do not change the last vowel of the verb. The suffix *-ni* is simply added to the final vowel. Here are some examples:

Sameheni! – Forgive! (pl.)
Jaribuni! – Try! (pl.)

Fikirini! – Think!(pl.)
Jibuni! – Answer! (pl.)

Since Monosyllabic verbs are also Bantu verbs, we change the last vowel of the verb to the letter *e* followed by the suffix *-ni*. Note that in Monosyllabic verbs, the *ku-* infinitive is prefixed to the verb to make it a command. Here are some examples:

Kuleni! – Eat! (pl.)
Kunyweni! – Drink! (pl.)

Practice Exercise A

Translate the following into Swahili.

1. Love! (sing)
2. Cook! (pl.)
3. Thank! (sing.)
4. Sweep! (sing.)
5. Swim! (sing.)
6. Speak! (pl.)
7. Look! (sing.)
8. Touch! (pl)
9. Smell! (sing.)
10. Choose! (pl.)

Section B: Singular and Plural Requests

Both singular and plural commands are changed into requests by following two simple steps: the prefix and suffix steps. These steps are:

- The prefix *u-* is used for 2nd person singular and the prefix *m-* for 2nd person plural.
- The suffix *e* replaces the last vowel of Bantu verbs and Monosyllabic verbs while the Arabic verbs retain their last vowel.

Ufanye! – Would you (sing.) do!
Mfanye! – Would you (pl.) do!

Ukate! – Would you (sing.) cut!
Mkate! – Would you (pl.) cut!

Ungoje! – Would you (sing.) wait!
Mngoje! – Would you (pl.) wait!

Uandike! – Would you (sing.) write!
Mandike! – Would you (pl.) write!

In the above examples, the second person prefixes are pronounced as a separate syllable. For example, the verb *mandike* would contain four syllables and be pronounced as *m-a-ndi-ke*.

Arabic verbs:
Usamehe! – Would you (sing.) forgive!
Msamehe! – Would you (pl.) forgive!
Ufikiri! – Would you (sing.) think!
Mfikiri! – Would you (pl.) think!

Monosyllabic verbs:
Ule! – Would you (sing.) eat!
Mle! – Would you (pl.) eat!
Unywe! – Would you (sing.) drink!
Mnywe! – Would you (pl.) drink!

Note that the *ku-* infinitive is not prefixed to the verb in Monosyllabic requests.

Practice Exercise B

Translate the following into English.

11. *Mseme!*
12. *Uchague!*
13. *Mkubali!*
14. *Utabasamu!*
15. *Ungoje!*

Section C: The Negations of Commands & Requests

When a command is negated, it is automatically changed to a request, having the meaning of "would you not." Both commands and requests are negated by following the same 3 simple steps: the prefix, infix and suffix steps. Note that the prefix and the suffix steps are the same as the ones we used in Section B to change commands into requests. Now, in order to change singular and plural commands and requests into their negations, we use a third step, which is the infix step. These three steps are listed below:

- The prefix *u-* is used for 2nd person singular and the prefix *m-* for 2nd person plural.
- The infix *-si-* is used to denote negation.
- The suffix *e* replaces the last vowel of Bantu and Monosyllabic verbs while the Arabic verbs retain their last vowel.

Here are some examples of negative singular and plural commands and requests.

Bantu verbs:
   Usifanye! – Would you (sing.) not do!
   Msifanye! – Would you (pl.) not do!
   Usikate! – Would you (sing.) not cut!
   Msikate! – Would you (pl.) not cut!
   Usingoje! – Would you (sing.) not wait!
   Msingoje! – Would you (pl.) not wait!

Arabic verbs:
   Usisamehe! – Would you (sing.) not forgive!
   Msisamehe! – Would you (pl.) not forgive!
   Usifikiri! – Would you (sing.) not think!
   Msifikiri! – Would you (pl.) not think!

Monosyllabic verbs:
   Usile! – Would you (sing.) not eat!
   Msile! – Would you (pl.) not eat!

Usinywe! – Would you (sing.) not drink!
Msinywe! – Would you (pl.) not drink!

Note that the *ku-* infinitive is not prefixed to the verb in negative Monosyllabic verbs.

Practice Exercise C

Translate the following into English.

16. *Msipende!*
17. *Msipike!*
18. *Msishukuru!*
19. *Usifagie!*
20. *Usiogelee!*
21. *Usiseme!*
22. *Usiangalie!*
23. *Usiguse!*
24. *Msinuse!*
25. *Usichague!*

Section D: Exception Verbs

There are only three exception verbs that do not use the verb stem for a singular command. These verbs are *leta* (bring), *enda* (go) and *ja* (come). The first two are Bantu verbs and the last one is a Monosyllabic verb.

When changing the verb *leta* into a singular command, we would expect it to become *Leta!* – Bring! (sing.) but it is instead *Lete!* – Bring! (sing.)

When changing the verb *enda* into a singular command, we would expect it to become *Enda!* – Go! (sing.) but it is instead *Nenda!* – Go!(sing.)

When changing the verb *ja* into a singular command, we would expect it to become *Kuja!* – Come! (sing.) but it is instead *Njoo!* – Come! (sing.)

When changing singular commands to become plural commands, all three verbs follow the rules listed in Section A. However, the verb *leta* behaves as a regular Bantu verb while *enda* and *ja* continue to behave as exception verbs:

Leteni! – Would you (pl.) bring!
Nendeni! – Would you (pl.) go!
Njooni! – Would you (pl.) come!

These three verbs behave as regular verbs when singular and plural commands are changed into requests:

Ulete! – Would you (sing.) bring!
Mlete! – Would you (pl.) bring!
Uende! – Would you (sing.) go!
Mende! – Would you (pl.) go!
Uje! – Would you (sing.) come!
Mje! – Would you (pl.) come!

These three verbs also behave as regular verbs when singular and plural commands and requests are negated, here are some examples:

Usilete! – Would you (sing.) not bring!
Msilete! – Would you (pl.) not bring!
Usiende! – Would you (sing.) not go!
Msiende! – Would you (pl.) not go!
Usije! – Would you (sing.) not come!
Msije! – Would you (pl.) not come!

Section E: Imperatives with objects

When singular and plural commands are used with objects, the object infix is used as a prefix. If the verb is of Bantu origin, the last vowel changes from *a* to *e*.

Example:

Nunua ua! – You (sing.) buy a flower!
Linunue! – You (sing.) buy it!
Nunueni ua! – You (pl.) buy a flower!
Linunueni! – You (pl.) buy it!

If the verb is of Arabic origin, the last vowel is unchanged:

Jaribu tunda! – You (sing.) try the fruit!
Lijaribu! – You (sing.) try it!

Jaribuni tunda! – You (pl.) try the fruit!
Lijaribuni! – You (pl.) try it!

If the verb is Monosyllabic, the *ku-* infinitive is dropped and the last vowel changes from *a* to *e*:

Kula ndizi! – You (sing.) eat a banana!
Ile! – You (sing.) eat it!
Kuleni ndizi! – You (pl.) eat a banana!
Ileni! – You (pl.) eat it!

Note that when commands are used with objects whose object infixes are "*-u-*" or "*-m-*," the resulting sentence can be mistaken for polite imperatives.

Example:
Piga mpira! – You (sing.) hit the ball!
Upige! – You (sing.) hit it!

As discussed in Section B, the word *upige* is also the singular request "Would you (sing.) hit." This is different from *upige* in the above example which is an order to hit something (in this case, the ball). The context of the situation determines which of the two possible meanings *upige* stands for.

When singular and plural requests are used with objects, the object infix is inserted between the prefix and the verb.

Example:
Ununue ua! – Would you (sing.) buy a flower!
Ulinunue! – Would you (sing.) buy it!
Mnunue ua! – Would you (pl.) buy a flower!
Mlinunue! – Would you (pl.) buy it!
Ujaribu tunda! – Would you (sing.) try the fruit!
Ulijaribu! – Would you (sing.) try it!
Mjaribu tunda! – Would you (pl.) try the fruit!
Mlijaribu! – Would you (pl.) try it!
Ule ndizi! – Would you (sing.) eat a banana!
Uile! – Would you (sing.) eat it!
Mle ndizi! – Would you (pl.) eat a banana!
Mile! – Would you (pl.) eat it!

When a command or request is negated, it is automatically changed to a request, having the meaning of "would you not."

Usinunue ua! – Would you (sing.) not buy a flower!
Usilinunue! – Would you (sing.) not buy it!
Msinunue ua! – Would you (pl.) not buy a flower!
Msilinunue! – Would you (pl.) not buy it!
Usijaribu tunda! – Would you (sing.) not try the fruit!
Usilijaribu! – Would you (sing.) not try it!
Msijaribu tunda! – Would you (pl.) not try the fruit!
Msilijaribu! – Would you (pl.) not try it!
Usile ndizi! – Would you (sing.) not eat a banana!
Usiile! – Would you (sing.) not eat it!
Msile ndizi! – Would you (pl.) not eat a banana!
Msiile! – Would you (pl.) not eat it!

Practice Exercise D

Translate the following into Swahili.

26. You all read it! (the book)
27. Choose him! (the president)
28. Would you (sing.) burn it! (the letter)
29. Burn them! (the letters)
30. You (pl.) don't cut it! (the bread)

New Vocabulary

chagua: choose, elect
gusa: touch
tabasamu: smile

Key to Exercises

Answers to Practice Exercise A

1. *Penda!*
2. *Pikeni!*
3. *Shukuru!*
4. *Fagia!*
5. *Ogelea!*

6. *Semeni!*
7. *Angalia!*
8. *Guseni!*
9. *Nusa!*
10. *Chagueni!*

Answers to Practice Exercise B

11. Would you (pl.) speak!
12. Would you (sing.) choose!
13. Would you (pl.) agree!
14. Would you (sing.) smile!
15. Would you (sing.) wait!

Answers to Practice Exercise C

16. Would you (pl.) not love!
17. Would you (pl.) not cook!
18. Would you (pl.) not thank!
19. Would you (sing.) not sweep!
20. Would you (sing.) not swim!
21. Would you (sing.) not speak!
22. Would you (sing.) not look!
23. Would you (sing.) not touch!
24. Would you (pl.) not smell!
25. Would you (sing.) not choose!

Answers to Practice Exercise D

26. *Kisomeni!*
27. *Mchague!*
28. *Uichome!*
29. *Zichome!*
30. *Msiukate!*

Chapter 31

-KA- Tense and Negation

The -KA- Tense has three different uses. Firstly, when someone is narrating a story or reporting an incident that happened in the past, we use the Narrative Past Tense. Secondly, when someone is going to do something, we use the Consecutive Subjunctive Tense. Finally, when it is used for newspaper headlines, we use the "Headline" Tense. In Narrative Past Tense and Consecutive Subjective, the -ka- tense marker is used as an infix while in the "Headline" Tense, it is used as the prefix ka-.

Section A: The Narrative Past Tense

When the -ka- tense is used for narratives, it is introduced by the simple past -li- tense marker. After the -li- tense marker is used for introduction, the -ka- tense marker is subsequently used to narrate the story. For example:

Nilinunua samaki, nikapika kutumia mafuta, tukala.
I bought fish, (and) cooked it with oil, (and) we ate.

As you can see from the above example, the -ka- tense marker is preceded by the -li- tense marker. Also note that the -ka- tense marker has the built in meaning "and" so we do not need to use the Swahili word *na*.

When used as a narrative past tense, the -ka- tense marker is used as a regular tense marker (follows the STV Rule).

Personal Subject Prefix + -KA- Tense Marker + Verb

When using the *-ka-* tense marker with Bantu, Arabic and Monosyllabic verbs, the STV Rule taught above applies. Here are examples using each kind of verb:

> *Alisoma barua, akamwonyesha mama yake, wakalia.*
> He/She read the letter, (and) showed it to his/her mother (and) they cried.
> *Mlirudi safari, mkawaletea wenzangu zawadi, mkasahau kuniletea mimi.*
> You (pl.) returned from the trip, (and) brought gifts for my companions (and) forgot to bring me (a gift).
> *Tulichuma nyanya kutoka shambani, tukazisafisha, tukazipika, tukazila.*
> We picked tomatoes from the farm, (and) washed them, (and) cooked them (and) ate them.

Please note, as in the final example above, that Monosyllabic verbs drop their infinitive *ku-* marker when used with the *-ka-* tense marker. Also, object infixes can be used with the *-ka-* tense marker.

If one would like to emphasize the chronological order of events, it is possible to use the word *halafu* which means "then." For example:

> *Alisoma barua, halafu akamwonyesha mama yake, halafu wakalia.*
> He/She read the letter, (and) then showed it to his/her mother (and) then they cried.

Practice Exercise A

Translate the following sentences into English.

1. *Tulikwenda Marekani, tukatembelea Disney World, tukafurahi.*
2. *Walinialika nyumbani, wakapika muhogo na maharagwe, tukala.*
3. *Mmilikaji aliagana na mhandisi kutengeneza mashua, mhandisi akaisanifu, akanunua vifaa kutoka Urusi, akamaliza mradi katika miezi miwili.*
4. *Mto ulifurika, ukaharibu mazao yetu, tukapata hasara?*
5. *Soko la hisa lilianguka, watu wengi wakapoteza kazi zao, wakaamua kupunguza matumizi yao.*
6. *Rubani aliwatahadharisha abiria, akabadili mwendo na mwinuko, akaendelea kusafiri wakati wa tufani.*

7. *Ndege aliruka, akatua juu ya mti, akajenga kiota, akaimba, akalala.*
8. *Mweka wa kitega uchumi alipanda mahindi kuyatumia kama mazao, akaweka nia yake, akapata pesa nyingi.*
9. *Zeruzeru alipata kazi ya kuendesha treni, halafu akafanya kazi kwa muda wa miaka ishirini, halafu akastaafu.*
10. *Lori lilimwaga shehena yake, likaangukia katika korongo, likashika moto.*

Section B: Negation of the Narrative Past Tense

When the narrative past tense is negated, the *-ka-* tense is replaced using the negative tense marker *-si-*. In addition, the verb must be in its subjunctive form (see Chapter 37 for more on Subjunctives).

Personal Subject Prefix + -SI- Tense Marker + Subjunctive Verb

For example:

Nilinunua samaki, nikapika kutumia mafuta, tusile.
I bought fish, (and) cooked it with oil, (and) did not eat (it).

In the example above, since the *-si-* negative tense marker is being used to negate the narrative past tense, the built in meaning "and" remains, so we do not need to use the Swahili word *na*.

Please note when *-si-* negative tense marker is used, the Monosyllabic verbs drop their infinitive *ku-* marker. Also, object infixes can be used with the *-si-* negative tense marker.

Practice Exercise B

Translate the following sentences into English.

11. *Tulikwenda Marekani, tukatembelea Disney World, tusifurahi.*
12. *Walinialika nyumbani, wasipike muhogo na maharagwe, tusile.*
13. *Mmilikaji aliagana na mhandisi kutengeneza mashua, mhandisi akaisanifu, akanunua vifaa kutoka Urusi, asimalize mradi katika miezi miwili.*
14. *Mto ulifurika, ukaharibu mazao yetu, tusipate hasara?*
15. *Soko la hisa halikuanguka, watu wengi wasipoteze kazi zao, wasiamue kupunguza matumizi yao.*

16. *Rubani aliwatahadharisha abiria, akabadili mwendo na mwinuko, asiendelee kusafiri wakati wa tufani.*
17. *Ndege aliruka, akatua juu ya mti, akajenga kiota, akaimba, asilale.*
18. *Mweka wa kitega uchumi alipanda mahindi kuyatumia kama mazao, akaweka nia yake, asipate pesa nyingi.*
19. *Zeruzeru alipata kazi ya kuendesha treni, halafu akafanya kazi kwa muda wa miaka ishirini, halafu asistaafu.*
20. *Lori lilimwaga shehena yake, likaangukia katika korongo, lisishike moto.*

Section C: Consecutive Subjunctive (going to do something)

When used as a consecutive subjunctive, the *-ka-* tense denotes the meaning of "going and" doing something. This does not have anything to do with the future tense but rather refers to the aspect of the action i.e. the action is going to take place. Since the consecutive subjunctive has the meaning of "going" to do something, it cannot be used with verbs that indicate "coming near" such as *ja, sogea, karibia* and *rudi*.

Before using the *-ka-* tense marker as a consecutive subjunctive, one must be familiar with the verbal construction of the singular and plural requests as taught in Chapter 30. The *-ka-* tense marker is inserted as an infix in the verbal construction as follows:

Personal Subject Prefix + -KA- Tense Marker + Subjunctive Verb

Nikanunue shampuu.
Let me go (and) buy shampoo.
Wakalime shamba la mboga.
Let them go (and) cultivate the vegetable farm.

As you can see from the examples above, unlike the singular and plural requests which are only directed to the 2nd person singular and plural, the consecutive subjunctive can use any Subject Prefix from any Noun Class.

Ndege ikachukue abiria.
Let the plane go and carry passengers.

Consecutive subjunctive can be used as an object infix from any noun class. Here are some examples:

Nikainunue.
Let me go (and) buy it.
Wakalilime.
Let them go (and) cultivate it.
Ikawachukue.
Let it (the plane) go (and) bring them (the passengers).

Also, the verb *enda* can be used in its command form or request form in conjunction with the *-ka-* tense marker to emphasize the action of going. For example:

Nenda ukasome.
Go and read. (or simply *ukasome*)
Uende ukasome.
Would you (sing.) go and read. (or simply *ukasome*)

Practice Exercise C

Translate the following sentences into English.

21. *Nikamalize kusoma shairi.*
22. *Mkawape wananchi wa Kenya dawa hizi.*
23. *Akawaambie tumerudi safari.*
24. *Nendeni mkalipe faini ya kosa la kuegesha gari.*
25. *Nikazongoe zawadi za Krismasi.*
26. *Mkauzime moto sasa hivi.*
27. *Mende mkamsaidie kufyatua matofali.*
28. *Wakanong'one usiku mzima.*
29. *Twende tukamtembelee bibi yetu.*
30. *Akamlishe mamba yule.*

Section D: Negation of the Consecutive Subjunctive (not going to do something)

When the consecutive subjunctive is negated, the *-ka-* tense is replaced using the negative tense marker *-si-*. In addition, the verb remains in its subjunctive form.

Personal Subject Prefix + -SI- Tense Marker + Subjunctive Verb

For example:

> *Nisinunue shampuu.*
> Let me not buy shampoo.
> *Ndege isichukue abiria.*
> Let the plane not carry passengers.
> *Wasililime.*
> Let them not cultivate it.

As you can see from the examples above, when the consecutive subjunctive is negated, the meaning of "going and" doing something does not apply. Also, the verb *enda* cannot be used with negative consecutive subjunctive since it also carries the meaning of going.

Please note when *-si-* negative tense marker is used, the Monosyllabic verbs drop their infinitive *ku-* marker. Also, object infixes can be used with the *-si-* negative tense marker.

Practice Exercise D

Translate the following sentences into English.

31. *Nisimalize kusoma shairi.*
32. *Msiwape wananchi wa Kenya dawa hizi.*
33. *Asiwaambie tumerudi safari.*
34. *Msilipe faini ya kosa la kuegesha gari.*
35. *Nisizongoe zawadi za Krismasi.*
36. *Msiuzime moto sasa hivi.*
37. *Msimsaidie kufyatua matofali.*
38. *Wasinong'one usiku mzima.*
39. *Tusimtembelee bibi yetu.*
40. *Asimlishe mamba yule.*

Section E: The "Headline" Tense

When used as a "headline" tense by the media, the -KA- tense marker can only be used with 3rd person singular in M-/WA- noun class. In this case, the *ka* tense marker is used without any subject prefix and without altering the verb in order to make the headline brief and catchy.

~~Personal Subject Prefix~~ + -KA- Tense Marker + Verb

For example:

Mtu kaiba saa ya mkono ya Rais.
Person steals President's watch.

If the example above was not used as a headline, the sentence would be written without the *ka-* tense as follows:

Mtu aliiba saa ya mkono ya Rais.
A person stole the President's watch.

Practice Exercise E

Translate the following sentences in English.

41. *Mbunge aliyepo kachaguliwa tena.*
42. *Paka kaua panya saba katika dakika kumi.*
43. *Tausi dume kaibwa kutoka zu.*
44. *Msafishaji madirisha kaanguka ghorofa thelathini.*
45. *Kiongozi wa watalii kaepuka poromoko la theluji.*

New Vocabulary

agana: agree with
aliyepo: He/She who is there (incumbent)
amua: decide
chuma: pick
dume/ma-: male animal(s)
epuka: avoid, escape
faini ya/za kosa la kuegesha gari: parking fine(s)
fyatua tofali/ma-: make brick(s)
ghorofa: floor(s)
halafu: then
haragwe/ma-: kidney bean(s)
hasara: loss
karibia: come close
kiota/vi-: nest(s)
korongo/ma-: ditch(es), channel(s)

Krismasi: Christmas(es)
matumizi: spending, expenditure(s)
msafishaji/wa-: cleaner(s)
mweka/waweka wa kitega uchumi: investor(s)
mwendo/mi-: speed(s)
mwinuko/mi-: altitude(s), slope(s)
nia: intention(s), aim(s)
nong'ona: whisper
poromoko/ma- la/ya theluji: avalanche(s)
sanifu: design
shampuu: shampoo(s)
shehena: cargo(es)
sogea: come close
soko/ma- la/ya hisa: stock market(s)
tahadhari: warn, caution
tausi: peacock(s)
tua: land, settle
tufani: storm(s)
zeruzeru/ma-: albino(s)
zima: whole, good, extinguish
zongoa: unwrap

Key to Exercises

Answers to Practice Exercise A

1. We went to America, (and) visited Disney World, (and) we were happy.
2. They invited me to the house, (and) they cooked cassava and kidney beans, (and) we ate.
3. The owner contracted the engineer to manufacture a boat, the engineer designed it, (and) bought the materials from Russia, (and) completed the project in two months.
4. The river flooded, (and) it destroyed our crops, (and) we incurred a loss?
5. The stock market collapsed, (and) many people lost their jobs, (and) decided to reduce their spending.
6. The pilot warned the passengers, (and) changed his speed and altitude, (and) continued to travel during the storm.

7. The bird flew, (and) landed on top of a tree, (and) built a nest, (and) sang, (and) slept.
8. The investor planted maize to use it as a crop, (and) kept his/her intention, (and) got a lot of money.
9. The albino got a job to drive the train, (and) then he/she worked for a period of twenty years, (and) then retired.
10. The truck spilled its cargo, (and) went into the ditch, (and) caught fire.

Answers to Practice Exercise B

11. We went to America, (and) visited Disney World, (and) we were not happy.
12. They invited me to the house, (and) they did not cook cassava and kidney beans, (and) we did not eat.
13. The owner contracted the engineer to manufacture a boat, the engineer designed it, (and) bought the materials from Russia, (and) did not complete the project in two months.
14. The river flooded, (and) it destroyed our crops, (and) we did not incur a loss?
15. The stock market did not collapse, (and) many people did not lose their jobs, (and) decided not to cut down on their spending.
16. The pilot warned the passengers, (and) changed his speed and altitude, (and) did not continue o travel during the storm.
17. The bird flew, (and) landed on top of a tree, (and) built a nest, (and) sang, (and) did not sleep.
18. The investor planted maize to use it as a crop, (and) kept his/her intention, (and) did not get a lot of money.
19. The albino got a job to drive the train, (and) then he/she worked for a period of twenty years, (and) then did not retire.
20. The truck spilled its cargo, (and) went into the ditch, (and) did not catch fire.

Answers to Practice Exercise C

21. Let me go (and) finish reading the poem.
22. Would you (pl.) go and give the Kenyan citizens these medicinal drugs.
23. Let him/her go and tell them that we have returned from the trip.

24. You (pl.) go and pay the fees for the parking infraction.
25. Let me go and unwrap the Christmas gifts.
26. Would you (pl.) go and extinguish the fire right now.
27. Would you (pl.) go and help him/her make bricks.
28. Let them go and whisper the whole night.
29. Let us go and visit our grandmother.
30. Let him/her go and feed that crocodile.

Answers to Practice Exercise D

31. Let me not finish reading the poem.
32. Would you (pl.) not give the Kenyan citizens these medicinal drugs.
33. Let him/her not tell them that we have returned from the trip.
34. Would you (pl.) not pay the fees for the parking infraction.
35. Let me not unwrap the Christmas gifts.
36. Would you (pl.) not extinguish the fire right now.
37. Would you (pl.) not help him/her make bricks.
38. Let them not whisper the whole night.
39. Let us not visit our grandmother.
40. Let him/her not feed that crocodile.

Answers to Practice Exercise E

41. The incumbent parliament member was elected again.
42. Cat kills seven mice in ten minutes.
43. Male peacock stolen from zoo.
44. Window cleaner falls thirty floors.
45. Tour guide escapes avalanche.

Chapter 32

Conditional Tenses: *-nge-*, *-ngali-* and *-ki-* Tenses and Their Negations

In this chapter, we will learn how to use conditional tenses: the *-nge-*, *-ngali-* and *-ki-* tenses. These tenses indicate a condition, hypothesis or an assumption. The *-nge-* tense shows a condition in the present tense eg: If I were to study, etc. while the *-ngali-* tense shows a condition in the past tense eg: If I had studied, etc. We will also discuss the *-ki-* tense which shows a condition in the present tense which has future implications eg: If I study, etc. Also, the word *kama* can be used with both the affirmative and negative conditional tenses to emphasize the conditionality. In addition, the *-ki-* tense can also be used as a present participle tense which will also be discussed in this chapter.

Note that in conditional clauses, past tense shows a present condition, a past perfect tense shows a past condition while a present tense shows a future condition.

Section A: *-nge-* Tense

The *-nge-* tense is used to show a hypothesis in the present tense. Similar to other tense markers, sentences using *-nge-* tense markers are constructed in the following manner.

Subject Prefix + *-nge-* Tense Marker + Verb

Example:
Ningesoma vizuri, ningefaulu.
If I were to study well, I would pass.

As you can see from the example above, the *-nge-* tense is always followed by another conditional tense. The first *-nge-* is used as a condition, while the second *-nge-* is used more like a hypothesis. If the sentence includes the *-nge-* tense, it indicates a real condition i.e. the action has the possibility to occur.

Also note that all verbs whether Bantu, Arabic or Monosyllabic are treated in the same way when using *-nge-* and *-ngali-* tenses and their negations, with Monosyllabic verbs retaining their -KU- infinitive in both affirmative and negative sentences.

Practice Exercise A

Translate the following sentences in Swahili.

1. If I were rich, I would marry you.
2. If he were honest, I would lend him my car.
3. If they were ready, we would travel at 8 am.
4. If we were to travel, we would go to Canada.
5. If I were chosen to choose a colour for the walls, I would choose white.

Section B: *-ngali-* Tense

The *-ngali-* tense is used to show a hypothesis in the past tense. Similar to other tense markers, sentences using *-ngali-* tense markers are constructed in the following manner.

Subject Prefix + *-ngali-* Tense Marker + Verb

Example:
Ningalisoma vizuri, ningalifaulu.
If I had studied well, I would have passed.

As you can see from the example above, the *-ngali-* tense is always followed by another conditional tense. The first *-ngali-* is used as a condition, while the second *-ngali-* is used more like a hypothesis. If the sentence includes the *-ngali-* tense, it indicates an unreal condition i.e. the possibility of the action occurring has passed and it cannot occur.

Practice Exercise B

Translate the following sentences in Swahili.

6. If I had been rich, I would have married you.
7. If he had been honest, I would have lent him my car.
8. If they had been ready, we would have travelled at 8 am.
9. If we had to travel, we would have gone to Canada.
10. If I had been chosen to choose a colour for the walls, I would have chosen white.

Section C: Mixing of *-nge-* and *-ngali-* Tenses

It is possible to use both *-nge-* and *-ngali-* tenses in the same sentence. When we want to show that a past condition has an effect in the present, the first condition is denoted by
  -ngali- and the second condition by *-nge-*.

Example:
  Ningalisoma vizuri, ningefaulu.
  If I had studied well, I would pass.

In some cases, when we want to show that a present condition could have had an effect in the past, the first condition is denoted by *-nge-* and the second condition by *-ngali-*.

Example:
  Ningekuwa daktari, ningalikutibu.
  If I were a doctor, I would have treated you.

Practice Exercise C

Translate the following sentences in Swahili.

11. If I were eighteen years old, I would have joined the military.
12. If you had been a scientist, you would discover the cure for AIDS.
13. If we were friends, I would help her.
14. If I had been a potter, I would make clay vessels.
15. If she had studied hard, she would pass.

Section D: Negation of *-nge-* and *-ngali-* Tenses

The most common way of negating *-nge-* and *-ngali-* tenses is by adding the infix *-si-* between the Subject Prefix and the *-nge-* or *-ngali-* Tense marker as shown below:

Subject Prefix + *-si-* + *-nge-* or *-ngali-* Tense Marker + Verb

Examples:
Nisingesoma vizuri, nisingefaulu.
If I were not to study well, I would not pass.
Nisingekuwa daktari, nisingalikutibu.
If I were not a doctor, I would not have treated you.

Practice Exercise D

Translate the following sentences in Swahili.

16. If I had not been rich, I would not have married you.
17. If he had not been honest, I would have lent him my car.
18. If they had not been ready, we would not have travelled at 8 am.
19. If we were not to travel, we would have saved money.
20. If I had not been chosen to choose a colour for the walls, I would have been angry.

Section E: *-ki-* tense and Negation

The *-ki-* tense can be used in two ways. It can be used as a conditional tense and a present participle tense. Similar to other tense markers, sentences using *-ki-* tense markers are constructed in the following manner.

Subject Prefix + *-ki-* Tense Marker + Verb

When used as a conditional tense, the *-ki-* tense is used to show a hypothesis in the present tense, similar to the *-nge-* tense. The only difference is that it is invariably followed by a future tense or an imperative which has a future implication. Also, when used as a conditional tense, the *-ki-* tense appears in the subordinate conditional clause.

Examples:

Nikisoma vizuri, nitafaulu.
If I study well, I will pass.
Akija darasani, ataleta karatasi za mtihani.
If he/she comes to class, he/she will bring the examination papers.

Also, as per the last example above, Monosyllabic verbs do not retain their *ku-* infinitive in affirmative sentences using the *-ki-* tense marker.

When used as a negative conditional tense, the *-ki-* tense can be negated in two ways:

1. By substituting the *-ki-* tense marker with the infix *-sipo-*. The Subject Prefix and the verb remain unchanged.

Examples:

Nisiposoma vizuri, sitafaulu.
If I do not study well, I will not pass.
Asipokuja darasani, hataleta karatasi za mtihani.
If he/she does not come to class, he/she will not bring the examination papers.

When negating the conditional tense sentences, one can negate the subordinate clause or the main clause or both clauses depending on the intent of the sentence. Also, as per the last example above, Monosyllabic verbs retain their *ku-* infinitive in negative sentences using the *-ki-* tense marker.

2. Use of *kama* with present tense negation.

Example:

Kama sisomi vizuri, sitafaulu.
If I do not study well, I will not pass.

In addition to being used as a conditional tense, the *-ki-* tense marker is also used as a present participle tense. When used as a present participle tense, it expresses a continuous or incomplete action. The English translation of the verb using the *-ki-* tense can be translated in two ways: the gerund form and the infinitive form. Also, when used as a present participle tense, the *-ki-* tense can be replaced by the *-na-* present tense marker. In addition, instead of occurring in the first verb of the sentence, the *-ki-* tense marker is found in the subsequent verb.

Examples:
Tuliwaona wakipika.
We saw them cooking.
Nilikuwa ninapenda kuona jua likichwa.
I used to like to see the sun (to) set.

Also, as per the last example above, Monosyllabic verbs do not retain their *ku-* infinitive in affirmative sentences using the *-ki-* tense marker.

When used as a present participle tense, the *-ki-* tense can be negated in two ways:

1. By negating the first verb of the sentence and leaving *ki-* tense marker in the subsequent verb unchanged.

Example:
Hatukuwaona wakipika.
We did not see them cooking.

2. Use of present tense negation.

Example:
Tuliwaona hawapiki.
We saw them not cooking.

When negating the present participle sentences, one can negate either of the verbs depending on what the speaker wishes to convey.

Practice Exercise E

Translate the following conditional sentences in Swahili.

21. If he/she converses on the phone while driving, he/she will get into an accident.
22. If the economy does not plummet, many people will have jobs.
23. If the computer does not work, I will use the typewriter.

24. If it rains heavily, the crops will not grow.
25. If I marry a rich man, he will not care about me.

Translate the following present participle sentences in Swahili.

26. I heard the frog croaking.
27. We did not expect to see them rushing.
28. We expected to see them not rushing.
29. She was carrying her grandmother's bags.
30. Her assistant did not continue to come on time.

New Vocabulary

azimia: lend
dunduiza: save up, accumulate
jeshi/ma-: army(ies), military
karatasi: paper(s)
koroma: croak, snore
mashine ya/za chapa: typewriter(s)
mfinyanzi/wa-: potter(s)
msaidizi/wa-: assistant(s)
mwaminifu/wa-: honest person(s)
mwanasayansi/wa-: scientist(s)
ongea: converse, speak with
poromoka: plummet, slip, slide
umri: age(s)
unga (na): join (up), connect (with)

Key to Exercises

Answers to Practice Exercise A

1. *Ningekuwa tajiri, ningekuoa.*
2. *Angekuwa mwaminifu, ningemwazimia gari langu.*
3. *Wangekuwa tayari, tungesafiri saa mbili asubuhi.*
4. *Tungesafiri, tungekwenda Kanada.*
5. *Ningechaguliwa kuchagua rangi ya kuta, ningechagua nyeupe.*

Answers to Practice Exercise B

6. *Ningalikuwa tajiri, ningalikuoa.*
7. *Angalikuwa mwaminifu, ningalimwazimia gari langu.*
8. *Wangalikuwa tayari, tungalisafiri saa mbili asubuhi.*
9. *Tungalisafiri, tungalikwenda Kanada.*
10. *Ningalichaguliwa kuchagua rangi ya kuta, ningalichagua nyeupe.*

Answers to Practice Exercise C

11. *Ningekuwa na umri wa miaka kumi na nane, ningalijiunga na jeshi.*
12. *Ungalikuwa mwanasayansi, ungegundua tiba ya Ukimwi.*
13. *Tungalikuwa rafiki, ningemsaidia.*
14. *Ningalikuwa mfinyanzi, ningetengeneza vyombo vya udongo wa kinamu.*
15. *Angalisoma kwa bidii, angefaulu.*

Answers to Practice Exercise D

16. *Nisingalikuwa tajiri, nisingalikuoa.*
17. *Asingalikuwa mwaminifu, ningalimwazimia gari langu.*
18. *Kama wasingalikuwa tayari, tusingalisafiri saa mbili asubuhi.*
19. *Tusingesafiri, tungedunduiza pesa.*
20. *Nisingalichaguliwa kuchagua rangi ya kuta, ningalikasirika.*

Answers to Practice Exercise E

21. *Akiongea kwenye simu wakati anaendesha gari, atapata ajali.*
22. *Uchumi usipoporomoka, watu wengi watapata kazi. OR*
    Kama uchumi hauporomoki, watu wengi watapata kazi.
23. *Kompyuta isipofanya kazi, nitatumia mashine ya chapa. OR*
    Kama kompyuta haifanyi kazi, nitatumia mashine ya chapa.
24. *Mvua ikinyesha kwa nguvu, mazao hayataota.*
25. *Nikiolewa na mwanaume tajiri, hatanijali.*
26. *Nilimsikia chura akikoroma.*
27. *Hatukutegemea kuwaona wakiharakisha.*
28. *Tulitegemea kuwaona hawaharakishi.*
29. *Alikuwa akibeba mifuko ya bibi yake.*
30. *Msaidizi wake hakuendelea kuja kwa wakati.*

Chapter 33

Additional Tenses and Their Negations

In this Chapter, we will learn how to use the following additional tenses and their negations:

The Present Indefinite Tense
The Habitual Tense
The Already Tense
The *-nga-* and *-japo-* Tenses

The Present Indefinite Tense is used to state facts and ask questions without reference to a specific time. The Habitual Tense is used in contexts which imply usual practices or truths of a general order which have no specific time reference. In addition, we will cover The Already Tense which is used to show an action that has already taken place as well as learn the uses of the *-nga-* and *-japo-* Tenses.

Section A: The Present Indefinite Tense

The Present Indefinite Tense is similar to the Present Tense as they are both present tense markers. However, the Present Indefinite Tense which is denoted by *-a-* is used to show an action that takes place periodically. The Present Tense which is denoted by *-na-* shows an action that is in progress at the present moment. Sentences using Present Indefinite Tense markers are constructed in the following manner.

Personal Subject Prefix + Present Indefinite Tense + Verb

If we want to make a simple sentence such as "I play," we do it as follows. We take the Personal Subject Prefix for "I" which is *ni-*. We then attach this to the Present Indefinite Tense marker *-a-* and we get *nia-*. Finally, we attach this to the verb "play" which is *cheza* and we get *Niacheza*, conjugated to *Nacheza* which means "I play." Since the tense marker is a vowel, the conjugation of this tense is done as follows with the M-/WA- class Personal Subject Prefixes.

Niacheza becomes *Nacheza* – I play
Uacheza becomes *Wacheza* – You (sing.) play
Aacheza becomes *Acheza* – He/She plays
Tuacheza becomes *Twacheza* – We play
Macheza becomes *Mwacheza* – You (pl.) play
Waacheza becomes *Wacheza* – We play

The other noun classes follow the same pattern as above:

M-/MI- class
Uachoma becomes *Wachoma* – It burns
Iachoma becomes *Yachoma* – They burn

JI-/MA- class
Liachoma becomes *Lachoma* – It burns
Yaachoma becomes *Yachoma* – They burn

KI-/VI- class
Kiachoma becomes *Chachoma* – It burns
Viachoma becomes *Vyachoma* – They burn

N- class
Iachoma becomes *Yachoma* – It burns
Ziachoma becomes *Zachoma* – They burn

U- class
Uachoma becomes *Wachoma* – It burns
Ziachoma becomes *Zachoma* – They burn

PA- class

Paachoma becomes *Pachoma* – It/They (definite) burn(s)
Kuachoma becomes *Kwachoma* – It/They (indefinite) burn(s)
Machoma becomes *Mwachoma* – It/They (inside) burn(s)

KU- class

Kuachoma becomes *Kwachoma* – It/They burn(s)

Note that "u" changes to "w" and "i" changes to "y" in the chart above.

Below are examples of Present Indefinite Tense sentences with object prefixes and other Bantu verbs:

Ndege zaruka mbinguni. – The airplanes fly in the sky.
Magari yatumia petroli kwenda. – Cars use gas to go.
Roboti yakimbia mita saba. – The robot runs seven metres.

In the Present Indefinite Tense, Arabic verbs follow the same rules as Bantu verbs. Below are some examples of verbs of Arabic origin:

Twasahau kununua unga. – We forget to buy flour.
Setilaiti yarudi ardhini. – The satellite returns to the ground.

Monosyllabic verbs drop their infinitive marker *ku-* in sentences using Present Indefinite Tense markers:

Nala achari. – I eat pickled condiments.
Wanywa kahawa chungu. – You (sing.) drink strong coffee.

When negating a Present Indefinite Tense sentence, we negate it just as we would negate the Present Tense. For example:

Mimi napika. – I cook.
Sipiki. – I am not cooking.
Francis aja kanisani. – Francis comes to the church.
Francis haji kanisani. – Francis does not come to the church.

Practice Exercise A

Translate the following sentences into English.

1. *Napenda kunywa maji ya madafu.*
2. *Dubu yule hatishi watalii.*
3. *Zabibu zahitaji mwanga wa jua kuota.*
4. *Malkia wa Uingereza apenda mapazia ya zambarau.*
5. *Mahali pa kulipa dukani palindwa.*

Section B: The Habitual Tense

The Habitual Tense which is denoted by the tense marker *hu-* is used to show an action that takes place on a daily basis. It can be translated in English by any of the following adverbs: "usually," "generally," or "always." Unlike most other tenses, the *hu-* tense does not take a subject prefix. In addition, it can be used with a noun from any noun class. It is directly attached to the verb, and if required, an object infix can be inserted between the *hu-* tense marker and the verb. Sentences using *hu-* tense marker are constructed in the following manner.

~~Personal Subject Prefix~~ + Habitual Tense Marker + Verb

If we want to make a simple sentence such as "I usually play," we do it as follows. We take the *hu-* Habitual Tense marker and attach this to the verb "play" which is *cheza* and we get *hucheza* which could mean "I usually play." Since the *hu-* Habitual Tense marker is not prefix specific, the same sentence could be translated for any of the six Personal Subject Prefixes or a Prefix from any other Noun Class in Swahili. *Hucheza* could mean any of the following:

I usually play.
We usually play.
You (sing.) usually play.
You (pl.) usually play.
He/She usually plays.
They usually play.

We can specify the subject of the verb by using an appropriate noun or a Personal Pronoun. For example:

Mimi hupenda kupika. – I usually like to cook.

Mhandisi yule hujenga madaraja. – That engineer usually builds bridges.

Mafuriko husambaza magonjwa. – Floods usually spread diseases.

Arabic verbs are treated in the same manner as Bantu verbs above:

Wewe husahau kufunga mlango usiku. – You (sing.) usually forget to lock the door at night.

Monosyllabic verbs drop their *ku-* infinitive when used with the Habitual Tense.

Yeye hula samaki na mkate kila Ijumaa. – He/She usually eats fish and bread every Friday.

When negating a Habitual Tense sentence, we negate it just as we would negate a present tense negation. For example:

Mimi hupika. – I usually cook.
Sipiki. – I usually do not cook.
Francis huja kanisani. – Francis usually comes to the church.
Francis haji kanisani. – Francis does not usually come to the church.

The Habitual Tense is often used in Swahili proverbs, riddles and common sayings.

Example:
Haba na haba hujaza kibaba.
Literally:
Little and little fills the measure. Meaning: Small things, when added together, lead to big things.

Practice Exercise B

Translate the following sentences into English.

6. *Kinda la ng'ombe hunywa maziwa.*
7. *Mimi hula mboga mchana.*
8. *Shauku nyingi huondoa maarifa.*

9. *Gari hili hutumia petroli nyingi.*
10. *Gari hili halitumii petroli nyingi.*

Section C: The Already Tense

The Already Tense which is denoted by the tense marker *-mesha-* is used to show an action that has already taken place. Sentences using the *-mesha-* Tense are constructed in the following manner.

Personal Subject Prefix + The *-mesha-* Tense + Verb

If we want to make a simple sentence such as "I have already played," we do it as follows. We take the personal subject prefix for "I" which is *ni-*. We then attach it to the *-mesha-* Tense and we get *nimesha-*. Finally, we attach this to the verb "play" which is *cheza* and we get *Nimeshacheza* which means "I have already played."

Using the same method of construction with other Subject Prefixes and Bantu verbs, we get:

Nimeshamaliza ukurasa wangu. – I have already completed my page.
Imeshanyesha. – It has already rained.

Arabic verbs are treated in the same manner as Bantu verbs above:

Wao wameshakubali kumkaribisha mgeni. – They have already agreed to welcome the guest.

Monosyllabic verbs retain their *ku-* infinitive when used with the *-mesha-* Tense:

Jua limeshakuchwa. – The sun has already set.

Note that the *-mesha-* Tense is a contraction of the following:

-me- tense + *-isha* "finish" = *-meisha* which is contracted to *-mesha-* which literally means "have finished," in other words, "is already finished."

When negating a *-mesha-* Tense sentence, we negate it by using the *-ja-* tense marker as taught in the Past Perfect Tense Negation (see Chapter 6). For example:

Nimepika. – I have cooked.
Nimeshapika. – I have already cooked.
Sijapika. – I have not yet cooked.

Practice Exercise C

Translate the following sentences into Swahili.

  11. The wine glass is already broken.
  12. The laundry detergent is not yet finished.
  13. I have already finished paying my mortgage.
  14. My sister has already seen the financial advisor.
  15. The circus has already arrived in town.

Section D: The *-nga-* and *-japo-* Tense

The *-nga-* and *-japo-* Tenses are commonly translated as "though," "even though," "although," or "even if." They are not used as regular tense markers in today's Swahili, except for the specific construction of *ingawa* and *ijapokuwa*. Here are a few sentences using *ingawa* and *ijapokuwa*:

Ijapokuwa walicheka kwa sauti, mtoto hakuamka.
Even though they laughed loudly, the child did not wake up.
Ingawa mnanidharau ninawaheshimu.
Even though you (pl.) ignore me, I respect you (pl.).
Ingawa utampa mshahara mkubwa, ataacha kazi.
Even if you give him/her a large salary, he/she will quit the job.

Ingawa and *ijapokuwa* cannot themselves be negated; instead the rest of the sentence can be negated. For example:

Ingawa hamnidharau siwaheshimu.
Even though you (pl.) do not ignore me, I do not respect you (pl.).

Practice Exercise D

Translate the following sentences into Swahili.

16. Although he/she has not completed sewing the sweaters, the customer has already arrived.
17. Although the tree fell, it did not hurt me.
18. Although he is old, he is not yet retired.
19. Even if they win the lottery, they will not be happy.
20. Even though there was an earthquake, many people did not die.

New Vocabulary

achari: pickled condiment(s)
bilauri: drinking glass(es)
chungu: strong, bitter, sharp
dafu/ma-: unripe coconut(s) (with lots of milk)
dubu: bear(s)
fua: launder, forge (metal)
haba: little, few
heshimu: respect, honour
ijapokuwa: although, even though, even if
ingawa: although, even though, even if
kanisa/ma-: church(es)
karibisha: welcome, invite
kibaba/vi-: measuring tin(s)
kinda/ma-: young animal(s)
maarifa: knowledge, understanding
malkia: queen(s) *mbingu*: sky(ies)
mshauri/wa-: advisor(s)
mvinyo/mi-: wine(s)
mwanga/mi-: light(s)
pazia/ma-: curtain(s)
rehani: mortgage(s)
roboti: robot(s)
sambaza: spread
sarakasi: circus(es)
setilaiti: satellite(s)
shauku: eagerness, desire
ukurasa/kurasa: page(s), sheet of paper(s)

umiza: hurt
zabibu: grape(s), raisin(s)
zambarau: plum(s), plum colour (purple)

Key to Exercises

Answers to Practice Exercise A

1. I like to drink the water of the coconuts.
2. That bear does not threaten the tourists.
3. The grapes need sunlight to grow.
4. The queen of Great Britain likes purple curtains.
5. The checkout counter is guarded.

Answers to Practice Exercise B

6. A calf generally drinks milk.
7. I usually eat vegetables in the afternoon.
8. Too much eagerness generally removes understanding.
9. This car generally uses a lot of petrol.
10. This car does not generally use a lot of petrol.

Answers to Practice Exercise C

11. *Bilauri ya mvinyo imeshavunjika.*
12. *Sabuni ya kufulia haijamalizika.*
13. *Nimeshamaliza kulipa rehani yangu.*
14. *Dada yangu ameshamwona mshauri wa fedha.*
15. *Sarakasi imeshafika mjini.*

Practice Exercise D

16. *Ijapokuwa hajamaliza kushona sweta, mteja ameshafika.*
17. *Ingawa mti ulianguka, haukuniumiza.*
18. *Ijapokuwa yeye ni mzee, hajastaafu.*
19. *Ijapokuwa watashinda bahati nasibu, hawatafurahi.*
20. *Ingawa kulikuwa na tetemeko la ardhi, watu wengi hawakufa.*

Chapter 34

Prepositions and Conjunctions

In this Chapter, we will discuss some commonly used prepositions and conjunctions and how they are used in a sentence. A preposition describes a relationship between words in a sentence and it shows time, space, and logical relationship. A conjunction is a word that connects words, phrases and clauses. There are two kinds of conjunctions: coordinating conjunctions and subordinating conjunctions. A coordinating conjunction links words, phrases and independent clauses in a sentence. However, a subordinating conjunction connects independent clause(s) and dependant clause(s). Some words can be either a preposition or conjunction depending on the context.

Section A: Prepositions

Some Swahili words exist as prepositions, while other prepositions are constructed using the *-a* of Association or its derived phrases. Some common Swahili words that exist as prepositions are:

mpaka – until, as far as, up to
kutoka, toka, tokea – from, out of
hata – even, until
bila – without
kama – as, if, like
tangu – since
kisha – then, and then
hadi – until, as far as, up to

kwa – by, to/by means of, for, with, on
na – and, with, by

Examples:
Alisoma mpaka jioni. – He/She studied until evening.
Nimenunua kikapu kutoka Kenya. – I have bought a basket from
    Kenya.
Wanasafiri bila pasipoti. – They are travelling without passports.
Tutakwenda kwa miguu. – We will go by foot.

The preposition *katika* which commonly means "in" also belongs to
the list above. However, since it can be translated in different ways into
English depending on the context, we will go into further detail here.
Katika can be used in reference to both time and space. When used in
reference to space, it indicates location exactly as the locative *-ni*. For
example, the phrase below could be either:

katika soko – in the market
OR
sokoni – in the market

However, when an adjective or demonstrative is used with a noun, only
the construction with *katika* can be used. For example:

katika soko kubwa – in the big market
katika soko lile – in that market

Katika can also be used in reference to time, for example:

Katika safari yetu, tulimwona kichakuro. – During our journey, we
    saw a squirrel.

Here are more examples where the preposition *katika* is translated in
different ways.

Kuanguka katika shimo. – To fall into a hole.
Vikombe viko katika meza. – The cups are on the table.

Other prepositions called compound prepositions can be formed from nouns, adjectives and adverbs using *kwa*, *na* or the *-a* of Association. Some common compound prepositions are:

badala ya – instead of
kwa ajili ya – for the sake of
kwa sababu ya – because of
kabla ya – before
baada ya – after, afterwards
karibu na – near
mbali na – far from
zaidi ya – more than
mahali pa – instead of
nje ya – outside
katikati ya – among, middle
pamoja na – together with
sawa na – equal to, similar

As you can see from the above examples, some compound prepositions take *kwa* at the beginning and all compound preposition end with either *na* or the *-a* of Association.

Examples:
Mwalimu wa sayansi alikuja badala ya mwalimu wa jiografia.
The science teacher came instead of the geography teacher.
Pikipiki imepinduka katikati ya barabara.
A motorcycle has overturned in the middle of the road.

Compound prepositions using *na* are followed by personal pronouns, for example:

Alifuatana pamoja na mimi.
He/She came with me.

If a compound prepositions using *kwa* or the *-a* of Association is followed by a possessive, it must take "y" as a prefix, for example:

Alikuja badala yangu.
He/She came instead of me.

In Swahili, just as in English, the preposition is usually placed before the noun, pronoun or phrase that connects it to the rest of the sentence. Also note that some prepositions can be used as conjunctions as you will see in Section B.

Practice Exercise A

Translate the following sentences into Swahili.

1. Her salary is more than her husband's salary.
2. He sold his property which was outside of the city.
3. I will solve the problem together with my colleague.
4. The priest did not finish the prayers before 6 pm.
5. I know her uncle since 1990.
6. The celebrity went with that car to the concert.
7. He agreed to marry her because of me.
8. He ran until evening.
9. On this question, there is no answer.
10. The boyfriend went to the restaurant without his girlfriend.

Section B: Conjunctions

As mentioned in the introduction, there are two kinds of conjunctions in Swahili: coordinating conjunctions and subordinating conjunctions. A coordinating conjunctions links words, phrases and independent clauses in a sentence. These are further divided according to what they express as shown below:

i) Coordinating conjunctions that express addition are:
    na – and, also
    pia – also, too
    tena – again, furthermore, besides
    juu ya hayo – in addition, furthermore
    pamoja na hayo – in addition, furthermore
    zaidi ya hayo – in addition, furthermore

Examples:
    Alileta mkate na mchuzi.
    He/She brought bread and curry.
    Nyumba yake ya kupanga ni chafu, juu ya hayo iko mbali sana.
    His/her rental house is dirty, in addition it is very far.

ii) Coordinating conjunctions that express alternatives, including those that indicate choice are:

ama...ama – either...or
au...au – either...or
au – or
wala – neither
wala...wala – neither...nor

Examples:

Watapaka chumba chao rangi ya kijani au zambarau.
They will paint their room green or purple.
Haangalii wala televisheni wala hasomi magazeti.
He/She watches neither television nor does he/she read newspapers.
Wala is used with a negative verb as shown in the example above.

iii) Coordinating conjunctions that express contrast are:

lakini – but, nevertheless
ila – but, except, unless
bali – but rather, on the contrary

Examples:

Anafanya kazi lakini hawezi kuweka pesa akiba.
He/She is working but is unable to save money.
Alifaulu masomo yote ila usimamizi wa fedha.
He/She passed all the subjects except financial management.

iv) Coordinating conjunctions that express reason are:

kwa hivyo – because of this
kwa vile – because of this
kwa kuwa – for, because, the reason being
sababu, kwa sababu – for, because, the reason being
kwani – for, because, the reason being
kwa maana – for, because, the reason being
basi – enough, stop, well, then, so
kwa ajili ya hayo – therefore

Examples:

Je, ulichelewa kwani saa ya kukuamsha haikulia saa mbili asubuhi?
Were you late because the alarm did not go off at 8 am?

Dereva alikufa katika ajali kwa sababu hakuvaa mkanda wa usalama wa kiti.

The driver died in the accident because he/she was not wearing a seat belt.

A subordinating conjunction connects independent clause(s) and dependant clause(s). These are further divided according to what they express as shown below:

v) Subordinating conjunctions that express condition are:
    kama – if, whether
    kwamba – if, whether
    kama kwamba – as if
    iwapo – when, if, in case
    ilimradi – provided that

Examples:
    Nitakodi teksi kwenda kazini kama mvua itanyesha.
    I will hire a taxi to go to work if it rains.
    Mwuzaji atapata bonasi yake ilimradi anauza safari za utalii tatu wiki hii.
    The salesman will get his bonus provided he sells three tours this week.

vi) Subordinating conjunctions that express purpose are:
    ili – so that, in order that
    ili kwamba – so that, in order that
    kusudi – in order that, with the intention of
    kwa nia ya – with the intention of

Examples:
    Alisomea kozi ya cheti kwa nia ya kuwa mpiga picha.
    He/She studied for the certificate course with the intention of becoming a photographer.
    Tulisaga vitunguu saumu ili tuvitumie katika mchuzi.
    We ground garlic so that we can use it in the curry.

vii) Subordinating conjunctions that simply provide an introduction are:
   kwamba – that
   ya kuwa – that
   kama – that

Example:
   Ofisa mipango alisema kwamba ataendeleza huduma za jamii.
   The planning officer said that he/she would improve social services.

viii) Subordinating conjunctions that express unexpected results:
   ingawa – although, even though, even if
   japo/ijapo/ijapokuwa – although
   hata hivyo – even though
   bila kujali – inspite of
   licha ya – despite

Example:
   Ingawa hali ya uchumi ni mbaya, watu wanaendelea kununua kwa kadi za mkopo.
   Although the economy is bad, people continue to buy with credit cards.

Practice Exercise B

Translate the following sentences into English.

   11. *Alimwambia maneno mabaya zaidi ya hayo alimpiga na mkanda.*
   12. *Mkulima wa bustani anapanda nyanya au matango.*
   13. *Nilitarajia chakula cha moto bali nilipewa sandwichi.*
   14. *Alikuwa na ngozi kavu, kwa hivyo alilia.*
   15. *Nitawasilisha tasnifu yangu wiki hii ilimradi nikiandika kurasa kumi leo.*
   16. *Alinunua ardhi katikati ya mji kusudi ajenge kituo cha afya.*
   17. *Licha ya maonyo ataendelea kuvuta sigara.*
   18. *Jeshi la anga liliambiwa kama litapata vifaa vipya.*
   19. *Waya wa kompyuta umelegea, kwa vile kompyuta haichaji.*
   20. *Wamesafisha bafu pamoja na hayo wamepaka rangi jiko.*

New Vocabulary

ama...ama: either...or
anga: air, sky(ies)
au...au: either...or
badala ya: instead of
bafu: bath(s), bathroom(s)
bali: but, rather, on the contrary
bila: without
bila kujali: inspite of
chaji: charge(s)
cheti/vy-: chit(s), pass(es), certificate(s)
fuatana: go together
hadi: until, as far as, up to
hata: even, until
huduma: service(s), help
ila: but, except, unless
ili kwamba: so that, in order that
ilimradi: provided that
iwapo: when, if, in case
jamii: community(ies), family(ies)
japo/ijapo/ijapokuwa: although
jawabu/ma-: answer(s), reply(ies)
jiografia: geography
juu ya hayo: in addition, furthermore
kadi: card(s)
kama kwamba: as if
kavu: dry, disinteresting
kichakuro/vi-: squirrel(s)
kikapu/vi-: basket(s)
kipenzi/vi-: boyfriend(s), favourite(s)
kasha: then, and then
kitunguu/vi- saumu: garlic clove(s)
kozi: course(s)
kusudi: in order that, with the intention of
kwa ajili ya: for the sake of
kwa ajili ya hayo: therefore
kwa hivyo: because of this

kwa kuwa: for, because, the reason being
kwa maana: for, because, the reason being
kwa nia ya: with the intention of
kwa vile: because of this
kwani: for, because, the reason being
legea: relax, be loose, be weak
licha ya: despite
mahali pa: instead of
maonyesho: show(s), concert(s)
mbali na: far from
mkanda/mi-: belt(s)
mkopo/mi-: credit(s), loan(s)
mpango/mi-: plan(s)
mpiga/wa- picha: photographer(s)
mwuzaji/wa-: seller(s), salesperson(s)
ngozi: skin(s), leather(s), hide(s)
onyo/ma-: warning(s), advice
pamoja na hayo: in addition, furthermore
pasipoti: passport(s)
pia: also, too
pikipiki: motorcycle(s)
saa ya/za kukuamsha: alarm clock(s)
safari ya/za utalii: tour(s)
saga: crush, grind
sandwichi: sandwich(es)
sayansi: science(s)
shimo/ma-: hole(s)
tango/ma-: cucumber(s), gutter(s)
tasnifu: thesis/theses
tatua: solve
teksi/ma-: taxi(s)
usalama: safety, security
usimamizi: management
wala: neither
wala...wala: neither...nor
wasilisha: submit
waya/nyaya: wire(s)
zaidi ya hayo: in addition, furthermore

Key to Exercises

Answers to Practice Exercise A

1. *Mshahara wake ni zaidi ya mshahara wa mume wake.*
2. *Aliuza mali yake iliyokuwa nje ya mji.*
3. *Nitatatua tatizo pamoja na mwenzangu.*
4. *Mchungaji hakumaliza sala kabla ya saa kumi na mbili jioni.*
5. *Ninamjua mjomba wake tangu mwaka wa elfu moja, mia tisa na tisini.*
6. *Mtu maarufu alikwenda kwa gari lile maonyeshoni.*
7. *Alikubali kumwoa kwa ajili yangu.*
8. *Alikimbia mpaka jioni.*
9. *Katika swali hili, hakuna jawabu.*
10. *Kipenzi alikwenda hotelini bila mpenzi wake.*

Answers to Practice Exercise B

11. He/She said bad words to him/her in addition he/she beat him/her with a belt.
12. The gardener plants tomatoes or cucumbers.
13. I expected a hot meal on the contrary I was given a sandwich.
14. He/She had dry skin, because of that he/she cried.
15. I will submit my thesis this week provided that I write 10 pages today.
16. He/She bought land in the city centre with the intention of building a health station.
17. Despite the warnings he/she will continue to smoke.
18. The air force was told that it will get new equipment.
19. The computer wire has loosened, because of this the computer is not charging.
20. They have cleaned the bathroom in addition they have painted the kitchen.

Chapter 35

Common Swahili Questions and Answers

This Chapter presents dialogues using question words learned in the preceding chapters. Some of the common questions asked are people's names, where they live and work, the type of work they do, their families, where they were born, where they go to school and so forth. Below are some common questions and answers that are used in conversation.

Section A: Meeting Someone

Shopkeeper: *Habari za asubuhi?*

Tourist: *Nzuri sana bwana. Na wewe je?*

Shopkeeper: *Mimi sijambo. Jina lako nani?*

Tourist: *Jina langu ni Mike. Mimi ninatafuta hoteli ya Kilimanjaro. Je, unajua iko wapi?*

Shopkeeper: *Iko katika mtaa wa Kivukoni, mbele ya Bahari ya Hindi. Si mbali kutoka hapa.*

Tourist: *Asante sana kaka. Samahani, nimesahau kukuuliza jina lako.*

Shopkeeper: *Hakuna matatizo. Jina langu ni Musa. Je, una muda wa kuangalia vinyago katika duka langu?*

Tourist: *Hapana, asante sana. Ninafanya haraka sasa hivi, lakini nitakutembelea wakati mwingine. Asante sana tena.*

Shopkeeper: *Nimefurahi kukutana na wewe. Ninatarajia nitakuona tena. Safari njema!*

Tourist: *Kwa heri.*

Practice Exercise A

Answer the questions below in English.

1. Why did the tourist say *samahani*?
2. What did the shopkeeper sell?
3. What street is Hotel Kilimanjaro located on?
4. Why did the tourist not want to look at the shopkeeper's carvings?
5. What is the name of the tourist?

Section B: Conversation between neighbours

Malikia: *Shikamoo Bwana Ali.*

Ali: *Marahaba Malikia. Wewe hujambo?*

Malikia: *Mimi sijambo sana.*

Ali: *Unakwenda wapi saa hizi?*

Malikia: *Mimi ninakwenda shuleni. Tuna mtihani wa historia leo. Je, unakwenda kazini?*

Ali: *Ndiyo. Nimepata kazi mpya katika kampuni ya umeme. Nina mkutano na wafanyakazi wangu.*

Malikia: *Je, una cheo gani na una wafanyakazi wangapi?*

Ali: *Mimi ni Meneja wa Utumishi na nina wafanyakazi arobaini na watatu chini yangu. Wachache wanatoka sehemu mbalimbali ulimwenguni kama vile Marekani na Ulaya lakini wengi ni Wakenya.*

Malikia: *Je, wafanyakazi wa kigeni wanaishi wapi na wanafanya kazi gani?*

Ali: *Wafanyakazi wa kigeni wanaishi katika nyumba za kukodi karibu na makao makuu ya kampuni. Wao ni wataalamu wa teknolojia na wako hapa kwa mkataba wa miaka miwili.*

Malikia: *Sawa kabisa. Leo usiku tuna sherehe nyumbani kwetu. Je, umepata mwaliko?*

Ali: *Ndiyo. Nitakuja na familia yangu. Tutaonana jioni.*

Malikia: *Inshallah. Kwa heri.*

Ali: *Kwa heri ya kuonana.*

Practice Exercise B

Answer the questions below in English.

6. *Kuna nini leo usiku nyumbani kwa Malikia?*
7. *Je, wafanyakazi wa kigeni katika kampuni ya umeme wanafanya kazi gani?*
8. *Je, Malikia ana mtihani wa somo lipi leo?*
9. *Je, Bwana Ali amefanya kazi katika kampuni ya umeme kwa muda mrefu?*
10. *Je, wafanyakazi wa kigeni wana mkataba wa miaka mingapi?*
11. *Bwana Ali ana cheo gani?*
12. *Wafanyakazi wengi wa kampuni wanatoka wapi?*

Section C: At the Airport

Passenger 1: *Jambo. Habari za asubuhi?*

Immigration Officer: *Nzuri sana Karibu Tanzania Bwana. Je, umesafiri peke yako leo?*

Passenger 1: *Hapana. Nimefuatana na mke wangu, Mary.*

Immigration Officer: *Yuko wapi? Ninamhitaji hapa na ninaomba pasipoti yake.*

Passenger 1: *Mary, njoo hapa.*

Passenger 2: *Naam ninakuja. Je, unahitaji nini?*

Passenger 1: *Ofisa wa uhamiaji anakuhitaji hapa na anaomba pasipoti zetu.*

Immigration Officer: *Je, mnatoka wapi na mlipitia nchi gani?*

Passenger 1: *Tumetoka Jamaika na tumepitia Uswisi.*

Immigration Officer: *Ninyi ni raia wa nchi gani?*

Passenger 2: *Sisi ni raia wa Jamaika.*

Immigration Officer: *Kiswahili chenu ni kizuri sana. Je, mlijifunza wapi?*

Passenger 2: *Wazazi wangu walizaliwa Tanzania na walihamia Jamaika mwaka wa elfu moja, mia tisa, sitini na tisa. Tulizungumza Kiswahili nyumbani.*

Immigration Officer: *Vizuri sana. Na mume wako alijifunza wapi?*

Passenger 1: *Nilijifunza Kiswahili katika Chuo Kikuu cha Kingston, Jamaika.*

Immigration Officer: *Vizuri sana. Je, mnawatembelea ndugu zenu Tanzania au mko hapa kama watalii?*

Passenger 1: *Hapana, tuko hapa kwa shughuli.*

Immigration Officer: *Mna kiasi gani cha pesa?*

Passenger 1: *Tuna Dola elfu kumi za Kimarekani na Yuro elfu sita na mia tano.*

Immigration Officer: *Je, mna kitu cho chote kingine cha kuonyesha?*

Passenger 1: *Hapana. Tuna vitu vya kibinafsi tu.*

Immigration Officer: *Je, mtakaa wapi mjini na mtaondoka lini?*

Passenger 2: *Tutakaa na rafiki yetu katika mtaa wa Kisutu na tutarudi Jamaika tarehe ya kumi na nane, mwezi wa Oktoba.*

Immigration Officer: *Sawasawa. Nimeambatisha viza zenu za kuingia Tanzania katika pasipoti. Karibu tena Tanzania na safari njema.*

Passenger 1 and 2: *Asante sana!*

Practice Exercise C

Answer the questions below in Swahili.

13. *Msafiri wa pili anaitwa nani?*
14. *Wasafiri ni raia wa wapi?*
15. *Je, wasafiri wanatembelea Tanzania kwa ajili gani?*
16. *Je, wameleta kiasi gani cha pesa?*
17. *Je, nani alijifunza Kiswahili katika Chuo Kikuu cha Kingston, Jamaika?*
18. *Wasafiri walipitia katika nchi gani?*
19. *Je, wanatarajia kurudi Jamaika lini?*
20. *Je, Mary na mume wake watakaa wapi mjini?*

Section D: Travelling in East Africa

Tour Guide: Hello Sir!

John: *Jambo rafiki yangu. Habari ya kazi?*

Tour Guide: *Loo! Kumbe unajua Kiswahili? Mimi ni mzima lakini hali ya kazi si nzuri kwa sababu bei ya mafuta imepanda. Lakini habari nzuri kwa ajili yako ni kwamba kampuni hii ilitangaza jana kuwa watalii wawili wanaweza kusafiri kwenda mbuga za wanyama kwa bei ya mtu mmoja tu. Je, una mwenzako?*

John: *Hapana. Kwa bahati mbaya, nipo peke yangu. Pia, sitegemei kusafiri wakati huu.*

Tour Guide: *Mbona? Watu wawili wanaweza kusafiri kwa dola mia moja tu. Bei hii ni nzuri kuliko bei yo yote. Unaweza kuwaona simba chini ya miti, kiboko katika mabwawa, chui wakiwakimbiza swala, twiga wakila majani ya miti, tembo wakipunga masikio yao na kima wakiruka kutoka mti mmoja kwenda mti mwingine.*

John: *Ama! Ninapata hamu ya kwenda sasa. Je, safari itachukua siku ngapi?*

Tour Guide: *Ni safari ya siku moja tu. Basi letu litaondoka saa mbili na robo asubuhi na kurudi kati ya saa tatu na saa nne usiku.*

John: *Tatizo langu ni kwamba niko peke yangu. Je, nitalipa kiasi gani?*

Tour Guide: *Basi nipe dakika moja nimpigie simu bosi wangu.*

Tour Guide: *Shikamoo bosi. Nina Mzungu mmoja hapa na anataka kununua tiketi kwa ajili yake tu. Je, ninaweza kumwuzia kwa bei ya dola hamsini? Sawasawa. Asante sana.*

Tour Guide: *Nimeongea na bosi wangu na amekubali bei ya dola hamsini tu. Je, una pesa tayari?*

John: *Ndiyo. Dola hamsini hizi hapa.*

Tour Guide: *Asante. Tiketi yako ni hii hapa. Tafadhali ukumbuke kufika hapa saa mbili kasorobo asubuhi. Asante kwa kusafiri na sisi.*

John: *Hamna tabu. Kwa heri. Tutaonana kesho asubuhi.*

Practice Exercise D

Answer the following questions in Swahili.

21. *Basi litaondoka saa ngapi?*
22. *Kiongozi wa watalii alimwambia John kuwa kima watakuwa wanafanya nini?*
23. *Kwa nini hali ya kazi haikuwa nzuri?*
24. *Je, John anatarajia kusafiri peke yake?*
25. *Kiongozi wa watalii alimpigia simu nani?*
26. *Bei ya mwisho iliyokubaliwa ilikuwa kiasi gani?*
27. *Basi litarudi saa ngapi?*
28. *John aliambiwa ataona wanyama gani katika mbuga za wanyama?*
29. *Je, John alipata hamu ya kwenda katika safari lini?*
30. *Je, safari itachukua siku ngapi?*

New Vocabulary

ama!: Wow!
ambatisha: attach
binafsi: personal
funza: teach
-geni: strange, foreign
hamna tabu: no problem
hamu: desire(s)
historia: history(ies)
Inshallah: If God wills it
Jamaika: Jamaica
kati ya: between
kima: monkey(s)
kinyago/vi-: carving(s)
kumbe: I see
kutana na: meet with
loo!: Oh!
makao makuu: headquarter(s)
mbona?: Why, for God's sake?
mbuga ya/za wanyama: game park(s)
Mkenya/wa-: Kenyan(s)
msafiri/wa-: traveller(s)
mtaalamu/wa-: specialist(s)
mwaliko/mi-: invitation(s)
Mzungu/wa-: European(s)
naam: yes
punga: wave, flap
saa hizi: at this time
sawa kabisa: completely O.K
swala: gazelle(s)
uhamiaji: immigration
ulimwengu: world(s), universe(s)
Uswisi: Switzerland
utumishi: personnel, manpower
viza: visa(s)

Key to Exercises

Answers to Practice Exercise A

1. The tourist said *samahani* because he forgot to ask the shopkeeper's name.
2. The shopkeeper sold carvings.
3. Hotel Kilimanjaro is located on Kivukoni Street.
4. The tourist did not want to look at the shopkeeper's carvings because he was in a hurry.
5. His name is Mike.

Answers to Practice Exercise B

6. There will be a party at Malikia's house.
7. The foreign workers work as technology specialists.
8. Malikia has a history exam today.
9. No, Mr. Ali has not been working at the electricity company for a long time.
10. The foreign workers have a two year contract.
11. Mr. Ali is a manager of Human Resources.
12. Many of the workers in the company are from Kenya.

Answers to Practice Exercise C

13. *Msafiri wa pili anaitwa Mary.*
14. *Wasafiri ni raia wa Jamaika.*
15. *Wasafiri wanatembelea Tanzania kwa ajili ya shughuli.*
16. *Wameleta Dola elfu kumi za Kimarekani na Yuro elfu sita na mia tano.*
17. *Mume wa Mary (msafiri wa kwanza) alijifunza Kiswahili katika Chuo Kikuu cha Kingston, Jamaika.*
18. *Wasafiri walipitia Uswisi.*
19. *Wanatarajia kurudi Jamaika tarehe ya kumi na nane, mwezi wa Oktoba.*
20. *Mary na mume wake watakaa mtaa wa Kisutu.*

Answers to Practice Exercise D

21. *Basi litaondoka saa mbili an robo asubuhi.*
22. *Kiongozi wa watalii alimwambia John kuwa kima watakuwa wakiruka kutoka mti mmoja kwenda mti mwingine.*
23. *Hali ya kazi haikuwa nzuri kwa sababu bei ya mafuta imepanda.*
24. *Ndiyo, John anatarajia kusafiri peke yake.*
25. *Kiongozi wa watalii alimpigia simu bosi wake.*
26. *Bei ya mwisho iliyokubaliwa ilikuwa dola hamsini.*
27. *Basi litarudi kati ya saa tatu na saa nne usiku.*
28. *John aliambiwa ataona simba, kiboko, chui, swala, twiga, tembo na kima.*
29. *John alipata hamu ya kwenda katika safari baada ya kusikia habari za wanyama mbalimbali.*
30. *Safari itachukua siku moja tu.*

Chapter 36

Interjections, Idiomatic Expressions and Impersonal Subjects

Interjections, Idiomatic Expressions and Impersonal Subjects are used on a frequent basis by the Swahili people. Therefore, knowledge of these expressions indicates the learner has a better grasp of the Swahili language and culture.

Section A: Interjections

An interjection is a word used to convey an emotion or fill a pause in conversation. An Interjection can stand as a separate sentence or be added to a sentence. When added to a sentence, the Interjection does not change the meaning of the sentence, and is usually followed by an exclamation point.

In Swahili, there are two categories of Interjections.

1. Words used as Interjections only.

Aa! – Expresses surprise, joy or pain.
Ah! – Used to express grief, same as in English.
Aisee! – Expression used to attract someone's attention, taken from the British expression "I Say!"
Ala! – Exclamation for annoyance or impatience.
Ati! – Expression of surprise or for seeking someone's attention, similar to the English expression "Hey!"
Bee! – Response used by females when someone is calling them.

Ebu! or *Hebu!* – Usually expresses surprise or even disapproval.

Ewallah! – Expression used by inferiors to agree with superiors.

Haya! – Used for expressing agreement, same as the English expression "OK."

Inshallah! – If God wills it!

Lahaula! – Expresses inevitability that something bad has happened, such as a death, and it must now be accepted as nothing can be done about it.

Laiti! – Expression of disappointment or regret that something could have been done differently.

Loo! – "Oh!" Expresses surprise or astonishment, in a positive or negative way.

Makubwa! – Expresses unexpected important news.

Mbona! – "Why, for God's sake?" Expression of astonishment.

Mmm... – Used to fill a pause in conversation, same as the English expression "Ummm.."

Ng'o! – Expression to tell a child "Absolutely not."

Shhh! – Expression to keep quiet, as used in English.

Ya Allah! – Mostly expresses amazed frustration but can be used to express pleasant surprise, similar to the English expression "Oh God!"

2. Words that may have other uses but are also used as Interjections.

Astafurulahi! – This is an expression of seeking forgiveness from God, similar to the English expression "God forgive me."

Haki ya Mungu! or *Wallahi!* – This expression is used to take an oath, similar to the English expression "I swear to God."

Hata! – Expresses complete disagreement, with stress on the 2nd syllable.

Haraka! – Expresses hurry, similar to the English expression "Quickly!"

Jamani! – This is an expression of surprise, similar to the English expression "My goodness!"

Kweli! – When used with an exclamation point, it's an expression of affirmation similar to the English expression "Truly!" However, when *Kweli?* is used with a question mark, it expresses disbelief, similar to the English expression "Really?"

Mashallah! – Expression for gratitude to God mostly used to admire his creations.

Maskini! – This is an expression of sympathy, similar to the English expression "Poor fellow!"

Mawe! – Expression of strong disagreement, exactly as the English expression "That's garbage"

Naam! – "Yes" Response used by males when someone is calling them. Also used as a filler to keep conversation going, similar to the English expression "Uh-huh...!"

Samahani! or *Kumradhi!* – "Excuse me" or "sorry," used to ask for forgiveness or pardon.

Shabashi! or *Hongera!* – Expresses congratulations, exactly as the English expression "Congratulations!"

Subutu! – This is a challenge, similar to the English expression "I dare you!"

Vema! – This is an expression of acceptance, similar to the English expression "Good."

Section B: Idiomatic Expressions

An Idiomatic Expression is a set of words that when used together have a different meaning than the individual words when used by themselves. Like other languages, *Kiswahili* has many idiomatic expressions. Most idiomatic expressions begin with the infinitive *ku-* marker followed by the verb.

Listed below are the most popular ones.

Idiomatic Expression – Literal meaning – Idiomatic meaning
Ni mjamzito. – She is full/heavy. – She is pregnant.
Kuvimba kichwa. –To swell the head. – To become big-headed/arrogant.
Kufumba na kufumbua. – To close and to open. – In the blink of an eye.
Kichwa maji. – Head of water. – Stupid/dumb person.
Kumpa mtu kichwa. – To give someone a head. – To spoil or pamper someone.
Moja kwa moja. – One by one. – Straight ahead.
Mkia wa mbuzi. – The tail of a goat. – Totally useless person.

Kuuma meno. – To bite teeth. – To take a vow of revenge.
Kupiga mkasi. – To hit the scissors. – To expel from service.
Kushika sikio. – To hold an ear. – To reprimand.

Section C: Impersonal Subjects

In previous chapters, we have learnt about the STV rule, where the "S" denotes a Subject Prefix from any noun class, the "T" for the tense marker and "V" for the verb. However, there exists in Swahili a category of sentences which begin with an Impersonal Subject Prefix. The most common Impersonal Subject Prefix used is *i-*, which corresponds to "it" in English. The prefix *i-* refers to the subject prefix of the N- class in the singular, which is used as the default prefix since the "it" being referred to is unknown. The *i-* Impersonal Subject Prefix is commonly used with any of the following tenses: present, simple past, past perfect, future and occasionally, the *-ka-* tense.

Some verbs when used with the *i-* Impersonal Subject Prefix exist in their original form and could take Object Infixes. For example:

Verb stem – Impersonal Subject Sentence
   faa becomes *inatufaa* – it is useful to us
   pasa becomes *imekupasa* – it behooves you (sing.)
   dhuru becomes *inadhuru* – it harms
   bidi becomes *inatubidi* – it behooves us

Other verbs use a derived or stative form which does not allow the use of Object Infixes. For example:

Verb stem – Derived/Stative Verb – Impersonal Subject Sentence
   sema – *semekana* – *inasemekana* (it is said)
   weza – *wezekana* – *inawezakana* (it is possible)
   amini – *aminika* – *inaaminika* (it is believed)
   no stem – *dhihirika* – *imedhihirika* (it has become clear)

In addition to the *i-* Impersonal Subject Prefix, there exists another Impersonal Subject Prefix which is *ya-*. This also corresponds to "it" in English. The rules governing the usage of *ya-* are the same as taught above for *i-*, except that it cannot take tense markers and is assumed to be in present tense. For example:

Verb stem – *faa*
>   *i*- Impersonal Subject Sentence – *inatufaa* (it is useful to us)
>   *ya*- Impersonal Subject Sentence – *yatufaa* (it is useful to us)

Verb stem – *sema*
>   *i*- Impersonal Subject Sentence – *inasemekana* (it is said)
>   *ya*- Impersonal Subject Sentence – *yasemekana* (it is said)

Note that there is an exceptional impersonal construction which can only use the *i*- Impersonal Subject Prefix and does not take either a tense marker or an object infix and it is:

>   *ikawa* – and it was

Practice Exercise A

Translate into Swahili.

1. I say! Is it possible to get a cup of tea?
2. It behooved him/her to leave late at night.
3. It is disappointing to see him/her tortured again in the jail.
4. It is enough to know you love me very much.
5. It depends on the type of the work itself.

Section D: Negation of Impersonal Subject

When negating a sentence which uses an Impersonal Subject Prefix, we negate it just as we would negate the present, future, simple past and past perfect tense sentences as taught previously. For example:

>   *inatufaa* – it is useful to us
>   *haitufai* – it is not useful to us
>   *imekupasa* – it behooves you (sing.)
>   *haijakupasa bado* – it has not yet behooved you (sing.) OR
>   *haikukupasa* – it did not behoove you (sing.)
>   *yasemekana* – it is said
>   *haisemekani* – it is not said

Practice Exercise B

Translate into Swahili.

6. It is not taught that men are better than women.
7. It is not attractive to me when you smoke.
8. It is not useful for me to collect many shoes.
9. My goodness! It is not possible that he/she is a dumb person.
10. It is not enough to know you love me very much.

New Vocabulary

aa!: expresses surprise, joy, pain

ah!: expresses grief

aisee!: expression used to attract attention

ala!: expresses annoyance, impatience

astafurulahi!: expresses seeking forgiveness from God

ati!: expresses surprise, for seeking attention

bado: still, not yet

bee!: response used by females when someone is calling them

bidi: behoove

dhihirika: become evident

dhuru: harm

ebu!: expresses surprise, disapproval

ewallah!: expression used by inferiors to agree with superiors

haki ya Mungu!: expression used to take an oath

haraka!: hurry!

hata!: expresses complete disagreement

haya!: OK!

hebu!: expresses surprise, disapproval

hongera!: Congratulations!

ikawa: and it was

jamani!: expresses surprise

jela: jail(s)

kichwa maji: stupid/dumb person (idiom. expr.)

kufumba na kufumbua: in the blink of an eye (idiom. expr.)

kumpa mtu kichwa: to spoil or pamper someone (idiom. exp.)

kumradhi!: used to ask for forgiveness, pardon

kupiga mkasi: to expel from service (idiom. expr.)

kusanya: collect

kushika sikio: to reprimand (idiom. expr.)
kuuma meno: to take a vow of revenge (idiom. expr.)
kuvimba kichwa: to become big-headed, arrogant (idiom. expr.)
kweli!: truly!
lahaula!: expresses inevitability
laiti!: expresses disappointment, regret
makubwa!: expresses unexpected important news
mashallah!: expresses gratitude to God
maskini!: poor fellow!
mawe!: expresses strong disagreement
mkia wa mbuzi: totally useless person (idiom. expr.)
mmm...: used to fill a pause in conversation
moja kwa moja: straight ahead (idiom. expr.)
ng'o!: expression to tell a child "Absolutely not"
ni mjamzito: she is pregnant (idiom. expr.)
pasa: behoove
shabashi!: congratulations!
shhh!: expression to keep quiet
sikitisha: be disappointed
subutu!: to dare someone
tesa: torture
tosha: enough
vema!: good!
wallahi!: expression used to take an oath
Ya Allah!: expresses amazed frustration, pleasant surprise

Key to Exercises

Answers to Practice Exercise A

1. *Aisee! Inawezekana kupata kikombe cha chai?*
2. *Ilimbidi aondoke usiku wa manane.*
3. *Inasikitisha kumwona anateseka tena katika jela.*
4. *Inatosha kujua unanipenda sana.*
5. *Inategemea aina ya kazi yenyewe.*

Answers to Practice Exercise B

6. *Haifundishwi kuwa wanaume ni bora kuliko wanawake.*
7. *Hainivutii ambapo wewe unavuta sigara.*

8. *Hainifai kukusanya viatu vingi.*
9. *Jamani! Haiwezekani kuwa yeye ni kichwa maji.*
10. *Haitoshi kujua unanipenda sana.*

Chapter 37

Subjunctives

In Chapter 30 we learned about 2nd person singular and plural commands and requests. In this Chapter we will deal with Subjunctives (*Dhamira Tegemezi*) in all noun classes including 1st and 3rd person singular and plural in the M-/WA- class, and their object infixes whenever necessary. Note that Subjunctives do not use tense markers except for the tense marker *-ka-* which has been taught in Chapter 31. First we will show how affirmative and negative Subjunctives are formed with Bantu, Monosyllabic and Arabic verbs. Finally, we will show some of the common uses of the Subjunctive form.

Section A: Subjunctives with Bantu Verbs

Subjunctives with Bantu Verbs are formed by the Subject Prefix + Bantu verb, with the last vowel *a* changed to *e*. Below are the Subject Prefixes of all Noun Classes in their singular and plural forms.

Subjunctives with Bantu Verbs

Nianguke! – Let me fall!
Tuanguke! – Let us fall!
Uanguke! – Would you (sing.) fall!
Manguke! – Would you (pl.) fall!
Aanguke! – Let him/her fall!
Waanguke! – Let them fall!
Uanguke! – Let it fall!
Ianguke! – Let them fall!

Lianguke! – Let it fall!
Yaanguke! – Let them fall!
Kianguke! – Let it fall!
Vianguke! – Let them fall!
Ianguke! – Let it fall!
Zianguke! – Let them fall!
Uanguke! – Let it fall!
Zianguke! – Let them fall!
Paanguke! – Let it fall! (specific location)
Kuanguke! – Let it fall! (general area)
Manguke! – Let it fall! (inside location)
Kuanguke! – Let it fall!

Examples:
Makamanda wapate mafunzo. – Commanders should receive
    training
Mwanga uwake! – Let the light shine!
Mwalimu alituambia tuandike. – The teacher told us to write.

Negation of Subjunctives with Bantu Verbs

Subjunctives with Bantu Verbs are negated by using the negative infix -*si*- which is inserted between the Subject Prefix and the Bantu verb which retains the final vowel *e*.

Makamanda wasipate mafunzo. – Commanders should not receive
    training.
Mwanga usiwake! – Let the light not shine!
Mwalimu alisema tusiandike. – The teacher told us not to write.

Section B: Subjunctives with Monosyllabic Verbs

Subjunctives with Monosyllabic Verbs are formed by the Subject Prefix + Monosyllabic verb stem with the last vowel *a* changed to *e*.

Subjunctives with Monosyllabic Verbs

Nife! – Let me die!
Tufe! – Let us die!
Ufe! – Would you (sing.) die!

Mfe! – Would you (pl.) die!
Afe! – Let him/her die!
Wafe! – Let them die!
Ufe! – Let it die!
Ife! –Let them die!
Life! – Let it die!
Yafe! – Let them die!
Kife! – Let it die!
Vife! – Let them die!
Ife! – Let it die!
Zife! – Let them die!
Ufe! – Let it die!
Zife! – Let them die!
Pafe! – Let it die! (specific location)
Kufe! – Let it die! (general area)
Mfe! – Let it die! (inside location)
Kufe! – Let it die!

Examples:
   Wafamasi wanywe divai nyekundu! – Let the pharmacists drink red
      wine!
   Mkutubi aje asubuhi! – Let the librarian come in the morning!
   Jua lichwe! – Let the sun rise!

Negation of Subjunctives with Monosyllabic Verbs

Subjunctives with Monosyllabic Verbs are negated by inserting the negative infix *-si-* between the Subject Prefix and the verb stem which retains
the final vowel *e*.

   Wafamasi wasinywe divai nyekundu! – Let the pharmacists not drink
      red wine!
   Mkutubi asije asubuhi! – Let the librarian not come in the morning!
   Jua lisichwe! – Let the sun not rise!

Section C: Subjunctives with Arabic Verbs

Subjunctives with Arabic Verbs are formed by Subject Prefixes + Arabic Verbs. However, unlike Bantu Verbs, the last vowel of an Arabic
Verb remains unchanged as shown below.

Subjunctives with Arabic Verbs

Nisafiri! – Let me travel!
Tusafiri! – Let us travel!
Usafiri! – Would you (sing.) travel!
Msafiri! – Would you (pl.) travel!
Asafiri! – Let him/her travel!
Wasafiri! – Let them travel!
Usafiri! – Let it travel!
Isafiri! – Let them travel!
Lisafiri! – Let it travel!
Yasafiri! – Let them travel!
Kisafiri! – Let it travel!
Visafiri! – Let them travel!
Isafiri! – Let it travel!
Zisafiri! – Let them travel!
Usafiri! – Let it travel!
Zisafiri! – Let them travel!
Pasafiri! – Let it travel! (specific location)
Kusafiri! – Let it travel! (general area)
Msafiri! – Let it travel! (inside location)
Kusafiri! – Let it travel!

Examples:
Nirudi Kanada! – Let me return to Canada!
Meneja alisema mapambo yabaki. – The manager said the decorations should stay.
Kikapu kiketi karibu na jifya! – Let the basket sit near the hearth!

Negation of Subjunctives with Arabic Verbs

Subjunctives with Arabic Verbs are negated by using the negative infix -si- which is inserted between the Subject Prefix and the Arabic Verb.

Nisirudi Kanada! – Let me not return to Canada!
Meneja alisema mapambo yasibaki. – The manager said the decorations should not stay.
Kikapu kisiketi karibu na jifya! – Let the basket not sit near the hearth!

Section D: Uses of Subjunctives

This section discusses the different ways in which the Subjunctive is used with Bantu, Arabic and Monosyllabic Verbs.

1. The Subjunctive is used after some Prepositions such as the following:

   hadi (until, as far as, up to)
   hata (even, until)
   karibu (almost, nearly)
   mpaka (until, as far as, up to)
   tangu (since, from)

   Winchi isitengenezwe hadi nije.
   The winch should not be repaired until I come.

   Karibu nimalize kuchimba handaki.
   I have nearly finished digging the trench.

   Tangu wasafiri hawajaandika barua bado.
   Since they travelled, they have not yet written a letter.

2. The Subjunctive is used when the preceding verb is an auxiliary verb such the following:

   omba – beg, request
   taka – want
   ambia – tell
   amuru – demand
   shauri – advise
   kubali – accept
   pendekeza – recommend
   lazimisha – order, force
   acha – permit
   fanya – do
   panda – like
   agiza – order
   Mwache acheze na mchanga! – Let him/her play with sand!
   Nilikubali apasue puto langu. – I accepted that he/she bursts my balloon.
   Alinishauri ninunue hisa. – He/She advised me to buy stock(s).

3. The Subjunctive is used when the preceding verb is an imperative.

    Njoo ucheze! – Come and play!
    Rudi uanze kazi! – Return to start work!
    Soma ufanikiwe! – Study to be successful!

4. The Subjunctive is used after expressions of request, obligation and advice such as the following:

    tafadhali – please
    afadhali – it is better
    sharti – it is necessary
    heri – it is better
    yapasa – it is necessary
    lazima – it is necessary
    inabidi – it behooves
    inafaa – it is suitable
    bora – it is better

Examples:

    Inabidi mkurufunzi asome kwa bidii. – It behooves the trainee to study hard.
    Tafadhali ujibu barua yetu. – Please respond to our letter.
    Lazima wawape wagonjwa dawa. – It is necessary that they give the patients the medicine.

5. The Subjunctive is used to express purpose or intention. The word *ili* (so that, in order that) and *kusudi* (in order that, with the intention of) can be used for emphasizing such constructions.

    Wajiandae vizuri ili wafaulu mtihani!
    Let them prepare themselves well so that they may pass the exam!
    Aliomba pesa ili anunue chakula.
    He/She asked for money so that he/she can buy food.
    Walinitembelea kusudi niwadekeze.
    They visited me for the purpose of pampering them.

Please note that verbs of "going and coming" have two ways to express purpose or intention. The first way is to use them with the *ku-* infinitive which is not a subjunctive sentence. The second way is to use a subjunctive verb which must be proceeded by *ili* or *kusudi*.

Alirudi kucheza gitaa. – He/She returned to play guitar.
Alirudi ili acheze gitaa. – He/She returned to play guitar.

6. The Subjunctive is used to ask for permission, advice or approval and can use any verb.

    Waangalie sinema ipi? – Which movie should they watch?
    Wageni wale saa ngapi? – What time should the guests eat?
    Nikirudishe lini kitabu cha maktaba? – When should I return the library book?

7. The Subjunctive is used when the subject of the first verb in the sentence is different from the subject of the second verb. The first verb can be a regular verb or subjunctive verb.

    Baba alitaka mama asuke mkeka. – Father wanted mother to weave a mat.
    Mwuzaji hakutaka wateja waondoke. – The salesperson did not want the clients to leave.
    Tupange meza wageni wale. – Let us arrange the table for the guests to eat.

8. The Subjunctive is used to convey a request to oneself, as 1st person singular or plural.

    Niseme siri yangu! – Let me tell my secret!
    Twende sasa hivi! – Let us go now!
    Tusisahau kumwalika! – Let us not forget to invite him/her!

Note that requests to 2nd person singular and plural were taught in Chapter 30.

9. The Subjunctive is used to convey a request to a 3rd party singular or plural by asking a 2nd person singular or plural to convey the request. This must be done by using an object infix.

    Umwambie afunge akaunti! – Would you (sing.) tell him/her to close the account(s)!
    Mwaambie wasianze mdahalo! – Would you (pl.) tell them not to start the debate!
    Uwaombe wanipe kalenda! – Would you (sing.) beg them to give me a calendar!

Note: Negative Subjunctive of the verbs *ambia* and *sema* can be used to imply astonishment as in "No way!"

> *Usiniambie!* – Don't tell me!

10. When the same Subjunctive verb is used affirmatively and negatively in the same sentence, it forms a question with two possible opposite outcomes.

    Nimpige nisimpige? – Should I hit him/her or not?
    Ashindane asishindane? – Should he/she compete or not?

11. The Negative Subjunctive is used to convey the meaning of an intention or purpose which has failed.

    Tulimtafuta mbwa tusimwone. – We looked for the dog but could not find it.
    Aliwapikia chakula kingi wasile. – He/She cooked a lot of food for them but they did not eat.
    Waliandikiwa barua wasijibu. – They were written letters but did not respond.

12. The Negative Subjunctive is used after verbs of forbidding, refusing and preventing (*kataza, zuia, kataa, kanya* and *onya*).

    PolisiW waliwazuia waandamanaji wasipite. – The police prevented the protestors from passing.
    Kijana alikatazwa asicheze nje. – The youth was forbidden from playing outside.
    Mama alikataa watoto wasile usiku. – Mother refused to let the children eat at night.

Practice Exercise A

Translate the following into Swahili.

1. I will not lend to him/her until he/she pays you.
2. He/She ordered (forced) me to get him/her life insurance.
3. Stop and think.
4. It is necessary that I send my in-laws presents.
5. I called him/her so that he/she could come.

6. What movie should I watch?
7. His wife wanted him to become a lawyer.
8. Let me brush my teeth before sleeping!
9. Tell him/her to knit me a glove.
10. Should I stay or not?
11. They chased the thief but did not catch him/her.
12. The judge warned me not to drive when I am drunk.

New Vocabulary

agiza: order
akaunti: account(s)
amuru: demand
andaa: prepare
baki: stay
bima ya maisha: life insurance
dekeza: pamper
divai: wine(s)
fanikiwa: succeed
gitaa/ma-: guitar(s)
glavu: glove(s)
kalenda: calendar(s)
kanya: forbid, prevent
keti: sit
mafunzo: training
mchanga: sand(s)
mdahalo/mi-: debate(s)
mkurufunzi/wa-: trainee(s)
mkwe/wa-: in-law(s)
mswaki/mi-: toothbrush(es)
mwandamanaji/wa-: protestor(s)
pasua: burst
pendekeza: recommend
puto/ma-: balloon(s)
sharti: it is necessary
suka: weave
winchi: winch(es)

Key to Exercises

Answers to Practice Exercise A

1. *Sitamkopesha mpaka akulipe.*
2. *Alinilazimisha nimpatie bima ya maisha.*
3. *Simama na ufikiri.*
4. *Inabidi niwapelekee wakwe zangu zawadi.*
5. *Nilimpigia simu ili aje.*
6. *Niangalie sinema gani?*
7. *Mke wake alitaka awe mwanasheria.*
8. *Nipige mswaki kabla ya kulala!*
9. *Mwambie anifumie glavu.*
10. *Nibaki nisibaki?*
11. *Walimfukuza mwizi wasimkamate.*
12. *Jaji alinionya nisiendeshe nimelewa.*

Chapter 38

Diminutive, Augmentative and Collective Nouns

Some Swahili nouns can express Diminutives, Augmentatives and Collectives by changing prefixes. Diminutives take *ki-* and *vi-* prefixes from the KI-/VI- Noun Class for singular and plural nouns respectively. Augmentatives take *ji-* and *ma-* prefixes from the JI-/MA- Noun Class for singular and plural nouns respectively. Collectives only take the *ma-* prefix from the JI-/MA- Noun Class for plural nouns. Nouns denoting Diminutives and Augmentatives can come from any Noun Class except the PA- and KU- classes and abstract nouns from the U- class. When some nouns are changed into Diminutives or Augmentatives, they sometimes convey a pleasant or a derogatory connotation. Nouns denoting Collectives come from only the U- and N- classes. It is not easy to determine which nouns can or cannot be made Diminutive, Augmentative or Collective.

Section A: Diminutive Nouns

As pointed out in the Introduction, only some nouns can be made into Diminutives to express smallness. When a noun becomes a Diminutive, it belongs to the KI-/VI- class, and follows the agreement rules for this class even if the nouns involved belong to animate things such people, animals or insects. For example:

Regular – Diminutive Sing.
   tunda langu (my orange) – *kitunda changu* (my little orange)
   mbuzi huyu (this goat) – *kibuzi hiki* (this small goat)

Nouns can be made into Diminutive form using the following rules:

1. After removing the prefix, if the remaining part of the noun has a disyllabic or polysyllabic root stem, the *ki-* prefix is added for singular nouns and *vi-* prefix for plural nouns.

   Regular – Diminutive Sing. – Diminutive Pl.
   mtoto (child) – *kitoto* (small child) – *vitoto* (small children)
   msichana (girl) – *kisichana* (small girl) – *visichana* (small girls)
   mkono (hand) – *kikono* (small hand) – *vikono* (small hands)

For nouns with disyllabic or polysyllabic root stems which do not have a prefix, the *ki-* prefix is simply added to singular nouns and *vi-* prefix to plural nouns.

   Regular – Diminutive Sing. – Diminutive Pl.
   sakafu (floor) – *kisakafu* (small floor) – *visakafu* (small floors)
   tunda (fruit) – *kitunda* (small fruit) – *vitunda* (small fruits)
   inzi (fly) – *kiinzi* (small fly) – *viinzi* (small flies)

2. After removing the prefix, if the remaining part of the noun has a Monosyllabic root stem, the *ki-* prefix is added for singular nouns and *vi-* prefix for plural nouns followed by the *-ji-* infix.

   Regular – Diminutive Sing. – Diminutive Pl.
   mtu (person) – *kijitu* (small person) – *vijitu* (small persons)
   mto (river) – *kijito* (stream) – *vijito* (streams)
   mti (tree) – *kijiti* (small tree/stick) – *vijiti* (small trees/sticks)

Note that in the last example, *kijiti* can be a small tree or a stick depending on the context.

After removing the prefix, if the remaining part of the noun begins with a vowel, the *ki-* prefix is added for singular nouns and *vi-* prefix for plural nouns followed by the *-j-* infix.

   Regular – Diminutive Sing. – Diminutive Pl.
   mwizi (thief) – *kijizi* (petty thief) – *vijizi* (petty thieves)
   mwiko (serving spoon) – *kijiko* (spoon) – *vijiko* (spoons)

3. Nouns that already belong to the KI-/VI- Class and start with the prefix *ki-* are made diminutive by the insertion of *-ji-* between the prefix *ki-* and the rest of the noun.

    Regular – Diminutive Sing. – Diminutive Pl.
    kikapu (basket) – *kijikapu* (small basket) – *vijikapu* (small baskets)
    kidonda (wound) – *kijidonda* (small wound) – *vijidonda* (small wounds)
    kisu (knife) – *kijisu* (small knife) – *vijisu* (small knives)
    kitanda (bed) – *kijitanda* (small bed) – *vijitanda* (small beds)

This rule does not apply to KI-/VI- Class nouns which start with the prefix *ch-/vy-* as they are treated as regular disyllabic or polysyllabic nouns with no prefixes.

    Regular – Diminutive Sing. – Diminutive Pl.
    cheti (chit) – *kicheti* (small chit) – *vicheti* (small chits)

Also note that sometimes the prefix *ka-* is used instead of the *ki-* prefix. For example

    Katoto kazuri – A small nice child

4. As mentioned previously, once a noun becomes diminutive, it can also have a derogatory or pleasant connotation. For example:

    Kisichana kinasikia muziki. – The immature girl is listening to music.
    Kibuzi kimechinjwa. – The small pathetic goat has been slaughtered.

5. Some Diminutives can take the infix *-ji-* to add an extra level of smallness as well as show a derogatory or pleasant connotation. For example:

    Kijiduka hiki hakina faida. – This insignificant shop does not make a profit.
    Kijiua kinanukia. – The delicate flower smells good.

Also, there are some nouns that can be made into Diminutives without following the rules above. Some of these exceptions nouns are listed below.

Regular – Diminutive Sing. – Diminutive Pl.
ndege (bird) – *kidege* (small bird) – *videge* (small birds)
nyumba (house) – *kijumba* (small house) – *vijumba* (small houses)
nyoka (snake) – *kijoka* (small snake) – *vijoka* (small snakes)
mbwa (dog) – *kijibwa* (small dog) – *vijibwa* (small dogs)

Practice Exercise A

Change the nouns below into Diminutives

1. *koroboi*
2. *mdomo*
3. *chenezo*
4. *kitabu*
5. *mlima*

Section B: Augmentative Nouns

As pointed out in the Introduction, only some nouns can be made into Augmentatives to express largeness or character. When a noun becomes an Augmentative, it belongs to the JI-/MA- class, and follows the agreement rules for this class even if the nouns involved belong to animate things such people, animals or insects.

Regular – Augmentative Sing.
kisu changu (my knife) – *jisu langu* (my large knife)
mbuzi huyu (this goat) – *buzi hili* (this large goat)

Nouns can be made into Augmentative form using the following rules:

1. For nouns that are not in the JI-/MA- class, if after removing the prefix, the remaining part of the noun has a disyllabic or polysyllabic root stem, the remaining part of the noun stands alone as the augmented noun in the singular form. The *ma-* prefix is added to the already augmented singular noun to make the augmented plural noun.

    Regular – Augmentative Sing. – Augmentative Pl.
    kikapu (basket) – *kapu* (large basket) – *makapu* (large baskets)
    kidonda (wound) – *donda* (large wound) – *madonda* (large wounds)
    mtoto (child) – *toto* (large child) – *matoto* (large children)

For nouns with disyllabic or polysyllabic root stems which do not have a prefix, the *ma-* prefix is added to the root stem.

> Regular – Augmentative Sing. – Augmentative Pl.
> *paka* (cat) – *paka* (large cat) – *mapaka* (large cats)
> *kompyuta* (computer) – *kompyuta* (large computer) – *makompyuta* (large computers)

2. For nouns that are not in the JI-/MA- class, if after removing the prefix, the remaining part of the noun has a Monosyllabic root stem or begins with a vowel, the *j-* or *ji-* prefix is added for singular nouns. The *ma-* prefix is added to the already augmented singular noun to make the augmented plural noun.

> Regular – Augmentative Sing. – Augmentative Pl.
> *mtu* (person) – *jitu* (giant) – *majitu* (giants)
> *mto* (river) – *jito* (large river) – *majito* (large rivers)
> *mwiko* (serving spoon) –*jiko* (large spoon) – *majiko* (large spoons)
> *chungu* (pot) – *jungu* (large pot) – *majungu* (large pots)

3. Nouns that already belong to the JI-/MA- Class cannot be made into augmentatives by using any prefixes or infixes. Their largeness is instead emphasized by the use of adjectives.

> *tunda* (fruit) – *tunda kubwa* (large fruit) – *matunda makubwa* (large fruits)
> *jicho* (eye) – *jicho kubwa* (large eye) – *macho makubwa* (large eyes)

4. As mentioned previously, some nouns take the prefix JI-/MA- to emphasize largeness as well as show a derogatory or pleasant connotation. For example:

> *Jana linasikia muziki.* – The ill-mannered youth is listening to music.
> *Jizi liliiba dola milioni mbili.* – The experienced thief stole two million dollars.

Also, there are some nouns that can be made into Augmentatives without following the rules above. Some of these exceptions nouns are listed below.

Regular – Augmentative Sing. – Augmentative Pl.
ndege (bird) – *dege* (large bird) – *madege* (large birds)
nyumba (house) – *jumba* (large house) – *majumba* (large houses)
nyoka (snake) – *joka* (large snake) – *majoka* (large snakes)

Practice Exercise B

Translate the sentences below into English.

6. *Tafadhali niletee pande la keki.*
7. *Msichana mdogo alibeba maji katika majungu.*
8. *Tulipiga magoma mpaka mikono yetu ilitoka damu.*
9. *Familia ile ilihamia jijini kuwapatia watoto wao elimu bora.*
10. *Kaka yake huvaa masuruali.*

Section C: Collective Nouns

Only some nouns from the U- and N- classes can be made into collectives to represent a collection of living species, objects or concepts. Once a singular noun from the U- or N- class is changed into its plural, it is then made into a collective by adding the prefix *ma-* from the JI-/MA- Noun Class. Since both Augmentatives and Collectives use the prefix *ma-*, the context of the sentence is used to determine whether the noun is an Augmentative or a Collective. Once a noun is collectivized, it follows the agreement rules for the JI-/MA- Noun Class even if the nouns involved belong to animate things such people, animals or insects.

Singular – Plural – Collective
samaki (fish) – *samaki* (fishes) – *masamaki* (fishes in general)
rafiki (friend) – *rafiki* (friends) – *marafiki* (friends in general)
simba (lion) – *simba* (lions) – *masimba* (lions in general)
babu (grandfather) – *babu* (grandfathers) – *mababu* (grandfathers in general)
mama (mother) – *mama* (mothers) – *mamama* (mothers in general)
mia (hundred) – *mia* (hundreds) – *mamia* (hundreds in general)
wukuta (wall) – *kuta* (walls) – *makuta* (walls in general)

Practice Exercise C

Change the sentences below into Collectives.

11. *Twiga anamwogopa simba yule.*
12. *Alishona shuka kwa kutumia uzi wa rangi njano.*
13. *Ng'ombe alisafirishwa kutoka Dodoma.*
14. *Alinunua nguo za kazi kutoka duka la mitumba.*
15. *Bwana Ali anamiliki supamaketi karibu na mlima wa Kilimanjaro.*

New Vocabulary

chenezo/vy-: measure(s)
chinja: slaughter
elimu: education, knowledge
jitu/ma-: giant(s)
kidomo/vi-: small mouth(s) (adj. talkative)
kidonda/vi-: wound(s)
kijitabu/vi-: small book(s), pamphlet(s)
kijito/vi-: stream(s)
koroboi: paraffin lamp(s)
mdomo/mi-: mouth(s)
mtumba/mi-: bundle(s) of clothes, usually second hand from abroad
ogopa: be afraid
shuka: sheet(s)
supamaketi: supermarket(s)
suruali: trouser(s)

Key to Exercises

Answers to Practice Exercise A

1. *kikoroboi*
2. *kidomo*
3. *kichenezo*
4. *kijitabu*
5. *kilima*

Answers to Practice Exercise B

6. Please bring me a large piece of cake.
7. The little girl carried water in big pots.
8. We played the large drums until our hands bled.
9. That family moved to a large city to get their children a better education.
10. His/Her brother wears (habitually, HU- habitual tense) large trousers.

Answers to Practice Exercise C

11. *Matwiga yanayaogopa masimba yale.*
12. *Alishona mashuka kwa kutumia manyuzi ya rangi njano.*
13. *Mang'ombe yalisafirishwa kutoka Dodoma.*
14. *Alinunua manguo ya kazi kutoka duka la mitumba.*
15. *Bwana Ali anamiliki masupamaketi karibu na mlima wa Kilimanjaro.*

Chapter 39

Direct and Reported Speech

When someone wishes to give information about what someone else has said, one can use either Direct Speech (*Usemi Halisi*) or Reported Speech (*Usemi wa Taarifa*). Direct Speech is easy to grasp while Reported Speech will be dealt with in detail because it requires additional rules.

Section A: Direct Speech

Direct Speech is a form of speech in which the actual words of the original speaker are quoted. In writing, Direct Speech is indicated by the use of quotation marks. For example:

> *"Gari hili ni bluu," Hawa alisema.*
> "This car is blue," Hawa said.
> *"Mifuko mitano ya viazi iliibiwa," mwenye duka alisema.*
> "Five bags of potatoes were stolen," the shopkeeper said.
> *"Unakwenda shuleni?" mwalimu aliuliza.*
> "Are you going to school?" the teacher asked.

Section B: Reported Speech

Reported Speech (*Usemi wa Taarifa*) is a form of speech in which the actual words of the original speaker are paraphrased. The order of the words and the grammar of the original sentence are changed without changing the message of the original speaker. The changes that occur affect the following:

Changing Personal Subject Prefixes
Changing Tenses
Adding Reported Speech Indicators
Changing Verbs
Changing Demonstratives
Changing Adverbs of Time
Changing Possessive Suffixes and Personal Pronouns
Changing Imperatives

Before we continue, it is important to note that when using spoken English, it is sometimes difficult to know whether a sentence is in Direct or Reported Speech. This happens when there is not enough contextual information about that sentence, leading to ambiguity. For example:

Natasha said, I like to eat.

When the above sentence is spoken, the hearer of that sentence could have interpreted the pronoun "I" as referring to the speaker or to Natasha. This is because the above sentence could have been considered as either a Direct or Reported Speech. If it was a known that the sentence above is in Direct Speech, then the "I" in the sentence must be Natasha referring to herself. However, if it was a known that the sentence above is in Reported Speech, then the "I" in the sentence must refer to the speaker.

In order to avoid ambiguity, English speakers prefer to use Reported Speech. The original sentence would be reported as:

Natasha said she herself likes to eat.

In Swahili, both the Direct Speech and Reported Speech can be used when speaking as it does not cause ambiguity. For example,

Natasha alisema, ninapenda kula.
Natasha said, I (the speaker) like to eat.

When the sentence above is spoken, the hearer is sure that the Personal Subject Prefix *ni-* can only refer to the speaker. If we wanted to refer to Natasha being the one who likes to eat, we would use the Personal Subject Prefix *a-* and the sentence would be:

Natasha alisema, anapenda kula.
Natasha said that, she likes to eat.

The use of Subject Prefixes in Swahili eliminates the type of ambiguity that occurs in English.

Changing Personal Subject Prefixes

When Direct Speech is changed to Reported Speech any singular Personal Subject Prefix could remain the same or be changed to either of the other two singular Personal Subject Prefixes. For example, the Personal Subject Prefix *ni-* in Direct Speech could remain as *ni-* or become *u-* or *a-* in Reported Speech depending on who the reporter and/or hearer is. Here are a few examples that will illustrate this point.

If John was talking about Anna and said in Direct Speech, "She is cooking," then, it can be reported in the following ways.

If Anna is reporting what John said about her to a 3rd party, she would say:
He said I am cooking.
Alisema kwamba ninapika.

If Anna is reporting back to John what John said about her, she would say:
You said I am cooking.
Ulisema kwamba ninapika.

If John reports what John said about Anna to another person, he/she would say:
I said that she is cooking.
Nilisema kwamba anapika.

If John reports back to Anna what he said about her, he would say:
I said you are cooking.
Nilisema kwamba unapika.

If a 3rd party reports to Anna what John said about her, he/she would say:
He said that you are cooking.
Alisema kwamba unapika.

If a 3rd party reports to John what he said about Anna, he/she would say:
　　You said that she is cooking.
　　Ulisema kwamba anapika.

If a 3rd party reports to another person about what John said about Anna, he/she would say:
　　He said that she is cooking.
　　Alisema kwamba anapika.

As with the singular Personal Subject Prefixes above, the plural Personal Subject Prefixes follow the same format. When Direct Speech is changed to Reported Speech any plural Personal Subject Prefix could remain the same or be changed to either of the other two plural Personal Subject Prefixes. For example, the Personal Subject Prefix *tu-* in Direct Speech could remain as *tu-* or become *m-* or *wa-* in Reported Speech depending on who the reporter and/or hearer is.

Changing Tenses

When Direct Speech is changed to Reported Speech, it is important to know how much time has elapsed since the time of the original utterance. The tense does not change when, at the time of reporting, the utterance refers to an action that is still taking place or refers to an action that is still expected to take place in the future. However, tense changes must occur when the utterance refers to an action that took place or was supposed to take place in the past or an action that was expected to take place in the future and at the time of reporting the future has passed. When Direct Speech is changed to Reported Speech and a tense change occurs, it is referred to as "backshifting." If a Direct Speech sentence has a negative tense then backshifting occurs to the corresponding negative tense. Table 39.1 shows the tense changes from Direct to Reported Speech.

TABLE 39.1
Tense Changes with Direct to Report Speech

Direct Speech	Action still pending	Reported Speech
-na-	*-na-*	*-li-*
a-	*a-*	*-li-*
hu-	*hu-*	*-li-*
-ta-	*-ta-*	*-nge-*
-li-		*-likuwa -me-*
-me-		*-likuwa -mesha-*
-nge-	*-nge-*	*-ngali-*
-ngali-		*-ngali-*
-ki- (conditional)	*-ki-*	*-nge-*
-ki- (present participle)	*-ki-*	*-ki-*
-mesha-		*-likuwa -mesha-*

Note that when a sentence using the *hu-* tense marker is not proceded by a noun or a personal pronoun, it cannot be turned into Reported Speech. This is because it is unclear who or what the subject of the sentence is.

Reported Speech Indicators

When Direct Speech is changed to Reported Speech, speech indicators are used to introduce the original words that are being reported. There are different types of speech indicators depending on the type of sentence.

For declarative sentences, the most frequently used speech indicators are *kuwa*, *kwamba*, *ya kwamba* and *kama* which are all equivalent to "that" as used in Reported Speech in English. In addition, *eti* and *sijui* are used as speech indicators when the reporter doubts the intention of the original speaker. Furthermore, *eti* shows surprise as well as doubt as to the intention of the original speaker.

For interrogative sentences, the speech indicators used depend on the type of interrogatives. For YES/NO questions, there is only one speech indicator which is *kama* and is equivalent to "that" as used in

Reported Speech in English. For WH questions (questions using who, what, when, where, why and how), the speech indicator used depends on what the question is being asked. For example, the indicator will be *kwa nini* if the question is asking about the reason, *wapi* if the question is asking about the place, *vipi* if the question is asking about the manner in which something was done, *lini* if the question is asking about the time etc. WH questions can also use a relative pronoun as a speech indicator (See Chapter 28 for more information on Relatives Infixes).

Verbs in Reported Speech

When Direct Speech is changed to Reported Speech, two categories of verbs are used to introduce Reported Speech in declarative sentences. The first category of verbs simply states facts and does not necessarily require speech indicators. Examples of such verbs are *ambia* (tell), *sema* (speak) and *shauri* (advise). The second category of verbs provides explanation and elaboration and requires speech indicators. Examples of such verbs are *eleza* (explain) and *fahamisha* (inform).

When Direct Speech is changed to Reported Speech, interrogative sentences require the verb *uliza* (ask) or the verb phrase *taka kujua* (want to know) which must be used with the interrogative speech indicators.

Now that you have been taught Personal Subject Prefixes, Tenses, Reported Speech Indicators and verbs in Reported Speech, below are a few examples of Direct Speech and Reported Speech sentences.

> *"Ninasoma kitabu,"* baba alisema. – "I am reading a book," father said.
>
> *Baba alisema kwamba alisoma kitabu.* (if reference is not made to the hearer and reporter) – Father said that he read a book.
>
> *"Tulinunua peremende,"* watoto walimwambia mwalimu. – "We bought peppermint," the children told the teacher.
>
> *Watoto walimwambia mwalimu kwamba walikuwa wamenunua peremende.* (if reference is not made to the hearer and reporter) – The children told the teacher that they had bought peppermint.
>
> *"Utajitolea kujenga shule?"* waziri aliuliza. – "Will you volunteer to build the school?" the minister asked.
>
> *Waziri alitaka kujua kama ningejitolea kujenga shule.* (if reference made to the reporter) – The minister asked if I would volunteer to build the school.

"Mnakwenda Dar es Salaam lini?" wakala wa ndege aliuliza. – "When have you (pl.) gone to Dar es Salaam?" the airline ticket agent asked.

Wakala wa ndege alitaka kujua lini tulikwenda Dar es Salaam. (if reference made to the reporter) – The airline ticket agent wanted to know when we had gone to Dar es Salaam.

"Umeshamaliza kula chungwa?" mpokezi alimwuliza mkurugenzi. – "Have you already eaten the orange?" the receptionist asked the director.

Mpokezi alitaka kujua kama mkurugenzi alikuwa ameshamaliza kula chungwa. (if reference is not made to the hearer and reporter) – The receptionist wanted to know if the director had already eaten the orange.

"Nikiandika barua pepe nitapata jibu," mtalii alisema. – "If I write an email I will get an answer," the tourist said.

Mtalii alisema kwamba angeandika barua pepe angepata jibu. (if reference is not made to the hearer and reporter) – The tourist said that if he/she wrote an email he/she would get an answer.

"Ungesoma kwa bidii, ungefaulu," mshauri aliniambia. – "If you were to study with diligence, you would succeed," the counsellor told me.

Mshauri aliniambia kwamba ningalisoma kwa bidii, ningalifaulu. (if reference is made to the reporter) – The counsellor told me that if I would have studied with diligence, I would have succeeded.

"Ungalisoma kwa bidii, ungalifaulu," mshauri aliniambia. – "If you would have studied with diligence, you would have succeeded," the counsellor told me.

Mshauri aliniambia kwamba ningalisoma kwa bidii, ningalifaulu. (if reference is made to the reporter) – The counsellor told me that if I would have studied with diligence, I would have succeeded.

Practice Exercise A

Change the following sentences from Direct to Reported Speech and assume backshifting occurs.

1. *"Juma anacheza katika kiwanja cha michezo," Thomas alisema.* (if reference is not made to the hearer and reporter)
2. *"Nilitaka kujitolea hospitalini," msimamizi alieleza.* (if reference is not made to the hearer and reporter)

3. *"Tumekubali kuchanga pesa za kutengeneza mabomba, "mafundi bomba walifahamisha.* (if reference is not made to the hearer and reporter)
4. *"Mtaondoka lini kwenda Zimbabwe?" mama aliuliza.* (if reference is made to the reporter)
5. *"Ningekuwa rubani, ningesafiri dunia nzima, " mwombaji alinong'ona.* (if reference is not made to the hearer and reporter)

Changing Demonstratives

When Direct Speech is changed to Reported Speech, the following changes need to be made when demonstratives are used. (See Chapter 14 for Demonstratives)

- Demonstrative of Proximity becomes Demonstrative of Distance.
- Demonstrative of Reference for Proximity becomes Demonstrative of Reference for Distance.
- Demonstrative of Distance and Demonstrative of Reference for Distance remain unchanged.

Below are a few examples:

"Jino hili ni imara, " daktari wa meno alisema. – "This tooth is firm," the dentist said.
Daktari wa meno alisema jino lile lilikuwa imara. – The dentist said that tooth was firm.

"Jino hilo ni imara, " daktari wa meno alisema. – "This (referred to) tooth is firm," the dentist said.
Daktari wa meno alisema lile jino lilikuwa imara. – The dentist said that (referred to) tooth was firm.

Practice Exercise B

Change the following sentences from Direct to Reported Speech assuming that reference is not made to the hearer and reporter and backshifting occurs.

6. *"Mtu huyu anatengeneza milango ya gereji, " mwenyenyumba alisema.*

7. *"Mahali hapo patapendeza sana,"* mjenzi alieleza.
8. *"Je, simba yule amelala?"* meneja wa zu aliuliza.
9. *"Kitabu kile kimechanika,"* mkutubi aliwaambia wasomaji.
10. *"Ningalikula lile chungwa tamu ningalifurahi,"* mhakiki wa chakula alieleza.

Changing Adverbs of Time

When Direct Speech is changed to Reported Speech, it is important to know how much time has elapsed since the time of the original utterance. The adverb of time changes only when backshifting is required otherwise the same adverb of time used in Direct Speech is used in Reported Speech. Mentioned below are changes to adverbs of time when backshifting occurs, and then some examples.

leo – today
siku ile – that day
sasa – now
wakati ule – that time
jana – yesterday
siku iliyopita – the day that passed
kesho – tomorrow
siku iliyofuata – the day that followed
sasa hivi – right now
wakati ule ule – at that exact time.

"Mwanaanga atatua katika mwezi leo," msemaji alisema. – "The astronaut will land on the moon today," the spokesperson said.

Msemaji alisema mwanaanga angetua katika mwezi siku ile. – The spokesperson said the astronaut would land on the moon on that day.

"Tutaondoka kwenda sokoni sasa hivi," nyanya alisema. – "We shall leave for the market right now," grandmother said.

Nyanya alisema kwamba wataondoka kwenda sokoni sasa hivi. – Grandmother said that they would leave for the market right now.

Note that in the second example, backshifting did not occur, hence the tense and the adverb of time did not change.

Practice Exercise C

Change the following sentences from Direct to Reported Speech assuming that reference is not made to the hearer and reporter and backshifting occurs.

11. *"Mzungu yule atacheza mpira wa miguu leo," refa alitangaza.*
12. *"Mbwa alilala usiku mzima," mganga wa wanyama alieleza.*
13. *"Vikapu viwili vimeibiwa jana," polisi alisema.*
14. *"Ninataka aiskrimu sasa hivi," Hawa alisema.*
15. *"Bilauri ya maji ingemwagika sasa hivi," mpishi alisema.*

Section D: Possessive Suffixes and Personal Pronouns

When Direct Speech is changed to Reported Speech any singular Possessive Suffix could remain the same or be changed to either of the other two singular Possessive Suffixes. For example, the Possessive Suffix -*angu* in Direct Speech could remain as -*angu* or become -*ako* or -*ake* in Reported Speech depending on who the reporter and/or hearer is. Here are a few examples that will illustrate this point.

If John was talking about Anna and said in Direct Speech, "She is cooking her food.," then, it can be reported in the following ways.

If Anna is reporting what John said about her to a 3rd party, she would say:

He said I am cooking my food.
Alisema kwamba ninapika chakula changu.

If Anna is reporting back to John what John said about her, she would say:

You said I am cooking my food.
Ulisema kwamba ninapika chakula changu.

If John reports what John said about Anna to another person, he/she would say:

I said that she is cooking her food.
Nilisema kwamba anapika chakula chake.

If John reports back to Anna what he said about her, he would say:
    I said you are cooking your food.
    Nilisema kwamba unapika chakula chako.

If a 3rd party reports to Anna what John said about her, he/she would say:
    He said that you are cooking your food.
    Alisema kwamba unapika chakula chako.

If a 3rd party reports to John what he said about Anna, he/she would say:
    You said that she is cooking her food.
    Ulisema kwamba anapika chakula chake.

If a 3rd party reports to another person about what John said about Anna, he/she would say:
    He said that she is cooking her food.
    Alisema kwamba anapika chakula chake.

As with the singular Possessive Suffixes above, the plural Possessive Suffixes follow the same format. When Direct Speech is changed to Reported Speech any plural Possessive Suffix could remain the same or be changed to either of the other two plural Possessive Suffixes. For example, the Possessive Suffix *-etu* in Direct Speech could remain as -*etu* or become *-enu* or *-ao* in Reported Speech depending on who the reporter and/or hearer is.

Note that when the *-a* of Association is used as a possessive, no changes occur when Direct Speech becomes Reported Speech.

When Direct Speech is changed to Reported Speech any singular Personal Pronoun could remain the same or be changed to either of the other two singular Personal Pronouns. For example, the Personal Pronoun *mimi* in Direct Speech could remain as *mimi* or become *wewe* or *yeye* in Reported Speech depending on who the reporter and/or hearer is. Here are a few examples that will illustrate this point.

If John was talking about Anna and said in Direct Speech, "She is cooking her food.," then, it can be reported in the following ways.

If Anna is reporting what John said about her to a 3rd party, she would say:

He said I am cooking my food.

Alisema kwamba mimi ninapika chakula changu.

If Anna is reporting back to John what John said about her, she would say:

You said I am cooking my food.

Ulisema kwamba mimi ninapika chakula changu.

If John reports what John said about Anna to another person, he/she would say:

I said that she is cooking her food.

Nilisema kwamba yeye anapika chakula chake.

If John reports back to Anna what he said about her, he would say:

I said you are cooking your food.

Nilisema kwamba wewe unapika chakula chako.

If a 3rd party reports to Anna what John said about her, he/she would say:

He said that you are cooking your food.

Alisema kwamba wewe unapika chakula chako.

If a 3rd party reports to John what he said about Anna, he/she would say:

You said that she is cooking her food.

Ulisema kwamba yeye anapika chakula chake.

If a 3rd party reports to another person about what John said about Anna, he/she would say:

He said that she is cooking her food.

Alisema kwamba yeye anapika chakula chake.

As with the singular Personal Pronouns above, the plural Personal Pronouns follow the same format. When Direct Speech is changed to Reported Speech any plural Personal Pronoun could remain the same or be changed to either of the other two plural Personal Pronouns. For example, the Personal Pronoun *sisi* in Direct Speech could remain as *sisi* or become *ninyi* or *wao* in Reported Speech depending on who the reporter and/or hearer is.

Below are a few additional examples:

"Mimi nitakwenda kujenga kibanda kijijini," *mwuza gazeti alisema.*
- "I will go to build a kiosk in the village," the newspaper vendor said.

Mwuza gazeti alisema yeye angekwenda kujenga kibanda kijijini. - The newspaper vendor said that he would go to build a kiosk in the village.

"Sisi ni wafanyakazi wa kampuni hii," *mwakilishi wa wafanyakazi alisema.* - "We are employees of this company," the workers' representative said.

Mwakilishi wa wafanyakazi alisema kwamba wao walikuwa wafanyakazi wa kampuni ile. - The workers' representative said that they were workers for that company.

"Bangili yangu imepotea," *bibi harusi alinifahamisha.* - "My bangle is lost," the bride informed me.

Bibi harusi alinifahamisha kwamba bangili yake ilikuwa imeshapotea. - The bride informed me that her bangle was already lost.

"Magari yangu yamefika kutoka Dubai," *mfanyabiashara alisema.* - "My vehicles have arrived from Dubai," the businessperson said.

Mfanyabiashara alisema magari yake yalikuwa yameshafika kutoka Dubai. - The businessperson said that his vehicles had already arrived from Dubai.

Practice Exercise D

Change the following sentences from Direct to Reported Speech assuming backshifting occurs.

16. *"Sisi tumewadekeza watoto wetu kwa kuwapa kila wanachotaka,"* *mzazi alisema.* (if reference is made to the original speaker and the hearer).

17. *"Je, wewe ni mwalimu wa historia?"* *mgeni aliuliza.* (if reference is made to the reporter)

18. *"Nafasi ya ofisi ya Rais inahitaji kupangwa,"* *mnadhifishaji alilalamika mbele ya mwenzake.* (if reference not made to the hearer or reporter).

19. *"Simu yangu ya mkononi haifanyi kazi kwa sababu haina betri,"*
    mfamasi alifahamisha. (if reference not made to the hearer or
    reporter).
20. *"Shangazi yangu atarasimu viatu vya wasanii,"* Krystal alisema.
    (if reference not made to the hearer or reporter).

Imperatives in Reported Speech

When Direct Speech is an abrupt imperative, it is changed to a polite
imperative in the Reported Speech (see Chapter 30). In addition, in Reported Speech, the prefix *a-* is used for 2nd person singular and the prefix
wa- for 2nd person plural. Below are a few examples:

"Nenda sokoni!" mfanyakazi aliamriwa. – "Go to the market!" the
    worker was ordered.
Mfanyakazi aliamriwa aende sokoni. (if reference not made to the
    hearer or reporter) – The worker was ordered to go to the mar-
    ket.
"Jibuni maswali!" polisi aliwaamuru wezi. – "Answer the questions!"
    police ordered the thieves.
Tuliamriwa na polisi tujibu maswali. (if reference made to the re-
    porter) – We were ordered by the police to answer the questions.

Note that although the Reported sentences use the polite imperatives in
Swahili, they still carry the meaning of an abrupt order in English.

Practice Exercise E

Translate into Swahili and change to Reported Speech assuming
backshifting occurs.

21. "Let me solve the problem!" the supervisor ordered the techni-
    cians. (if reference not made to the hearer or reporter).
22. "Do not cut down the trees without the proper permit!" the town
    official warned the residents. (if reference not made to the hearer
    or reporter).

New Vocabulary

a kufaa: proper, suitable
aiskrimu: ice cream(s)
bangili: bangle(s), bracelet(s)
bibi harusi: bride(s)
bluu: blue
changa: contribute
eleza: explain
eti: indicates doubt about a following statement
gereji: garage(s)
idhini: permit(s)
-jitolea: volunteer
mhakiki/wa-: critic(s)
mjenzi/wa-: builder(s)
mnadhifishaji/wa-: organizer(s)
msanii/wa-: artist(s)
msemaji/wa-: spokesperson(s)
msimamizi/wa-: supervisor(s)
msomaji/wa-: reader(s)
mwakilishi/wa-: representative(s)
mwanaanga/wanaanga: astronaut(s)
mwuza/wa-: seller, vendor
peremende: peppermint(s)
rasimu: plan, design
ruhusu: permit, allow
siku iliyofuata: the day that followed
siku iliyopita: the day that passed
Usemi Halisi: Direct Speech
Usemi wa Taarifa: Reported Speech
wakala/ma-: agent(s)
wakati ule ule: at that exact time
ya kwamba: that

Key to Exercises

Answers to Practice Exercise A

1. *Thomas alisema kwamba Juma alicheza katika kiwanja cha michezo.*
2. *Msimamizi alieleza kwamba alikuwa ametaka kujitolea hospitalini.*
3. *Mafundi bomba walifahamisha kuwa walikuwa wameshakubali kuchanga pesa za kutengeneza mabomba.*
4. *Mama alitaka kujua tungeondoka lini kwenda Zimbabwe.*
5. *Mwombaji alinong'ona angalikuwa rubani, angalisafiri dunia nzima.*

Answers to Practice Exercise B

6. *Mwenyenyumba alisema mtu yule alitengeneza milango ya gereji.*
7. *Mjenzi alieleza kwamba pale mahali pangependeza sana.*
8. *Meneja wa zu alitaka kujua kama simba yule alikuwa ameshalala.*
9. *Mkutubi aliwaambia wasomaji kwamba kitabu kile kilikuwa kimeshachanika.*
10. *Mhakiki wa chakula alieleza kwamba angalikula lile chungwa tamu angalifurahi.*

Answers to Practice Exercise C

11. *Refa alitangaza kuwa Mzungu yule angecheza mpira wa miguu siku ile.*
12. *Mganga wa wanyama alieleza kwamba mbwa alikuwa amelala usiku mzima.*
13. *Polisi alisema vikapu viwili vilikuwa vimeshaibiwa siku iliyopita.*
14. *Hawa alisema alitaka aiskrimu wakati ule ule.*
15. *Mpishi alisema bilauri ya maji ingalimwagika wakati ule ule.*

Answers to Practice Exercise D

16. *Mzazi alisema kwamba sisi tulikuwa tumeshawadekeza watoto wetu kwa kuwapa kila wanachotaka.*
17. *Mgeni alitaka kujua kama mimi nilikuwa mwalimu wa historia.*
18. *Mnadhifishaji alikuwa amelalamika mbele ya mwenzake kuwa nafasi ya ofisi ya Rais* ilihitaji kupangwa.

19. *Mfamasi alifahamisha kwamba simu yake ya mkononi haikufanya kazi kwa sababu haikuwa na betri.*
20. *Krystal alisema shangazi yake angerasimu viatu vya wasanii.*

Answers to Practice Exercise E

21. *Msimamizi aliwaamuru mafundisanifu kwamba wamruhusu atatue tatizo.*
22. *Ofisa wa mji aliwaonya wakazi kwamba wasikate miti bila idhini ya kufaa.*

Chapter 40

Swahili Proverbs

Proverbs are short sayings that generally express words of wisdom or commonly held ideas. Proverbs exist in all spoken languages and originate from oral tradition. In modern times, Swahili proverbs are not only used orally, they are also written on Kanga. Often some proverbs are well known in different languages although variations do occur. Proverbs can be used in a variety of ways. They are used to teach and pass on knowledge to others, entertain and make conversations livelier as well gently point out mistakes and reinforce social behaviour. In addition, the knowledge of proverbs is usually a mark of someone who is familiar with the culture and language. In this chapter, we will introduce some well known Swahili proverbs as well as some proverbs from other languages which have been adopted into the Swahili language. Below are some common proverbs, their literal translations and their implied meaning(s). Of course, the meaning(s) of some proverbs have changed over time while the meaning of others has remained more or less the same.

Akiba haiozi.
> Savings do not decay.
> Savings (usually money) are never a bad thing. It is always good to save for the future.

Akili ni mali.
> Intelligence is wealth.
> If you use your intelligence, you will acquire wealth. If you have

wealth but do not use your intelligence, your wealth will soon diminish.

Akipenda chongo huita kengeza.
> Someone who loves a one-eyed person would call that condition only a squint.
> When you love someone, you overlook their faults. This is similar to the proverb "Beauty is in the eye of the beholder."

Aliye kando haangukiwi na mti.
> One who stands far away from a tree will not be hurt when the tree falls.
> We should stay away from dangerous people and situations to avoid getting hurt.

Amani haipatikani ila kwa ncha ya upanga.
> Peace cannot be obtained except by the point of a sword.
> It is by being prepared for war that you are most likely to be left in peace. This is similar to the proverb "If you want peace, prepare for war."

Anayeonja asali huchonga mzinga.
> Someone who tastes honey makes a beehive.
> One who has experienced success or luxury will strive to acquire more of it through hard work.

Asifuye mvua imemnyea.
> One who praises the rain does so because it has rained on him.
> One can only talk about what he/she has experienced.

Asiyefunzwa na mamaye, hufunzwa na ulimwengu.
> One who is not taught by his/her mother is taught by the world.
> If you are not taught at home, then you will learn it the hard way.

Asiyesikia la mkuu huvunjika guu.
> One who does not listen to the elderly suffers a broken leg.
> If you do not heed the counsel given by elders, you will experience difficulties.

Bandu! Bandu! huisha gogo.
> A log can be finished by chopping little pieces.
> If you continue to use up your resources little by little, eventually they will be depleted. Or it could be interpreted as if you do the work little by little eventually it will be done.

Bendera hufuata upepo.
> The flag follows the direction of the wind.
> This is directed towards opportunists who change sides depending on what they will gain.

Cha mlevi huliwa na mgema.
> What belongs to the drunkard is eaten by a wine maker.
> This proverb implies that addiction will cost you your wealth.

Chema chajiuza, kibaya chajitembeza.
> A good thing sells itself while a bad thing has to be advertised.
> If something is good, it will become well known. However, if something is bad, continuous effort(s) must be made to keep up its reputation.

Dalili ya mvua ni mawingu.
> The sign of the rain is clouds.
> If one knows where to look, there are always signs to indicate what is coming.

Damu nzito kuliko maji.
> Blood is heavier than water.
> People tend to favour family rather than people who are not related to them. This is similar to the proverb "Blood is thicker than water."

Dua la kuku halimpati mwewe.
> The curse of a hen will have no impact on an eagle.
> If less successful people complain about those who are successful, the complaints will not have an impact and will not lead to any change.

Haba na haba hujaza kibaba.
>Little by little fills the bucket.
>Great things are accomplished by small deeds.

Hapana siri ya watu wawili.
>There is no secret between two people.
>Once you have shared a secret with another person, it is no longer a
>   secret because chances are that more people will find out.

Haraka haraka haina baraka.
>Hurry hurry has no blessings.
>If you do things in a hurry, you are likely to make mistakes. This is
>   similar to the proverb "Haste makes waste."

Hasira hasara.
>Anger causes loss.
>If you do something when you are angry, you may regret it later.

Kidole kimoja hakivunji chawa.
>One finger cannot kill lice.
>It is possible to achieve greater success when you have the support of
>   others. This is similar to the proverb "United we stand, divided
>   we fall."

Kikulacho ki nguoni mwako.
>What eats you is in your clothes.
>Most of your problems are caused by yourself or someone close to
>   you.

Kipya kinyeme ingawa kidonda.
>A new thing attracts even though it is a wound.
>New things always attract even though they may have defects.

Kukopa ni arusi kulipa ni matanga.
>Borrowing is like a wedding , paying back is like mourning.
>Borrowing makes people happy but paying back makes people sad.

Kutoa ni moyo, usiseme utajiri.
> Giving depends on the heart don't say that it depends on wealth.
> Some people who are wealthy are not willing to help others while some who are poor are willing to help others.

Lisilokuwepo machoni na moyoni halipo.
> What is not seen by the eye is not in the heart.
> Those that are seen are remembered more than those who are not seen. This is similar to the proverb "Out of sight, out of mind."

Mafahali wawili hawakai zizi moja.
> Two bulls cannot reside in the same shed.
> If two people with strong personalities have to deal with each other, they will fight.

Maji yakimwagika hayazoleki.
> Spilled water cannot be gathered.
> It may be too late to salvage something which is already damaged. This is similar to the proverb "It is no use crying over spilt milk."

Maneno mazuri humtoa nyoka pangoni.
> Sweet words can make a snake come out of its cave.
> One is likely to convince someone by using sweet words. This is similar to the proverb "You catch more flies with honey than with vinegar."

Mbuzi wa maskini hazai.
> A poor man's goat does not reproduce.
> Poor people cannot overcome their poverty because you need wealth to generate more wealth.

Mchagua jembe si mkulima.
> One who chooses a hoe is not a farmer.
> If you are good at your job, then you can use any tool to accomplish your task and you do not have to be selective of which tool you need to get the job done.

Mchelea mwana kulia hulia yeye.

> He who is afraid to see a child cry will cry himself.
>
> If you don't discipline your child, they will cause you great sadness. This is similar to the proverb "Spare the rod, spoil the child."

Mchimba kisima huingia mwenyewe.

> The one who digs a well gets himself inside.
>
> If you are planning something with the intention of harming someone, you may be the one who ends up getting hurt instead.

Mgema akisifiwa sana tembo hulitia maji.

> If a wine-maker is praised too much, he/she is likely to dilute the wine.
>
> The proverb teaches people not to heap too much praise on people for the work they are doing. They might think too highly of themselves, and end up doing a poor job.

Mjumbe hauwawi.

> A messenger is not killed.
>
> It is no use blaming or hurting the one who brings the news. It is the one who caused the problem that should be blamed. This is similar to the proverb "Don't kill the messenger."

Mshika mawili, moja humpokonya.

> One who holds two things, one will slip away.
>
> One who is busy with too many things will not finish anything successfully.

Mstahimilivu hula mbivu.

> A patient person eats ripe fruits.
>
> Patience is always rewarded.

Mtaka cha uvunguni sharti ainame.

> One who wants to get something under the bed must bend.
>
> You must be willing to do what it takes to get what you want.

Mwenye njaa hana miiko.

> A hungry person does not have taboos.
>
> When you are in desperate need, you will do desperate things.

Mzigo wa mwenzio ni kanda la usufi.
> Your companion's luggage is a load of cotton wool.
> The burden is light when it is on another's shoulder.

Nazi mbovu haramu ya nzima.
> A rotten coconut is prohibited to the group of coconuts.
> One spoilt thing spoils other things around it. This is similar to the proverb "One bad apple spoils the bunch."

Shukrani ya punda ni mateke.
> The gratitude of a donkey is kicks.
> This is used to warn people to be cautious as there are some people who are selfish and will still treat you badly in return for a favour.

Tamaa mbele, mauti nyuma.
> Desire first, death afterwards.
> No one ever thinks of the dangers when concentrating on achieving a particular end.

Udugu wa nazi hukutania chunguni.
> The brotherhood of coconuts has its meeting in the cooking pot.
> This is used for people who do not cooperate until it is too late.

Usipoziba ufa utajenga ukuta.
> If you do not repair a crack you will build an entire wall.
> Fixing a small problem is easier than fixing a big one. This is similar to the proverb "A stitch in time saves nine."

Usitukane wagema na ulevi ungalipo.
> Don't insult wine makers while drinking is still there.
> Do not spoil a relationship which you may need later on.

Vita havina macho.
> War does not have eyes.
> War affects everyone.

Wapiganapo tembo wawili ziumiazo nyasi.
> When two elephants fight, it is the grass that gets trampled.
> When two powerful forces clash, others around them will be hurt.

Appendix

Important Charts

TABLE 41.1

Noun Class		Aff. Subject Prefix	Neg. Subject Prefix	Object Infix	Demonstrative Proximity	Demonstrative Distance	Demonstrative Reference
Sing. M-	1st person sing	ni-	si-	-ni-			
	2nd person sing	u-	hu-	-ku-			
	3rd person sing	a-	ha-	-m(w)-	huyu	yule	huyo
Pl. WA-	1st person pl	tu-	hatu-	-tu-			
	2nd person pl	m-	ham-	-wa-			
	3rd person pl	wa-	hawa-	-wa-	hawa	wale	hao
Sing.	M-	u-	hau-	-u-	huu	ule	huo
Pl.	MI-	i-	hai-	-i-	hii	ile	hiyo
Sing.	JI-	li-	hali-	-li-	hili	lile	hilo
Pl.	MA-	ya-	haya-	-ya-	haya	yale	hayo
Sing.	KI-	ki-	haki-	-ki-	hiki	kile	hicho
Pl.	VI-	vi-	havi-	-vi-	hivi	vile	hivyo
Sing.	N-	i-	hai-	-i-	hii	ile	hiyo
Pl.	N-	zi-	hazi-	-zi-	hizi	zile	hizo
Sing.	U-	u-	hau-	-u-	huu	ule	huo
Pl.	U-	zi-	hazi-	-zi-	hizi	zile	hizo
	PA-	pa-	hapa-	-pa-	hapa	pale	hapo
	KU-	ku-	haku-	-ku-	huku	kule	huko
	M-	m-	ham-	-m(w)-	humu	mle	humo
	KU-	ku-	kuto-	-ku-	huku	kule	huko

TABLE 41.2

Noun Class		Possessive Prefix	Relative Particle	-ote	-o -ote	-enye	Interrogative (which?)
Sing.	M- 1st person sing	w-	ye	wote		mwenye	
	2nd person sing	w-	ye	wote		mwenye	
	3rd person sing	w-	ye	wote	ye yote	mwenye	yupi
Pl.	WA- 1st person pl	w-	o	sote		wenye	
	2nd person pl	w-	o	nyote		wenye	
	3rd person pl	w-	o	wote	wo wote	wenye	wepi
Sing.	M-	w-	o	wote	wo wote	wenye	upi
Pl.	MI-	y-	yo	yote	yo yote	yenye	ipi
Sing.	JI-	l-	lo	lote	lo lote	lenye	lipi
Pl.	MA-	y-	yo	yote	yo yote	yenye	yapi
Sing.	KI-	ch-	cho	chote	cho chote	chenye	kipi
Pl.	VI-	vy-	vyo	vyote	vyo vyote	vyenye	vipi
Sing.	N-	y-	yo	yote	yo yote	yenye	ipi
Pl.	N-	z-	zo	zote	zo zote	zenye	zipi
Sing.	U-	w-	o	wote	wo wote	wenye	upi
Pl.	U-	z-	zo	zote	zo zote	zenye	zipi
	PA-	p-	po	pote	po pote	penye	papi
	KU-	kw-	ko	kote	ko kote	kwenye	kupi
	M-	mw-	mo	mote	mo mote	mwenye	mpi
	KU-	kw-	ko	kote	ko kote	kwenye	kupi

TABLE 41.3

Consonant and Vowel Stem Adjectives

	-zuri	-baya	-angavu	-ekundu	-ingine	-ororo	-unganifu
M-	mzuri	mbaya	mwangavu	mwekundu	mwingine	mwororo	munganifu
WA-	wazuri	wabaya	waangavu	wekundu	wengine	waororo	waunganifu
M-	mzuri	mbaya	mwangavu	mwekundu	mwingine	mwororo	munganifu
MI-	mizuri	mibaya	myangavu	myekundu	mingine	myororo	miunganifu
JI-	zuri	baya	langavu	jekundu	lingine	lororo	liunganifu
MA-	mazuri	mabaya	maangavu	mekundu	mengine	mororo	maunganifu
KI-	kizuri	kibaya	changavu	chekundu	kingine	chororo	kiunganifu
VI-	vizuri	vibaya	vyangavu	vyekundu	vingine	vyororo	viunganifu
N-	nzuri	mbaya	nyangavu	nyekundu	nyingine	nyororo	nyunganifu
N-	nzuri	mbaya	nyangavu	nyekundu	nyingine	nyororo	nyunganifu
U-	mzuri	mbaya	mwangavu	mwekundu	mwingine	mwororo	munganifu
U-	nzuri	mbaya	nyangavu	nyekundu	nyingine	nyororo	nyunganifu
PA-	pazuri	pabaya	pangavu	pekundu	pengine	pororo	punganifu
KU-	kuzuri	kubaya	kuangavu	kwekundu	kwingine	kororo	kuunganifu
M-	mzuri	mbaya	muangavu	mwekundu	mwingine	mororo	munganifu
KU-	kuzuri	kubaya	kuangavu	kwekundu	kwingine	kororo	kuunganifu

Swahili Vocabulary Dictionary

-a fahari kupita: stylish
-a kawaida: usual, average, normal
-a kike: female, feminine
-a kitoto: childish
-a kiume: male, masculine
-a kizamani: ancient
-a kizungu: European
-a kufaa: proper, suitable
-a kulia: right
-a kushoto: left
-a moto: hot
-a mwisho: last
-a plastiki: plastic
aa!: expresses surprise, joy, pain
abiria: passenger(s)
acha: stop, quit, permit
achari: pickled condiment(s)
achia: release
ada: fee(s)
adhuhuri: noon(s), midday(s)
adui/ma-: enemy(ies)
afadhali: better, it is better
afisa/ma-: officer(s), official(s)
Afrika: Africa
Afrika Kusini: South Africa
afya: health
agana: agree with
agiza: order

ah!: expresses grief
ahidi: promise
aina: kind(s), type(s) of
aisee!: expression used to attract attention
aiskrimu: ice cream(s)
ajali: accident(s)
Ajentina: Argentina
akaunti: account(s)
akiba: saving(s), deposit(s)
akili: intelligence
akina mama: women folk
ala!: expresses annoyance, impatience
alasiri: late afternoon(s)
alekum salam: I am well
alfajiri: dawn(s)
alika: invite
aliyepo: He/she who is there (incumbent)
almasi: diamond(s)
ama!: Wow!
ama...ama: either...or
ambaa: surf
ambatisha: attach
ambia: tell
Amerika: America
amini: believe
amka: wake up

amkia: greet
amua: decide
amuru: demand
andaa: prepare
andama: follow
andika: write
andikana: report each other
anga: air, sky(ies)
angalia: watch, look
-angalifu: watchful, careful
-angavu: clear, shining
anguka: fall
anguka pu: fall on the sand
anwani: address(es)
anza: start, begin
apa: swear (the truth)
Arabu/wa-: Arab(s)
ardhi: land(s), ground(s)
asante: thank you
asili: origin
asilimia: percent, originating out
    of a hundred
askari: guard(s), soldier(s)
astafurulahi!: expresses seeking
    forgiveness from God
asubuhi: morning(s)
ati!: expresses surprise, for
    seeking attention
au: or
au...au: either...or
aunsi: ounce(s) (U.S. unit of
    weight)
azima: borrow
azimia: lend
baa/ma-: bar(s)
baada: after
baada ya: after, afterwards
baadaye: after
baba: father(s)

babu: grandfather(s)
badala ya: instead of
badili: change
badilisha: exchange, change
bado: still, not yet
bafu: bath(s), bathroom(s)
bahari: sea(s), ocean(s)
Bahari ya Hindi: Indian Ocean
baharia/ma-: sailor(s)
bahasha: envelope(s)
bahati: luck
bahati nasibu: lottery(ies)
baiskeli: bicycle(s)
baki: stay
bali: but, rather, on the contrary
balozi/ma-: ambassador(s)
bangili: bangle(s), bracelet(s)
Bangladeshi: Bangladesh
barabara: road(s)
barabara ya/za ndege: runway(s)
barafu: ice
baridi: cold
barua: letter(s)
barua pepe: e-mail(s)
basi: enough, stop, well, then, so
basi/ma-: bus(es)
bawabu/ma-: doorman/doormen
-baya: bad
beba: carry
bee!: response used by females
    when someone is calling them
begi/ma-: bag(s)
bei: price(s)
bembeleza: sooth
bendera: flag(s)
benki/ma-: bank(s)
betri: battery(ies)
biashara: business(es), commerce
bibi: lady(ies), grandmother(s)

bibi harusi: bride(s)

bidhaa: product(s), merchandise

bidi: behoove

bidii: effort(s), diligence

bila: without

bila kujali: inspite of

bila samahani: No excuses needed

bilauri: drinking glass(es)

bili: bill(s)

bima: insurance

bima ya maisha: life insurance

binafsi: personal

binamu: cousin(s)

binti/ma-: daughter(s)

bisha: argue

-bivu: ripe

blanketi/ma-: blanket(s)

bluu: blue

boma/ma-: fort(s), compound(s)

bomba/ma-: pipe(s)

bondia/ma-: boxer(s)

bonasi: bonus(es)

bora: better, best

bosi/ma-: boss(es)

Brazili: Brazil

buluu: blue

bundi: owl(s)

bunduki: gun(s)

bunge/ma-: parliament(s)

bure: useless

burudisha: entertain, refresh

busara: wise

bustani: garden(s), park(s)

butu: blunt (referring to anything that can be sharpened: pencil, knife)

bwana/ma-: sir(s), gentleman(men)

bwawa/ma-: pool(s), swamp(s)

bweka: bark

cha: rising of the sun

-chache: few

chafu: dirty

chafua: make dirty

chagua: choose, elect

chai: tea

chaji: charge(s)

chakula/vy-: food(s)

chakula/vy- cha/vya mchana: lunch(es)

chama/vy-: political party(ies)

chamshakinywa/vy-: breakfast(s)

chana: tear

chandarua/vy-: mosquito net(s), veil(s)

changa: contribute

changanya: mix

cheka: laugh

chekeana: smile at each other

chelewa: be late

chelewesha: delay

chemka: boil

chenezo/vy-: measure(s)

cheo/vy-: position(s), title(s)

chepechepe: wet, moist, soaked

cheti/vy-: chit(s), pass(es), certificate(s)

cheza: play

chimba: dig

chini: below, under

chinja: slaughter

chipsi: chip(s), French fry(ies)

cho chote: any object at all

choka: tired

choma: roast, burn

chombo/vy-: vessel(s), tool(s), utensil(s)

chomoa: extract
choo/vy-: lavatory(ies)
chui: leopard(s), tiger(s)
chukua: take, carry
chuma: pick
chuma/vy-: steel, iron
chumba/vy-: room(s)
chumba/vy- cha/vya kulia: dining room(s)
chumvi: salt
chungu/vy-: pot(s)
chungu: strong, bitter, sharp
chungwa/ma-: orange(s)
chuo/vy-: college(s)
chuo/vy- kikuu/vi-: university(ies)
chupa: bottle(s)
chura/vy-: frog(s)
chwa: setting of the sun
dada: sister(s)
dafu/ma-: unripe coconut(s) (with lots of milk)
daima: always
dakika: minute(s)
daktari/ma-: doctor(s)
daladala/ma-: minibus(es)
damu: blood
danganya: cheat
daraja/ma-: bridge(s)
darasa/ma-: classroom(s), class(es), grade(s)
dawa: medicine(s), drug(s)
dawati/ma-: desk(s)
debe/ma-: tin(s), can(s)
dekeza: pamper
deni/ma-: debt(s)
dereva/ma-: driver(s)
dhahabu: gold
dharau: ignore, despise
dharura: emergency(ies)

dhihirika: become evident
dhuru: harm
digrii: degree(s)
diriki: manage
dirisha/ma-: window(s)
diski madhubuti: compact disk(s)
divai: wine(s)
-dogo: little, small
Dola: Dollar(s)
dubu: bear(s)
duka/ma-: shop(s)
dume/ma-: male animal(s)
dunduiza: save up, accumulate
duni ya: less than
dunia: world(s), the Earth
duriani/ma-: Durian fruit(s)
ebu!: expresses surprise, disapproval
eka/ekari: acre(s) (U.S. unit of measurement)
-ekundu: red
elekeza: direct, instruct
elewa: understand
eleza: explain
elezo/ma-: explanation(s)
elimu: education, knowledge
-ema: good, kind
-embamba: thin, narrow
embe/ma-: mango(es)
enda: go, move
endelea: continue, progress
endesha: drive
-enye: having, using
-enyewe: -self
-epesi: light (in weight), quick
epuka: avoid, escape
-erevu: clever
eti: indicates doubt about a following statement

-eupe: white

-eusi: black

ewallah!: expression used by inferiors to agree with superiors

fa: die

faa: suitable, useful

fagia: sweep

fahamisha: inform

fahamu: understand

faida: profit(s)

faini: fine(s)

faini ya/za kosa la kuegesha gari: parking fine(s)

familia: family(ies)

fana: succeed, prosper

fanana: resemble

fanikiwa: succeed

fanya: do, make

farasi: horse(s)

Farenihaiti: Fahrenheit

fariki: die

faulu: be successful, pass (a test)

fedha: money, silver

ficha: hide

fidia: compensation(s)

figa/ma-: hearth(s)

fika: arrive

fikia: stay at, reach

fikiri: think

fikisha: deliver

filamu: film(s)

fleti: apartment(s), flat(s)

forodha: customs, customs duty(ies)

freshi: fresh

friji: refrigerator(s)

fua: launder, forge (metal)

fuata: follow

fuatana: go together

fukuza: chase, terminate (from work)

fuma: weave, knit

fundi/ma-: craftsperson(s)

fundi/ma- bomba: plumber(s)

fundisanifu/ma-: technician(s)

fundisha: teach

funga: close, lock

funga goli/ma-: score goal(s)

fungua: open, unlock

funika: cover, disguise

funza: teach

-fupi: short

furahi: be happy

furika: overflow, flood

furiko/ma-: flood(s)

futa: delete, erase

futi: foot (feet)(U.S. unit of measurement)

fyatua risasi: fire a bullet

fyatua tofali/ma-: make brick(s)

gaidi/ma-: terrorist(s)

galoni: gallon(s) (U.S. unit of volume)

gani?: what?, which?, how?

gari/ma-: vehicle(s), car(s)

gauni/ma-: gown(s), dress(es)

gavana/ma-: governor(s)

gawa: distribute, divide

gazeti/ma-: newspaper(s), magazine(s)

-geni: strange, foreign

gereji: garage(s)

ghafla: suddenly

ghali: expensive

gharama: expense(s)

ghorofa: floor(s)

gitaa/ma-: guitar(s)

giza: dark, darkness

glavu: glove(s)

godoro/ma-: mattress(es)

gofu/ma-: ruin(s), wreck(s)

gogo/ma-: tree trunk(s)

gomba: quarrel

gramu: gram(s) (Metric unit of weight)

gubigubi: covered from head to toe (usually clothing or blanket)

-gumu: difficult, hard

gundua: discover

gurudumu/ma-: tire(s), wheel(s)

gusa: touch

gwaride: parade(s)

haba: little, few

habari: news, what news?

hadaa: deceive

hadi: until, as far as, up to

hadithi: story(ies)

haiba: personality(ies), appearance(s)

haki ya Mungu!: expression used to take an oath

halafu: then

hali: condition, state

hali ya hewa: weather

halijoto: temperature(s)

halmashauri ya/za mji/miji: town council(s)

hama: relocate, migrate

hamia: immigrate to, move to

hamna tabu: no problem

hamu: desire(s)

handaki/ma-: trench(es), tunnel(s)

hapa: here

hapana: no

haragwe/ma-: kidney bean(s)

haraka: quick, quickly, rush

haraka!: hurry!

harakati: activity(ies), struggle(s)

haramia/ma-: bandit(s), pirate(s)

haribu: destroy, spoil, damage

hasa: especially

hasara: loss

hasira: anger

hata: even, until

hata!: expresses complete disagreement

hata hivyo: even though, however

hatari: danger(s), emergency(ies)

hati: document(s), certificate(s)

haya!: OK!

hazina: treasure(s)

hebu!: expresses surprise, disapproval

hekta: hectare(s) (Metric unit of measurement)

helikopta: helicopter(s)

heri: better, it is better

heshima: honour(s), respect(s)

heshimu: respect, honour

hindi/ma-: grain(s) of maize/corn

hisa: stock(s), share(s)

hisi: feel

Hispania: Spain

historia: history(ies)

hitaji: need

hodari: clever, brave, serious

hodi?: may I come in?

hongera!: congratulations!

hospitali: hospital(s)

hoteli: hotel(s), restaurant(s)

hotuba: speech(es)

huduma: service(s), help

huku: while, meanwhile

hundi/ma-: cheque(s)

huruma: compassion
iba: steal
idhini: permit(s)
iga: imitate
igiza: act, stage
ijapokuwa: although, even though, even if
ijayo: next
ikawa: and it was
Ikulu: State House in Dar-es-Salaam
ila: but, except, unless
ili: so that, in order that
ili kwamba: so that, in order that
ilimradi: provided that
imara: firm, stable
imba: sing
inchi: inch(es)
ingawa: although, even though, even if
-ingi: many
ingia: enter
-ingine: another
Inshallah: If God wills it
inzi: fly(ies) (any sort)
-ipi?: which?
ishi: live
ita: call
iwapo: when, if, in case
ja: come
jaa: fill
jadili: discuss
jagi/ma-: jug(s)
jaji/ma-: judge(s)
jaji/ma- wa uraia: citizenship judge(s)
jali: care
jamaa: relative(s)
Jamaika: Jamaica

jamani!: expresses surprise
jambazi/ma-: gangster(s)
jambo/mambo: thing(s), matter(s), affair(s)
jamii: community(ies), family(ies)
jana: yesterday
jani/ma-: leaf(ves)
Japani: Japan
japo/ijapo/ijapokuwa: although
jaribu: try
jawabu/ma-: answer(s), reply(ies)
jaza: fill
je?: well, how about?
jela: jail(s)
jembe/ma-: hoe(s)
jenga: build
jengo/ma-: building(s)
jeshi/ma-: army(ies), military
jibu: answer
jibu/ma-: answer(s)
jicho/macho: eye(s)
jifya/ma-: hearth(s)
jiko/meko: stove(s), kitchen(s)
jimbo/ma-: province(s)
jina/ma-: name(s)
jini/ma-: spirit(s)
jino/meno: tooth/teeth
jinsi: the way that, how
jiografia: geography
jioni: evening(s)
jirani/ma-: neighbour(s)
-jitolea: volunteer
jitu/ma-: giant(s)
jiwe/mawe: stone(s)
jogoo/ma-: rooster(s)
joto: hot, heat
jua: know
jua/ma-: sun(s)
juisi: juice(s)

jumba/ma-: mansion(s)
juu: up, above, on top
juu ya: over, above, about
juu ya hayo: in addition, furthermore
juzi: the day before yesterday
juzijuzi: the other day
kaa: live, stay, sit
kaanga: fry
kabati/ma-: cupboard(s), locker(s)
kabisa: completely, thoroughly
kabla: before
kadhaa: several
kadi: card(s), one's ability
kahawa: coffee
kaka: brother(s)
kalamu: pen(s), pencil(s)
kale: ancient
kalenda: calendar(s)
kali: sharp, fierce
kama: as, if, like, "as...as", about
kama kwamba: as if
kama vile: such as
kamanda/ma-: commander(s)
kamata: arrest, catch
kamba: prawn(s), rope(s)
kame: barren, arid (referring to land)
kamera: camera(s)
kamili: exactly
kampuni: company(ies)
kamua: squeeze, wring
kamusi: dictionary(ies)
kana: refuse, reject, deny
Kanada: Canada
kandili: lamp(s), lantern(s)
kanisa/ma-: church(es)
kanya: forbid, prevent
karani/ma-: clerk(s)

karatasi: paper(s)
karibia: come close
karibisha: welcome, invite
karibu: near, nearby, nearly, close, welcome (sing.)
karibu na hapa: near here
karimu: generous
karo: fee(s)
karoti: carrot(s)
kasi: fast
kasirika: get angry
Kaskazini: North
kasoro: less, lack
kasorobo: less a quarter
kasri/ma-: palace(s)
kata: cut
kataa: refuse, reject, deny
katakata: completely
kataza: forbid, prohibit
kati ya: between
katika: in, into, inside, at
katikati: among, middle
kauka: dry
kavu: dry, disinteresting
kazi: work, job(s)
keki: cake(s)
kelele/ma-: noise(s)
kemikali: chemical(s)
Kenya: Kenya
kesho: tomorrow
kesho kutwa: day after tomorrow
keti: sit
khanga: piece of fabric
Kiajemi: Persian/Farsi, Persian/Farsi language
kiangazi/vi-: dry season(s)
Kiarabu: Arabic, Arabic language
kiasi: a bit
kiasi/vi-: amount(s), measure(s)

kiaskari: like a soldier

kiatu/vi-: shoe(s)

kiazi/vi-: potato(es)

kibaba/vi-: measuring tin(s)

kibanda/vi-: booth(s)

kibarua/vi-: labourer(s)

kibiriti/vi-: match(es) - for lighting a fire

kiboko/vi-: hippopotamus(mi)

kichakuro/vi-: squirrel(s)

Kichina: Chinese, Chinese language

kichwa/vi-: head(s)

kichwa maji: stupid/dumb person (idiom. expr.)

kidomo/vi-: small mouth(s) (adj. talkative)

kidonda/vi-: wound(s)

kidonge/vi-: pill(s)

kifaa/vi-: equipment, instrument(s), material(s), supply(ies)

Kifaransa: French, French language

kifaru/vi-: rhino(s)

kifedha: financial

kifundo/vi-: ankle(s)

kifurushi/vi-: parcel(s)

Kihindi: Hindi, Hindi language

Kihispania: Spanish, Spanish language

Kiingereza: English, English language

kijana/vi-: youth(s), young person(s)

kijani: green

Kijerumani: German, German language

kijiji/vi-: village(s)

kijiko/vi-: spoon(s)

kijitabu/vi-: small book(s), pamphlet(s)

kijiti/vi-: twig(s), stick(s), small tree(s)

kijito/vi-: stream(s)

kikao/vi-: meeting(s)

kikapu/vi-: basket(s)

kike: female, feminine

kiko/vi-: elbow(s)

kikombe/vi-: cup(s)

kikompyuta/vi-: laptop computer(s)

kikondoo: like a sheep

kila: each, every

kila kitu: everything

kilo: kilogram(s) (Metric unit of weight)

kilomita: kilometre(s) (Metric unit of measurement)

kima: monkey(s)

Kimaasai: Maasai, Maasai language

kimbia: run

kimbiza: chase

kimilikishi/vi-: possessive(s)

kimondo/vi-: meteor(s)

kinanda/vi-: piano(s)

kinda/ma-: young animal(s)

king'ora/vi-: alarm(s)

kinyago/vi-: carving(s)

kinyozi/vi-: barber(s)

kiongozi/vi-: guide(s), leader(s)

kiongozi/vi- wa watalii: tour guide(s)

kioo/vi-: glass, mirror(s)

kioski: kiosk(s)

kiota/vi-: nest(s)

kipande/vi-: piece(s)

kipenzi/vi-: boyfriend(s), favourite(s)

kipofu/vi-: blind person(s)

kipumbavu: like an idiot

Kireno: Portuguese, Portuguese language

Kirusi: Russian, Russian language

kisasa: modern, up-to-date

kasha: then, and then

kisirisiri: secretly

kisu/vi-: knife(ves)

Kiswahili: Swahili, Swahili language

kitabu/vi-: book(s)

kitambaa/vi-: cloth(s)

kitanda/vi-: bed(s)

kiti/vi-: chair(s)

kito/vi-: jewel(s), precious stone(s)

kitoto/vi-: infant(s)

kitu/vi-: thing(s)

kitunguu/vi-: onion(s)

kitunguu/vi- saumu: garlic clove(s)

kituo/vi-: station(s), stop(s)

kiumbe/vi-: organism(s)

kiume: like a man

kiungo/vi-: body joint(s)

kiuno/vi-: waist(s)

kiunzi/vi-: hurdle(s)

kiwanja/vi- cha/vya michezo: stadium(s)

kizee: like an old man

kiziwi/vi!: deaf person(s)

kizungu: like a European

kizunguzungu: dizzy

klabu: club(s)

kocha/ma-: coach(es)

kochi/ma-: couch(es)

kodi: hire, rent

kodoa macho: stare

kofia: hat(s), crown(s)

komboa: rescue

kompyuta: computer(s)

kopa: borrow

kopesha: lend

kopo/ma-: can(s)

koroboi: paraffin lamp(s)

koroma: croak, snore

korongo/ma-: ditch(es), channel(s)

kosa: miss, fail

kosa/ma-: mistake(s), fault(s), offence(s)

kosana: quarrel, disagree

kozi: course(s)

Krismasi: Christmas(es)

kua: grow

kubali: accept, agree

-kubwa: big, large

kufa fofofo: stone dead

kufumba na kufumbua: in the blink of an eye (idiom. expr.)

kuhusu: concerning, about

kuku: chicken(s)

kuliko: more, ... than, where something exists

kumbe: I see

kumbuka: remember

kumpa mtu kichwa: to spoil or pamper someone (idiom. expr.)

kumradhi!: used to ask for forgiveness, pardon

kuna: there is/are

kupiga mkasi: to expel from service (idiom. expr.)

kura: vote(s)

kusanya: collect

kushika sikio: to reprimand (idiom
    expr.)

kusudi: in order that, with the
    intention of

kuta: meet

kutana na: meet with

kutoka: from

kutosha: enough

kutwa: all day

-kuu: main

kuuma meno: to take a vow of
    revenge (idiom. expr.)

kuvimba kichwa: to become big-
    headed/arrogant (idiom.
    expr.)

kuwa: that

kuwako: to be in a place

kwa: by, to/by means of, for,
    with, on

kwa ajili: for, because

kwa ajili ya: for the sake of

kwa ajili ya hayo: therefore

kwa heri: goodbye (sing.)

kwa hivyo: because of this

kwa kifupi: in short

kwa kusudi: intentionally

kwa kuwa: for, the reason being

kwa kweli: really, truly

kwa maana: for, because, the
    reason being

kwa mia: from/out of a hundred

kwa nia ya: with the intention of

kwa nini?: Why?

kwa sababu: by reason of,
    because

kwa sauti: loudly

kwa vile: because of this

kwamba: if, whether, that

kwani: for, because, the reason
    being

kweli: true, truth(s)

kweli!: truly!

la: eat

lahaula!: expresses inevitability

laini: soft

laiti!: expresses disappointment,
    regret

lakini: but, nevertheless

lala: sleep

lalamika: complain

lango/ma-: gate(s)

lazima: obligation

lazimisha: order, force

lea: raise, bring up

legea: relax, be loose, be weak

lengo/ma-: goal(s)

leo: today

leta: bring

lewa: to be intoxicated

lia: cry

licha ya: despite

likizo: holiday(s), vacation(s)

lima: cultivate

limbika: set aside, invest

linda: guard

lingana: match, harmonize

lini?: when?

lipa: pay

lita: litre(s) (Metric unit of
    volume)

loo!: Oh!

lori/ma-: truck(s), from the
    English "lorry"

lugha: language(s)

maalumu: special

maarifa: knowledge, understand-
    ing

maarufu: famous
madhubuti: precise, reliable
madini: mineral(s)
mafanikio: success(es)
mafunzo: training
mafuriko: flood(s)
mafuta: fat, oil
mafutaghafi: crude oil
magharibi: late evening(s)
mahakama: law court(s)
mahali: place(s)
mahali pa: instead of
maili: mile(s) (U.S. unit of measurement)
maisha: life(ves)
maji: water
maji ya machungwa: orange juice
majira ya baridi: winter(s)
majira ya pukutiko la majani: autumn(s)
majivu: ashes
makao makuu: headquarter(s)
makasi: shears, scissors
makasiya kunyolea: haircutting scissors
maktaba: library(ies)
makubwa!: expresses unexpected important news
mali: wealth, property(ies), possession(s)
maliza: complete, finish
malkia: queen(s)
mama: mother(s)
mama wa kambo: stepmother(s)
mamba: crocodile(s)
Mandela: Nelson Mandela
maonyesho: show(s), concert(s)
mara: time(s), occasion(s)
mara pale pale: just then

marahaba: hello, delightful
marathoni: marathon(s)
Marekani: The United States of America
masalkheri: good evening
mashallah!: expresses gratitude to God
mashine: machine(s)
mashine ya/za ATM: ATM machine(s)
mashine ya/za chapa: typewriter(s)
mashua: small boat(s)
mashuhuri: famous, important
maskini: poor
maskini!: poor fellow!
matata: trouble
matengenezo: repair(s)
matumizi: spending, expenditure(s)
mauaji: massacre(s)
mawasiliano: communication(s)
mawe!: expresses strong disagreement
mazingira: environment(s)
maziwa: milk
mazungumzo: conversation(s)
mbali: far, far away
mbali na: far from
mbalimbali: different, differently
mbao: wood, timber
mbegu: seed(s)
mbele: front, in front
mbingu: sky(ies)
mboga: vegetable(s)
mbona?: Why, for God's sake?
mbu: mosquito(es)
mbuga ya/za wanyama: game park(s)

mbunge/wa-: member(s) of Parliament

mbuni: ostrich(es)

mbuyu/mi-: baobab tree(s)

mbuzi: goat(s)

mbwa: dog(s)

mchana: daytime(s), afternoon(s)

mchanga: sand(s)

mchango/mi-: contribution(s), donation(s)

mchekeshaji/wa-: comedian(s)

mchele: uncooked rice

mchemraba/mi-: cube(s)

mchezaji/wa-: actor(s), dancer(s), player(s), athlete(s)

mchezo/mi-: game(s), play(s)

mchezo/mi- wa kikapu: basketball

Mchina/wa-: Chinese person(s)

mchinjaji/wa-: butcher(s)

mchoraji/wa-: artist(s)

mchungaji/wa-: priest(s), shepherd(s)

mchuzi/mi-: curry(ies), sauce(s)

mdahalo/mi-: debate(s)

mdhamini/wa-: sponsor(s)

mdomo/mi-: mouth(s)

mdudu/wa-: insect(s)

meli: ship(s)

meneja/ma-: manager(s)

menejimenti: management

meremeta: shine, glitter

meya: mayor(s)

meza: table(s)

mfalme/wa-: king(s)

mfamasi/wa-: pharmacist(s)

mfano/mi-: model(s), example(s)

mfanyabiashara/wa-: businessperson(s)

mfanyakazi/wa-: worker(s)

mfanyakazi/wa- wa huduma za jamii: social worker(s)

Mfaransa/wa-: Frenchperson(s)

mfereji/mi-: ditch(es)

mfinyanzi/wa-: potter(s)

mfugo/mi-: farm animal(s)

mfuko/mi-: bag(s), pocket(s), sack(s)

mfumko: inflation

Mfumo wa Metriki: Metric System

mfungwa/wa-: prisoner(s)

mfupa/mi-: bone(s)

mganga/wa-: doctor(s), shaman(s)

mgeni/wa-: visitor(s), guest(s)

Mgiriki/wa-: Greek(s)

mgomo/mi-: strike(s)

mgonjwa/wa-: sick person(s), patient(s)

mguu/mi-: leg(s), by foot

mhakiki/wa-: critic(s)

mhalifu/wa-: criminal(s)

mhamahamaji/wa-: nomad(s)

mhamiaji/wa-: immigrant(s)

mhandisi/wa-: engineer(s)

mhariri/wa-: editor(s)

mhasibu/wa-: accountant(s)

mhifadhi/wa- wa wanyama: game keeper(s)

Mhindi/wa-: Indian(s)

Mhispania/wa-: Hispanic(s)

Mholanzi/wa-: Dutch person(s)

miliki: own

mililita: millilitre(s)

milimita: millimetre(s)

Misri: Egypt

mita: metre(s)

miwani: eyeglasses

mjanja: cunning, sly

mjenzi/wa-: builder(s)
mji/mi-: city(ies), town(s)
mjomba/wa-: maternal uncle(s)
mjukuu/wa-: grandchild(ren)
mkalimani/wa-: interpreter(s)
mkanda/mi-: belt(s)
mkataba/mi-: contract(s)
mkate/mi-: bread(s)
mkazi/wa-:
    resident(s),inhabitant(s)
mke/wa-: wife(ves)
mkeka/mi-: mat(s)
Mkenya/wa-: Kenyan(s)
mkia wa mbuzi: totally useless
    person (idiom. expr.)
mkimbizi/wa-: refugee(s)
mkoa/mi-: region(s)
mkokoteni/mi-: cart(s)
mkono/mi-: hand(s)
mkopo/mi-: credit(s), loan(s)
mkulima/wa-: farmer(s)
mkurufunzi/wa-: trainee(s)
mkurugenzi/wa-: director(s)
mkutano/mi-: meeting(s)
mkutubi/wa-: librarian(s)
mkuu/wa-: elder(s)
mkwe/wa-: in-law(s)
mlango/mi-: door(s)
mlemavu/wa-: disabled person(s)
mlima/mi-: mountain(s)
mlimaji/wa-: farmer(s)
mlinzi/wa-: guard(s)
mmea/mi-: plant(s)
mmilikaji/wa-: owner(s)
mnadhifishaji/wa-: organizer(s)
mnamo: about
mnara/mi-: tower(s)
Mnijeria/wa-: Nigerian(s)
mno: a lot

mnyama/wa-: animal(s)
moja kwa moja: straight ahead
    (idiom. expr.)
mojamoja: one by one
moto/mi-: fire(s)
motokaa: car(s)
moyo/mi-: heart(s)
mpaka: until, as far as, up to
mpanda/wa- mlima:
    mountaineer(s)
mpango/mi-: plan(s)
mpeketevu/wa-: arrogant
    person(s)
mpenzi/wa-: dear(s), loved
    one(s), girlfriend(s)
mpiga/wa- kura: voter(s)
mpiga/wa- picha: photographer(s)
mpigamuziki/wa-: musician(s)
mpira/mi-: football(s)
mpira wa miguu: soccer
mpishi/wa-: cook(s), chef(s)
mpokezi/wa-: receptionist(s)
mraba/mi-: square(s)
mradi/mi-: project(s)
Mrusi/wa-: Russian(s)
msaada/mi-: assistance
msafiri/wa-: traveller(s)
msafirishaji/wa-: courier(s)
msafishaji/wa-: cleaner(s)
msaidizi/wa-: assistant(s)
msanii/wa-: artist(s)
msemaji/wa-: spokesperson(s)
mshahara/mi-: salary(ies)
mshauri/wa-: advisor(s)
mshikaki/mi-: skewered meat(s)
mshitakiwa/wa-: accused
    person(s)
mshonaji/wa-: tailor(s)
msichana/wa-: girl(s)

msikilizaji/wa-: listener(s)
msikiti/mi-: mosque(s)
msimamizi/wa-: supervisor(s)
msitu/mi-: forest(s)
msomaji/wa-: reader(s)
Msumbiji: Mozambique
msumeno/mi-: saw(s)
mswada/mi-: manuscript(s),
    legislative bill(s)
Mswahili/wa-: Swahili person(s)
mswaki/mi-: toothbrush(es)
mtaa/mi-: street(s)
mtaalamu/wa-: specialist(s)
mtafiti/wa-: researcher(s)
mtalii/wa-: tourist(s)
mtandao: the internet
mtazamaji/wa-: spectator(s),
    viewer(s)
mteja/wa-: customer(s)
mteswa/wa-: victim(s)
mti/mi-: tree(s)
mtihani/mi-: examination(s)
mto/mi-: pillow(s), river(s)
mtondo: three days from now
mtondogoo: four days from now
mtoto/wa-: child(ren)
mtu/wa-: person(s)
mtu/wa- anayeleta/wa- barua:
    mailman/mailmen
mtu/wa- wa posta: postal
    worker(s)
mtukufu/wa-: dignitary(ies)
mtumba/mi-: bundle(s) of clothes,
    usually second hand from
    abroad
mtumishi/wa-: servant(s),
    steward(s)
muda: period(s), time(s)
muhimu: important, urgent

muhogo/mi-: cassava root(s)
muhula/mihula: term(s), period(s)
mume/waume: husband(s)
muziki: music
mvinyo/mi-: wine(s)
mvua: rain(s)
mvulana/wa-: boy(s)
Mwafrika/wa-: African(s)
mwaga: spill, pour
mwaka/mi-: year(s)
mwaka jana: last year
mwaka ujao: next year
mwakilishi/wa-: representative(s)
mwaliko/mi-: invitation(s)
mwalimu/wa-: teacher(s)
Mwamerika/wa-: American(s)
mwaminifu/wa-: honest person(s)
mwana/wa-: child(ren)
mwanaanga/wanaanga:
    astronaut(s)
mwanafunzi/wa-: student(s)
mwanagenzi/wa-: apprentice(s)
mwanajeshi/wa-: soldier(s)
mwanakijiji/wa-: villager(s)
mwanakwaya/wa-: choir
    member(s)
mwanamichezo/wa-: athlete(s)
mwanamke/wanawake: woman/
    women
mwanamuziki/wa-: musician(s)
mwananchi/wa-: citizen(s)
mwanasayansi/wa-: scientist(s)
mwanasemina/wa-: seminar
    participant(s)
mwanasheria/wa-: lawyer(s)
mwanasiasa/wa-: politician(s)
mwanaume/wa-: man/men
mwandamanaji/wa-: protestor(s)
mwandiko/mi-: handwriting(s)

mwandishi/wa-: writer(s), author(s)

mwandishi/wa- wa habari: reporter(s)

mwanga/mi-: light(s)

Mwarabu/wa-: Arab(s)

mwavuli/mi-: umbrella(s)

mweka/waweka wa kitega uchumi: investor(s)

mwelekeo/mi-: attitude(s), tendency(ies)

mwembe/mi-: mango tree(s)

mwendesha/wa- mashtaka: prosecutor(s)

mwendo/mi-: speed(s)

mwenye duka/wenye duka: shopkeeper(s)

mwenyeji/wa-: inhabitant(s), host(s)

mwenyembwa/wenyembwa: dog owner(s)

mwenyenyumba/wenyenyumba: houseowner(s)

mwenyewe/wenyewe: owner(s)

mwenzi/wenzi: friend(s), colleague(s), companion(s)

mwezi/mi-: month(s), moon(s)

mwiba/mi-: thorn(s)

mwigizaji/wa-: actor(s)

mwiko/mi-: serving spoon(s)

mwili/mi-: body(ies)

mwimbaji/wa-: singer(s)

mwindaji/wa-: hunter(s)

mwinuko/mi-: altitude(s), slope(s)

Mwirani/wa-: Iranian(s)

mwisho/mi-: end(s), conclusion(s)

Mwitaliano/wa-: Italian(s)

mwizi/wezi: thief(ves)

mwoga/wa-: swimmer(s), coward(s)

mwogeleaji/wa-: swimmer(s)

mwombaji/wa-: beggar(s)

mwuguzi/wa-: nurse(s)

mwuza/wa-: seller, vendor

mwuzaji/wa-: seller(s), salesperson(s)

mzazi/wa-: parent(s)

mzee/wa-: elder(s), old person(s)

mzigo/mi-: luggage(s)

mzimamoto/wa-: firefighter(s)

Mzungu/wa-: European(s)

na: and, with, by, also

naam: yes

nabii/ma-: prophet(s)

nadhifu: clean, neat, tidy

nafasi: space(s), opportunity(ies)

namna: type(s), kind(s)

nanasi/ma-: pineapple(s)

nani?: who?

nauli: fare(s)

nawa: wash

nazi: coconut(s)

nchi: country(ies), state(s)

ndani: inside

ndege: plane(s), bird(s)

ndiyo: yes

ndizi: banana(s)

ndoo: bucket(s)

ndugu: relative(s)

nene: fat

neno/ma-: word(s)

nesi/ma-: nurse(s)

ng'aa: shine

ng'o!: expression to tell a child "Absolutely not"

ng'oa: extract

ng'ombe: cow(s), cattle

-ngapi?: how many?

ngazi: ladder(s), stair(s)

ngoja: wait

ngoma: dance(s), drum(s)

ngozi: skin(s), leather(s), hide(s)

nguo: cloth(es), clothing, garment(s)

nguruwe: pig(s)

nguvu: strength, power, force

ni: is/are

ni mjamzito: she is pregnant (idiom. expr.)

nia: intention(s), aim(s)

nini?: what?

nishani: ceremonial medal(s)

njaa: hunger(s), famine(s)

njano: yellow

nje: outside

njia: way(s), method(s), road(s), path(s)

njiwa: dove(s)

njoo: come

nong'ona: whisper

nuka: smell bad, stink

nuka fee: smell badly

nukia: smell good, scent

nukta: point(s), decimal(s), dot(s), period(s)

nunua: buy

nusa: smell

nusu: half(ves) (as a fraction)

nya: rain

nyama: meat

nyang'anya: take away (force-fully)

nyangumi: whale(s)

nyani: baboon(s)

nyanya: tomato(es), grandmother(s)

nyasi/ma-: grass(es)

nyati wa kufugwa: water buffalo(es)

nyatunyatu: stealthily

nyekundu: red

nyesha: rain

nyoka: snake(s)

nyosha: straighten

nyuma: behind

nyumba: house(s)

nywa: drink

-o -ote: any

oa: marry (for men only)

ofisa/ma-: officer(s), official(s)

ofisa/ma- tawala: administrative officer(s)

ofisi: office(s)

oga: bathe, wash

ogelea: swim, wash

ogopa: be afraid

okoa: rescue

olewa: get married (for women only)

omba: ask, beg

ombi/ma-: request(s), application(s)

ona: see, feel

onana: meet/see each other

ondoa: remove

ondoka: leave, depart

onekana: be seen, appear

ongea: converse, speak with

ongeza: increase

onya: warn

onyesha: show, demonstrate

onyo/ma-: warning(s), advice

opereta/ma-: operator(s)
orodha: list(s)
orodhesha: register
-ororo: soft, smooth
osha: wash
ota: grow, dream
-ote: all, whole
-ovu: wicked, evil
ovyo: carelessly
oza: rot, give in marriage (for women only)
pa: give
paa: raise, fly
pacha/ma-: twin(s)
painti: pint(s) (U.S. unit of volume)
paka: cat(s)
paka rangi: apply colour(s) (paint)
pakua: serve, unload
palilia: weed, hoe
pambo/ma-: ornament(s), decoration(s)
pamoja: together
pamoja na hayo: in addition, furthermore
-pana: wide, flat
panda: climb, plant
panda: crossing(s), fork(s)
pandisha: promote
panga: rent, arrange
panua: widen
panya: mouse(s), rat(s)
pasa: behoove
pasha: inform
pasipoti: passport(s)
pasua: burst
pata: get, receive
patana: haggle, bargain

pato/ma-: revenue(s)
Pauni: Pound(s) (British currency)
pazia/ma-: curtain(s)
peke: -self, alone
peleka: send
penda: love, like
pendekeza: recommend
pendelea: favour
pendeza: beautiful, pleasant, attractive, fancy
penseli: pencil(s)
pera/ma-: guava(s)
peremende: peppermint(s)
pesa: money
pete: ring(s)
petroli: petrol, gasoline
-pevu: ripe
-pi?: which?
pia: also, too
picha: picture(s)
piga: hit, kick, play (music)
piga chapa: type, print
piga kura: cast a vote
pika: cook
pikipiki: motorcycle(s)
pilipili: pepper(s)
pinda: bend
pinduka: overturn
pipa/ma-: barrel(s)
piramidi/ma-: pyramid(s)
pita: pass, exceed
pitia: pass through, transit through
pitisha: approve
poa: cool, calm, peaceful, feel better
pogoa: prune
pointi: point(s), decimal(s)

pokea: accept, receive
pole: sorry (sing.)
polepole: slowly
polisi: police
pona: cure, heal
ponda: crush
pori: wilderness
poromoka: plummet, slip, slide
poromoko/ma- la/ya theluji:
     avalanche(s)
posta: post, post office(s)
potea: lose, disappear
poteza: lose, waste
poza: cool off
pua: nose(s), nozzle(s)
pumzi: breath(s)
pumzika: rest
pumzika fofofo: resting soundly
pumziko/ma-: break(s), rest
     period(s)
pundamilia: zebra(s)
punga: wave, flap
pungua: reduce, become less
puto/ma-: balloon(s)
pwani: coast(s)
-pya: new
rafiki: friend(s)
rahisi: easy, simple, cheap
raia: citizen(s)
rais/ma-: president(s)
Ramadhani: Ramadan
Randi: South African Rand
rangi: colour(s)
rasimu: plan, design
ratili/ratli: pound(s) (U.S. unit of
     weight)
redio: radio(s)
refa: referee(s)
-refu: tall, long

rehani: mortgage(s)
reli: rail(s), railway(s)
riba: interest (financial)
robo: quarter(s) (as a fraction)
roboti: robot(s)
roho: spirit(s), soul(s)
roketi: rocket(s)
roshani: balcony(ies)
rubani/ma-: pilot(s)
rudi: return, come back
ruhusu: permit, allow
ruka: jump, fly
Rupia: Indian Rupee
rusha: fly
Rwanda: Rwanda
saa: time(s), hour(s), clock(s)
saa hizi: at this time
saa ngapi?: What time is it?
saa ya/za kukuamsha: alarm
     clock(s)
saa ya/za ukuta: clock(s)
sababisha: cause
sababu: cause, reason
sabalkheri: good morning
sabuni: soap(s), detergent(s)
sadaka: charity(ies)
safari: journey(s), safari trip(s)
safari ya/za utalii: tour(s)
safi: clean
safari: travel
safisha: clean
saga: crush, grind
sahani: plate(s)
sahau: forget
saidia: help
sakafu: floor(s)
sala: prayer(s)
salam alekum: How are you?
salama: peaceful, safe

salimu: greet
samahani: excuse me, sorry
samaki: fish(es)
sambaza: spread
samehe: forgive, pardon
sana: very
sanaa: art(s), craft(s)
sanaa umbuji: fine art(s)
sanduku/ma-: box(es), suitcase(s)
sandwichi: sandwich(es)
sanifu: design
sarakasi: circus(es)
sasa: now
sasa hivi: right now
sauti: voice(s), sound(s)
sawa: equal (to/in)
sawa kabisa: completely O.K.
sawa na: equal to, similar
sawasawa: same, O.K.
sayansi: science(s)
sayari: planet(s)
sehemu: part(s), fraction(s), area(s), portion(s)
sekondari: secondary
sekunde: second(s) (unit of time)
Selsiasi: Celsius
sema: speak, say
sentimita: centimetre(s) (Metric unit of measurement)
seremala/ma-: carpenter(s)
serikali: government(s)
setilaiti: satellite(s)
shabashi!: congratulations!
shairi/ma-: poem(s)
shajara: diary(ies)
shamba/ma-: farm(s)
shampuu: shampoo(s)
shangazi: paternal aunt(s)
sharti: it is necessary

shati/ma-: shirt(s)
shauku: eagerness, desire
shauri: advise
shehena: cargo(es)
shemeji: brother/sister-in-law(s)
sherehe: celebration(s), party(ies)
shiba: be full
shida: trouble(s),difficulty(ies), hardship(s)
shika: catch, hold
shikamoo: Hello (said to an elder)
Shilingi: Shilling(s) (name of currencies used by Kenya, Tanzania and Uganda)
shimo/ma-: hole(s)
shinda: pass, defeat, win
shindana: compete
shindano/ma-: competition(s)
shirika/ma- la/ya uma: public institution(s)
shiriki: share, participate
shirikiana: co-operate
shoka: axe(s)
shona: stitch, sew
shughuli: business(es), activity(ies)
shujaa: brave
shuka: descend, fall
shuka: sheet(s)
shukuru: thank
shule: school(s)
si: is not/are not
sifa: quality(ies), praise(s), characteristic(s)
sigara: cigarette(s)
sijambo: I am fine
sikia: listen, hear, feel
sikio/ma-: ear(s)
sikitika: regret

sikitiko/ma-: regret(s)
sikitisha: be disappointed
siku: day(s)
siku iliyofuata: the day that
    followed
siku iliyopita: the day that passed
siku ya/za kuzaliwa: birthday(s)
Siku ya Uhuru: Independence Day
sikukuu: holiday(s)
silaha: weapon(s)
simama: stand
simba: lion(s)
simu: telephone(s)
simu ya/za mkono: cell phone(s)
    (literally a telephone of the
    hand)
simulia: narrate, tell a story
sindano: needle(s)
sinema: cinema(s)
siri: secret
sogea: come close
soko/ma-: market(s)
soko/ma- la/ya hisa: stock
    market(s)
soksi: sock(s)
soma: read, study
somana: spy on each other
somo/ma-: academic subject(s)
spana: spanner(s), wrench(es)
staafu: retire
stawi: prosper
stempu: stamp(s)
subutu!: to dare someone
suka: weave
sukari: sugar
sukuma: push
sumbua: disturb, annoy
supamaketi: supermarket(s)
sura: face(s), appearance(s)

suruali: trouser(s)
swala: gazelle(s)
swali/ma-: question(s)
sweta: sweater(s)
swila: cobra(s)
taabu: troubled, distressed
tabasamu: smile
tabia: behaviour(s)
tafadhali: please
tafuta: look for, search
tahadhari: warn, caution
taifa/ma-: nation(s)
tajiri: rich
tajiri/ma-: wealthy person(s)
tajirika: become rich
taka: want
takataka: garbage
takiwa: require, need
tamasha: festival(s), show(s)
tamu: sweet, delicious
tangaza: advertise, announce
tangazo/ma-: notice(s),
    advertisement(s)
tangi/ma-: tank(s), reservoir(s)
tango/ma-: cucumber(s), gutter(s)
tangu: since, from
tani: tonne(s) (Metric unit of
    weight) also a "ton(s)" as
    U.S. unit of weight
Tanzania: Tanzania
tarajia: expect to
taratibu: slowly
tarehe: date(s)
tasnifu: thesis/theses
tatizo/ma-: problem(s)
tatua: solve
taulo: towel(s)
tausi: peacock(s)
tawi/ma-: branch(es)

tayari: ready

tazama: look at, watch, stare

tegemea: depend, rely on, expect

teknolojia: technology(ies)

teksi/ma-: taxi(s)

televisheni: television(s)

tembea: walk

tembelea: visit

tembo: elephant(s)

tena: again, furthermore, besides

tenda: do, treat

tengeneza: fix, repair, manufacture

tesa: torture

tetemeko/ma- la/ya ardhi: earthquake(s)

thamani: price, value, worth

thamini: value, appraise

theluji: snow(s)

theluthi: third(s) (as a fraction)

thurea: chandelier(s)

tia: put

tiara: kite(s)

tiba: treatment(s), cure(s), medicine(s)

tibu: treat, cure

tiketi: ticket(s)

timia: complete

timu: team(s)

tisha: scare, threaten

toa: give, deliver, remove

tochi: flashlight(s)

tofali/ma-: brick(s)

toka: come from, until

toka nje: go outside

tokea: happen, come out

tokeo/ma-: consequence(s)

tosha: enough

trekta/ma-: tractor(s)

treni: train(s)

tu: only

tua: land, settle

tufaha/ma-: apple(s)

tufani: storm(s)

tulivu: quiet

tuma: send, employ

tumaini/ma-: hope(s)

tumbuiza: entertain

tumia: use, spend, exploit

tunda/ma-: fruit(s)

tundu/ma-: hole(s), nest(s)

tupa: throw away, abandon

tupu: empty

twiga: giraffe(s)

ua: kill

ua/ma-: flower(s)

ua/ny-: courtyard(s)

uamuzi/maamuzi: decision(s), judgement(s)

uangalizi/maangalizi: management, management styles

uangilifu: care

Uarabuni: Arabia

ubainisho/bainisho: clear evidence

ubalozi: embassy(ies)

ubao/m-: plank(s), board(s)

ubavu/m-: rib(s)

ubawa/m-: wing(s)

ubinja/m-: whistle(s)

uboho: bone marrow

ubongo: brain matter

uchaguzi: election(s)

uchaguzi mkuu: general election(s)

uchi: bare, naked

Uchina: China

uchofu: tiredness

uchoyo: greed
uchumi: economy(ies)
udanganyifu: trickery
udevu/ndevu: beard(s)
udongo: dirt, soil
udongo wa kinamu: clay (literally "soil of flexibility")
uduvi/nduvi: shrimp(s)
ufa/ny-: crack(s), fault(s)
ufagio/fagio: brush(es), broom(s)
ufalme: kingship
Ufaransa: France
ufunguo/funguo: key(s)
ugali: corn meal porridge
ugimbi/ngimbi: beer(s)
ugonjwa/magonjwa: disease(s)
ugua: feel sick
ugunduzi: discovery(ies)
uhamiaji: immigration
Uhindi: India
Uholanzi: The Netherlands, Holland
uhuru: freedom, independence
Uingereza: Great Britain
Uislamu: Islam
ujamaa: relationship, socialism
ujana: youthfulness
Ujerumani: Germany
uji: porridge
ukali: fierceness
ukimwi: AIDS
ukingo/kingo: riverbank(s)
ukoja/koja: necklace(s)
ukoo/koo: family(ies)
ukosefu: deficit, shortage(s)
Ukristo: Christianity
ukumbi/kumbi: lounge(s), meeting hall(s)

ukurasa/kurasa: page(s), sheet of paper(s)
ukuta/kuta: wall(s)
ulaghai: deceitfulness
Ulaya: Europe
ulimi/ndimi: tongue(s)
ulimwengu: world(s), universe(s)
ulinganifu: harmony
ulinzi: security, defence
uliza: ask
uma: bite, hurt
uma/ny-: fork(s)
Umaasai: Maasailand
umeme: electricity, lightning
umia: get hurt
umiza: hurt
umoja: unity
umri: age(s)
unga: flour
unga (na): join (up), connect (with)
-unganifu: connecting
ungua: burn
Unguja: Zanzibar
unyang'anyi: robbery(ies)
unyoya/manyoya: feather(s)
unywele/nywele: hair(s)
upana: width
upande: sideways
upendo: love
upesi: fast
upya: new
urafiki: friendship(s)
urefu: length, depth, height, distance
Urusi: Russia
usalama: safety, security
Usemi Halisi: Direct Speech

Usemi wa Taarifa: Reported Speech

ushanga/shanga: bead(s)

Ushuru wa Forodha: Duties and Customs Department

usiku: night(s)

usiku kucha: all night

usiku wa manane: late at night, dead of night

usimamizi: management

uso/ny-: face(s)

Uswisi: Switzerland

utajiri: wealth

utambi/tambi: wick(s)

utamu: sweetness, tastiness

utata: complication, complexity

utoto: childhood

utumishi: personnel, manpower

uvivu: laziness

uwanja/nyanja: field(s), open area(s)

uwanja/nyanja wa/za ndege: airport(s)

uwingu/mbingu: sky(ies)

uwongo: lie(s)

uza: sell

uzani: weight

uzee: old age

uzi/ny-: thread(s), string(s)

uzito: weight(s)

vaa: wear, put on

vema!: good!

vibaya: badly

vigumu: difficult

vilevile: also, equally

vingine: in another way

vipi?: how?

vita: war(s)

Vita vya Pili vya Dunia: The Second World War

vivu: lazy

viza: visa(s)

vizuri: nicely, well

vuja: leak, spill out

vuma: make noise

vunja: break

vuta: pull, smoke

vutia: attract, interest

wa: be, exist

-wa na: be with, have

waadhi/nyaadhi: sermon(s)

wadhifa/nyadhifa: position(s)

wahi: be on time

waka: burn, shine, light

wakala/ma-: agent(s)

wakati/nyakati: time(s), moment(s)

wakati ule ule: at that exact time

wakili/ma- mtetezi/wa-: defence counsellor(s)

wala: neither

wala...wala: neither...nor

wali: rice

wallahi!: expression used to take an oath

wapi?: where?

waraka/nyaraka: document(s)

waridi/ma-: rose(s)

washa: switch on

wasilisha: submit

wavu/nyavu: net(s)

waya/nyaya: wire(s)

wazi: obvious, self evident

waziri/ma-: minister(s)

waziri/ma- mkuu/wa-: prime minister(s)

wazo/ma-: thought(s)
weka: keep, save, set aside
wekwa: put in, install
wenyewe kwa wenyewe: each other
weza: able
wika: crow
wiki: week(s)
wikiendi: weekend(s)
wima: upright
wimbo/nyimbo: song(s)
winchi: winch(es)
winda: hunt
wingi: plenty
wingu/ma-: cloud(s)
wino: ink
Ya Allah!: expresses amazed frustration, pleasant surprise
ya kwamba: that
yadi: yard(s) (U.S. of measurement)
yai/ma-: egg(s)
yaya/ma-: nanny(ies)
Yuro: Euro currency
zaa: bear, produce
zabibu: grape(s), raisin(s)
zaidi: more
zaidi ya: more than
zaidi ya hayo: in addition, furthermore

zaliwa: born
zamani: long ago, old (for non-living things)
zambarau: plum(s), plum colour (purple)
zao/ma-: crop(s)
zawadi: present(s), gift(s)
zeeka: old, worn out
zeruzeru/ma-: albino(s)
ziara: visit(s)
zidi: increase, more than
zima: whole, good, extinguish
zimia: faint
-zito: heavy, severe
ziwa/ma-: lake(s), pond(s)
zoa: pick up
zoea: be used to
zoezi/ma-: exercise(s)
zoezi/ma- la/ya viungo: physical exercise(s)
zongoa: unwrap
zu: zoo(s)
Zuhura: Venus
zuia: hold, stop, prevent
zulia/ma-: carpet(s), rug(s)
zungumza: converse
-zuri: good, beautiful
zurura: wander around aimlessly

About the Authors

Oswald Almasi was born in Tanzania and educated at the University of Dar-es-Salaam. He received his Ph. D. in 1993 from the University of Toronto. He has been an educator for more than 40 years, in the last 19 years as a Professor of Swahili at the University of Toronto and also at York University since 2005.

Michael David Fallon graduated from the University of Toronto as an African Studies Specialist. While at the University of Toronto he studied several languages including Portuguese, Arabic and also Swahili under the tutelage of Dr Almasi. He has also lived and travelled in East Africa, as well as the Far East.

Nazish Pardhan-Wared was born in Tanzania and educated at Aga Khan Mzizima Secondary School in Dar-es-Salaam. She moved to Canada in 2001 for her undergraduate studies and graduated with an Honours Degree in Biology from the University of Toronto. She has also studied advanced Swahili under Dr. Almasi and speaks Swahili fluently.

Milton Keynes UK
Ingram Content Group UK Ltd.
UKHW021942060824
446621UK00020B/413